Carbon Societies

Carbon Societies

The Social Logic of Fossil Fuels

Peter Wagner

polity

First published in 2024 by Polity Press

Polity Press
65 Bridge Street
Cambridge CB2 1UR, UK

Polity Press
111 River Street
Hoboken, NJ 07030, USA

ISBN-13: 978-1-5095-5708-0
ISBN-13: 978-1-5095-5709-7(pb)

A catalogue record for this book is available from the British Library.

Library of Congress Control Number: 2024935058

Typeset in 10.5 on 13pt Swift
by Cheshire Typesetting Ltd, Cuddington, Cheshire
Printed and bound in Great Britain by CPI Group (UK) Ltd, Croydon

For further information on Polity, visit our website:
politybooks.com

Table of Contents

Detailed Table of Contents

List of Figures

List of Abbreviations

BCE	before the common era
BRICS	association of Brazil, Russia, India, China and South Africa
CBDR	common but differentiated responsibilities
CDR	carbon dioxide removal
CE	common era
CO_2	carbon dioxide
COMECON	Council for Mutual Economic Assistance
COP	Conference of Parties
COVID-19	coronavirus disease originating in 2019
EU	European Union
IPCC	Intergovernmental Panel on Climate Change
NATO	North Atlantic Treaty Organization
NIEO	New International Economic Order
OECD	Organisation for Economic Co-operation and Development
OPEC	Organisations of Petroleum Exporting Countries
SDG	Sustainable Development Goals
SRM	Solar Radiation Management
UK	United Kingdom
UN	United Nations
UNCTAD	United Nations Conference on Trade and Development
UNFCCC	United Nations Framework Convention on Climate Change
US	United States of America

Preface

This book has two main concerns, one of which is more intellectual, the other one more practical or political: On the one side, it aims to contribute to understanding the dynamics of long-term social change, which needs to be studied in global terms, in terms of world-history. On the other side, its writing was driven by the urgency of global warming, of the climate crisis, which has come to be experienced more strongly than ever before during the work on this book. The two concerns indeed come together when we consider the climate emergency as the most recent turn of world-history. Then, the task is to understand if and how the preceding history of human societies and their engagement with non-human nature has led – unavoidably, contingently, irreversibly? – to the current situation. This is a big task, and the hope is that this book can make a small contribution to accomplish it.

Looking back, I can say that these concerns were both already important for me when I started studying the social sciences. But they became separated, and for extended periods the scholarly interests in long-term social change overtook the practical ones in thinking about how to sustain the conditions for human life on the planet. To bring them together again, a stay at the Humanities Centre for Advanced Studies 'Futures of sustainability' at the University of Hamburg in 2019–20 has been very fruitful. Between 2016 and now, furthermore, I have been able to present the ideas, at early and at more advanced stages, that have crystallized in this book at Ural Federal University and at the Yeltsin Centre, Yekaterinburg; the Institute of Philosophy and Law of the Ural Branch of the Russian Academy of Sciences; the 4th International Symposium on Philosophy, Education, Arts and History of Science, Mugla; the Congress of the Swiss Sociological Association, Geneva; the conference 'Global history and the modern world' at the Wenner-Gren Foundation, Stockholm; on various occasions at the University of Central Asia; the Centre for the Study of Culture, Politics, and Society (CECUPS) at the University of Barcelona; the University of Tours; and the Congress of the Catalan Association for Sociology, Barcelona. I am grateful for these occasions that have allowed me to further develop my thoughts and would like to thank all those who made comments and expressed criticism.

During the final stage of writing, I have benefitted from discussions in an informal research group on environmental sociology in the Department of Sociology at the University of Barcelona and would like to thank Anna Clot Garrell, Oriol Batalla, and Iris Hilbrich, visiting fellow from Hamburg for some time, for their comments. Special thanks go to Angelo Pichierri, who read the whole draft manuscript and made numerous suggestions that certainly have helped improve the book. All remaining errors and misconceptions are my sole responsibility.

Last but certainly not least, I would like again to express my thanks to John Thompson and his collaborators at Polity Press for the continued confidence in my work and a smooth and highly competent interaction from first ideas to the published book. This expression of thanks includes the reviewers for Polity for comments and suggestions on both the initial proposal and the final draft that helped to clarify the argument and its presentation.

Barcelona, August 2023

Part I

Setting the Agenda: Biophysical Resources and Societal Self-Understandings

1

Climate Change, Modernity and Capitalism

The year is 1889. There had been ongoing debate about the consequences of industrialization for the climate on the earth. The burning of coal led to carbon dioxide emissions that accumulated in the atmosphere and were likely to make the average temperature rise across the globe. No clear hypothesis had been formulated yet. But the reasoning showed strong plausibility, and the amount of coal being burnt increased quickly year by year. In the moderate climate of the North, where industrialization took place, this prospect did not cause much concern. Rising temperatures could be an opportunity rather than a threat. After a tense international negotiation between the northern powers, a US-based hedge fund supported by its government acquired the right to exploit any resources that would be found in the Arctic. Once the ice shelf had melted, this would be the business opportunity of the next century. The engineering company working on behalf of the investors was actively developing geo-engineering measures to speed up global warming. The first experiment was scheduled to be undertaken later this same year.

This occurrence is largely forgotten. And maybe rightly so because it never happened. It only took place in Jules Verne's novel *Sans dessus dessous*, published in 1889 (in English translation entitled *The Purchase of the North Pole*). Verne may have invented the first case of climate change as intentional human action.

The plot of the novel had many of the elements we see today in debates about fossil fuels and climate change. A company driven by the profit motive acts internationally with the support of its government while hiding the detail of its planned actions and their possible consequences. An international negotiation takes place in which the great powers as well as other concerned northern states are represented. But no southern country is present, even though the geo-engineering device is to be stationed in East Africa, on the territory of the current state of Tanzania. In the end, the project fails due to a measurement error, demonstrating human hubris.

Climate change as problem solving

There is no shortage of books about climate change. The standard introduction goes as follows: climate change is one of the greatest challenges that human societies have ever faced. It has been internationally recognized as such for more than three decades, at least since the Earth Summit in Rio de Janeiro in 1992. Adequate action, however, has not been taken. The atmosphere continues warming towards unsustainable levels; extreme weather events become more frequent; the need for drastic action increases; and time is running out (for a most recent update, see Forster et al. 2023).

This is all true. But it has also often been said, even in very similar ways, and increasingly so. Over the past decade, numerous books, articles and speeches have started with sentences closely resembling the ones above. So why should there be another book?

In much of public debate, a great discrepancy between the available knowledge about climate change, on the one hand, and the lack of action, on the other, is identified and deplored. This discrepancy is often seen as the core of the issue, and this is so because climate change is considered as a highly urgent problem. Very rightly so. What is missing, though, is a convincing explanation for the persistent discrepancy. And maybe the reason why we fail to understand precisely how climate change can be combatted is exactly because from the start it has been seen as an unsolved problem that somehow emerged and with which we are confronted. This book will provide a new perspective by turning the question around. To put it provocatively: before climate change became a problem, it was a solution.

A bit more concisely: before becoming the highly urgent problem that it is today, those actions that we now know as generating climate change were, on the contrary, intentional problem-solving actions. Humankind did not ‘stumble’ or ‘slide’ into the

Anthropocene, as Dipesh Chakrabarty (2021: 40) had rather infelicitously put it. Only by understanding precisely which problems human beings intended to solve when they increasingly resorted to CO_2-emitting fossil fuels, and under which circumstances they embarked on the resource-intensive trajectory at the likely endpoint of which we now stand, will we be able to change our socio-ecological trajectory. In other words, we need to understand how our societies became so dependent on fossil fuels that we may well refer to them as carbon societies and how a social logic unfolded that made fossil fuels evermore entrenched in the fabric of these societies. To enhance this understanding is the objective of this book.

This agenda may, initially, open up more questions than it answers. To name just the most important ones:

- We agree today that current climate change is human-made, but what exactly does it entail to analyse climate change as a social phenomenon?
- Thanks to the Intergovernmental Panel on Climate Change (IPCC), we operate with a very clear connection between carbon dioxide emissions and the warming of the atmosphere, but how is this connection embedded in the broader issue of the human use of biophysical resources and the human need for non-human sources of energy?
- There has long been an opposition in our societies, often unacknowledged, between those who hold that there are 'limits to growth' (Meadows et al. 1972) and those who consider human innovativeness as opening an 'endless frontier' (Bush 1945). Has the insight into climate change altered the terms of this debate, and if so how?
- And last but not least: if we analyse climate-changing actions as attempts at problem solving, were these problems of humanity at large or problems of specific categories of human beings, defined by class, gender, 'race', location on the globe or otherwise?

The remainder of this introduction will, first, explore these questions in more detail and explain how they will be tackled and, second, give a brief outline of the way the analysis and argument will proceed.

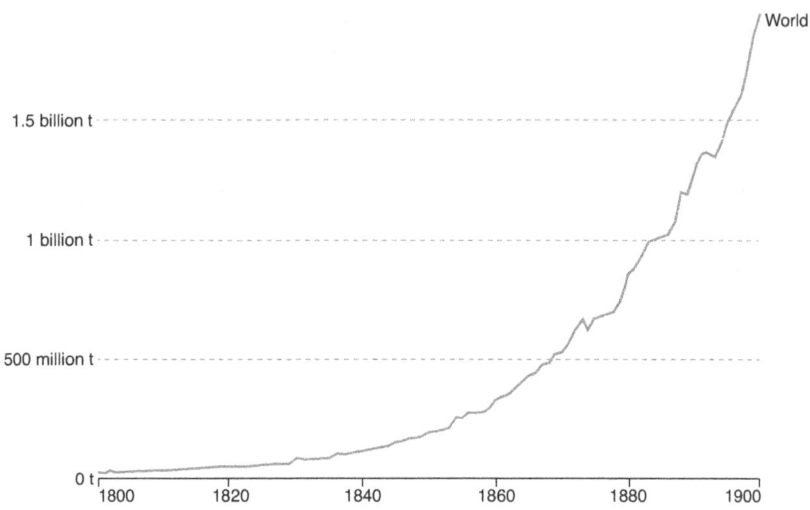

Figure 1.1 Global CO_2 emissions during the nineteenth century

Source: Hannah Ritchie, Max Roser and Pablo Rosado, 2020, *CO_2 and Greenhouse Gas Emissions*. Published online at OurWorldInData.org. at https://ourworldindata.org/co2-and-greenhouse-gas-emissions

Climate change as a social phenomenon

That human action may cause the climate of the planet to change is not a new thought. The hypothesis was first raised in the nineteenth century and directly related to the rapidly increasing burning of coal (Figure 1.1).

However, the evidence was insufficient to convincingly support the claim that a continuation on this trajectory would have catastrophic consequences for the habitability of the planet for human beings. This latter insight is due to advances in the climate and earth sciences over the past few decades, as they are now regularly assembled and interpreted by the IPCC. In due course, the new planetary knowledge has given rise to a debate about the need for a radical rethinking in the humanities and the social sciences, in which two strands of thought converge. First, it is argued that the 'modern' humanities and social sciences have been built on a radical separation from the natural sciences and that this separation needs to be undone (Descola 2005; Latour 1991; these works precede the intensification of the climate change debate but are increasingly referred to in the current context). Second, the new knowledge about the planet is seen as requiring us to reframe our search for social and historical knowledge in articulation with the planetary condition (e.g., Chakrabarty 2021).

These are fundamental questions, but they are not at the centre of this book. Rather, the following analysis is based on two quite straightforward assumptions regarding these questions, which need to be made explicit: first, human life has at all times been part of what we call 'nature' and has necessarily engaged with non-human nature. The ways in which human beings conceived of 'nature' and have engaged with non-human nature have undergone radical historical transformations, some of which will be the centre of attention in what follows. However, the view that there has at one point been a radical separation of the human and social from the natural and the concomitant rise of an instrumental relation to nature is misleading and unhelpful. In particular, this view jumps to the conclusion that there is today a need for either a return to or the creation of a more harmonious relation with nature instead of a critical analysis of the changing forms of engagement. Second, there is no doubt that the new knowledge of the planet changes our view of the 'human condition'. Not least, the insight into the dependence of human life on the state of the planet and the dangers of engaging in any action that risks altering the planetary condition without knowing the consequences, while not entirely new, has become much more concrete and specific. However, this knowledge does not profoundly alter the concepts and methods of the humanities and social sciences, provided that human beings, as just emphasized, are seen as part of 'nature' and engaged with non-human nature. Rather, it provides them with the new task of understanding phenomena of which they were not fully aware until recently.

Having said this, this book will analyse climate change as a social and historical phenomenon. But is this more than merely stating the obvious? Who speaks about climate change today means human-made climate change. Without bowing to the decreasing number of people who hold against all evidence that current climate change happens without human intervention, it is worthwhile to contemplate this possibility for a moment. It is conceivable that the temperature of the atmosphere rises due to non-human, planetary changes. This has happened before and may happen again. If current climate change were of this nature, which it is not, humankind would be employing all its available tools, including social science knowledge, to search for measures of mitigation and adaptation – just as it should be doing now. But it would not look at history and society for explanations because none would be found there. Humankind would just be trying to react to something that is happening to it. This, though, is not the situation with current climate change.

We have made it, and we need to understand why and how we have made it. (The problems that may arise when one uses the collective personal pronoun 'we' to refer to humankind will be discussed later.) This is a quite common, indeed fundamental, assumption of the social sciences. There is no reason to deviate from it in the case of human-made climate change. In turn, there is reason to reflect on the specific conceptual and methodological obstacles that pose themselves with regard to this phenomenon.

Climate change is a social phenomenon of large scale and long duration. Its scale is global or planetary. Its duration is more contested, depending on the definition, but a plausible conceptualization would date its beginning in the early to mid-nineteenth century (another issue to which we will need to return). Importantly, anthropogenic climate change is considered to be a phenomenon that, once it exists, perpetuates itself and cannot be easily undone.

These features make climate change a relatively rare, but not an exceptional, social phenomenon. Nations, civilizations and states are large-scale, long-lasting phenomena that, once created, tend to persist, even though they may also 'decline' and disappear. But in contrast to climate change, they have limited spatial extension and they exist in plurality. Coming closer, 'modernity' and 'capitalism' are large-scale, long-lasting phenomena that tend towards being global. Indeed, they are often considered as not only persisting but even expanding – in space, time and also in social permeation (see chapter 2 for more detailed discussion). Furthermore, a question to be explored in detail throughout this book, modernity and capitalism are often – though in competing ways – seen to coincide with, maybe even be causally related to, climate change.

The origins of all such social phenomena of large scale and long duration are difficult to determine; this question has occupied much of the historical social sciences (e.g., Tilly 1984). While debates are ongoing and unlikely to ever be fully resolved, it is often possible to point to some agents and arguments that supported the emergence of those large-scale, long-lasting social phenomena. Let us just recall Albert Hirschman's (1977) expression that there were 'arguments for capitalism before its triumph'. In contrast, for climate change this was not the case. While technologies of weather making have been experimented with for quite some time, nobody ever wanted to explicitly bring about climate change as we know it today, as far as my knowledge extends (or should Jules Verne's *Sans dessus dessous* make us think otherwise?).

But even such a situation is not alien to the social sciences. There are social phenomena that have been created through human agency without any human being having ever intended to create precisely this phenomenon. Max Weber's (2002 [1904/5]) analysis of the rise of modern capitalism out of an entrepreneurial spirit that emerged from the Protestant ethics is the prime example of such an approach: 'The Puritan wanted to work in a calling; we are forced to do so' (let us note in passing that he mentioned the exhaustion of fossil fuel reserves in this context). To put it briefly, we can analyse social phenomena as being created through meaningful human actions and – often spatio-temporally widely extended – chains of interaction, while acknowledging that the outcome of such actions and interactions may deviate strongly from the meaning and intention with which any of the human agents involved in it endowed their actions. For phenomena emerging over a long duration, furthermore, earlier sets of action create interim constellations, which provide different conditions and frameworks for later sets of action. Over time, thus, a trajectory of interim outcomes emerges that can be reconstructed as a causal narrative of interaction chains. It is from such a conceptual and methodological perspective that climate change will be analysed in this book (for the notion of 'unintended consequences', see Merton 1936; for its use for analysing long-term social change, see van Parijs 1982).

Climate change, energy, biophysical resources

'Climate change' is the current term for a social phenomenon that became known as such only during the second half of the twentieth century but has much earlier origins and a longer duration (e.g., Weart 2008). Due to the steady work of the IPCC since the late 1980s, we currently have a rather concise view of the issue: the rise in temperature is mostly due to the accumulation of CO_2 in the atmosphere. CO_2 levels continue rising because the gas keeps being emitted, in some settings even increasingly so, despite international agreements on emission reduction. Most of current CO_2 emissions stem from the burning of fossil fuels, in particular coal, oil and gas. For this reason, the reduction of fossil fuel use, ideally its phasing out, has become a key target of climate policy.

At the same time, the connection of climate change with fossil fuels provides the basis for the longer history of the issue. Coal was more intensely exploited from the late eighteenth century onwards, oil and gas from the late nineteenth century onwards, with their use increasing rapidly after the middle of the twentieth century when in turn the use of coal started to decline (e.g., Smil 2021; for detail, see chapters 4 and 5 below). While this framing is broadly convincing (we will raise specific queries later), it takes the form of the history of a problem. Here, though, we are interested in understanding what intensified fossil fuel use was (seen as) a solution to.

Human beings, like all living beings, need energy. In contrast to other animals, though, they have learned how to harvest energy. They have used the energy stored in wood for cooking and heating; they have used wind for transportation on the sea – and, less successfully, in the air – and for grinding wheat; and they have also used the energy of falling water for grinding grain and, later, for generating electricity. Until recently, it has remained difficult to directly transform the energy coming from the sun, the ultimate source of most energy on the earth. In contrast to wood, wind, sun and water, fossil fuels provide for a highly condensed and, at the same time, relatively easily transportable storage of energy. This can be seen as the main functional reason for the rising share of fossil fuels in human energy consumption, as most standard accounts of history would have it, not free of technical determinism. However, there have been alternatives that were not obviously functionally inferior. This is the case for dammed water, still today a main source of electricity and in many so-called developing countries a core part of energy policy after the middle of the twentieth century. Furthermore, the so-called civilian use of nuclear energy, after its military use in the Second World War, held the promise of a long-term cheap supply of energy for some time from the 1950s to the 1980s. Today, some argue for returning to that promise, given that nuclear energy does not contribute to climate change (see chapter 7 below on alternatives to fossil fuels). But it is only after the threat of climate disaster became imminent that work on improving the harvesting of wind and solar energy has seriously been undertaken. Given these alternatives, the question reasonably arises why, beyond the functional argument, our societies embarked on a fossil fuel-intensive trajectory two centuries ago and accelerated on this path until at least the end of the twentieth century. Andreas Malm (2016) developed a politico-economic argument on 'fossil capital', focusing on coal, and Timothy Mitchell (2011) had earlier elaborated a sociopolitical argument on 'carbon democracy', focusing on oil (see also DiMuzio 2015 on 'carbon capitalism'). These analyses will be critically assessed later (see chapters 4 and 5 respectively; Victor Seow's [2021] 'carbon technocracy' will be addressed in chapter 7). Let it just be said at this point that the aim of the current analysis is to be socio-historically more comprehensive. That is why we speak of 'carbon societies'.

However, the socio-ecological trajectory over the past two centuries should not exclusively be analysed as a switch from other to fossil energy sources. The period witnessed an overall growth in energy consumption, to a considerable extent enabled by resorting to the condensed energy in fossil fuels. Part of this growth can be attributed to an increasing population. But in the early industrializing countries, which carried the lion's share of energy use, energy consumption per capita also increased, in particular during the twentieth century (which is why it is mostly more appropriate to think of 'energy additions' rather than 'energy transitions'; see York and Bell 2019). The second half of that century has been labelled the age of the 'Great Acceleration' (Steffen et al. 2015), referring to exponential growth not only of energy use but of consumption of biophysical resources in general as well of the burden on the environment which goes along with it.

These brief introductory reflections show that a longer historical perspective on climate change goes along with a widening of the framework of issues. Under its current denomination, climate change appears to be an issue of the last three decades. But it refers back to the turn towards fossil fuels two centuries ago. And the switch to fossil fuels had recast the ways – in quantity and quality – in which human societies employ and exploit biophysical resources. Based on this insight, the book will first consider transformations in the ways in which human societies engaged non-human nature in the pre-fossil fuel age (chapters 2 and 3). This is a necessary step for two reasons: first, to understand the socio-ecological dynamics of human societies in general; and, second, to concisely grasp the nature of the transformation of those societies towards the intensive use of fossil fuels.

Boundaries, frontiers, hierarchies

The current debate about climate change is closely aligned with the theme of planetary boundaries. It is argued that the warming of the atmosphere is one key indicator showing that the way in which human beings inhabit this planet has limits, and that these limits are identifiable and some of them are close to being reached, if they are not even already exceeded. Bringing together a larger set of indicators, so the argument goes, one can define the 'safe operating space of humanity' (Rockström et al. 2009; most recently, see Rockström et al. 2023) and determine how far humankind can go, and no further. Moreover, a differentiated analysis can show in which world-region boundaries are already exceeded, in the sense of going beyond the average amount conceded to every inhabitant of the earth with a view to staying within the boundaries (O'Neill et al. 2018).

While the reasoning is new in the current form and in terms of the evidence by which it is sustained, it has had predecessors, of which two stand out. The 1972 Club of Rome report *The Limits to Growth* (Meadows et al. 1972) rang alarm bells in the very middle of what we now recognize as the Great Acceleration. It focused on limited availability of biophysical resources at a moment when consumption of these resources rapidly accelerated and at the same time the global population was still growing quickly. The report argued that the continuation of resource use was not sustainable, given planetary boundaries – already using the first but not literally the second of these two expressions, which became core components of ecological thinking later. *The Limits to Growth* was the first such reasoning at planetary scale, but a similar argument had already been elaborated by Thomas Robert Malthus (1798) at the very end of the eighteenth century, at smaller scale but with the ambition of demonstrating a general law. Living still largely in the pre-fossil fuel age, Malthus saw available soil for food production as the limit. From his angle, human industriousness was fully deployed, and without further natural resources available on a planet that was 'already possessed' (Malthus 1798: 63), no further growth of population was possible.

We shall look later in more detail at the contexts in which these analyses emerged and the fate they met (in chapters 3 and 8 respectively). Let it just be noted now that their findings and predictions appear to have been invalidated over time and by future human action. What was seen as a limit turned out not to be such a firm boundary at all. Such experience – or, rather, interpretation of an experience – feeds into a different view of the relation between human societies and biophysical resources: Rather than having boundaries, human existence on earth encountered frontiers that can be transgressed. The term 'frontier', today widely used in economic and environmental history, entered into the language of the historical social sciences through Frederick Jackson Turner's (2014 [1893]) thesis about the role of the western frontier in the history of the United States, which, interestingly even though problematically, links changing recourse to biophysical resources with sociopolitical change. (The term 'frontier' will be further explored and used in chapter 2 below.) In US history, it was prominently reappropriated in the 1945 report to the president entitled *Science: The Endless Frontier* (discussed in chapter 8 below).

This preceding experience of seemingly fixed boundaries having been overcome has opened the possibility of also seeing the current planetary boundaries as less firm than they are claimed to be. There is no reason to assume, so it is argued, that human ingenuity could not find ways to transgress this frontier and open up new horizons. In current debate, this view is held by many economists who use their standard toolkit to argue that the transformative power of 'innovation' will effectively mitigate climate change and create new sustainable growth paths (e.g., Aghion, Antonin and Bunel 2021 [2020]). Such supposedly expert advice is appreciated by politicians eager to claim that they can combat climate change while avoiding rocking the boat of the established resource-intensive way of life. The distinction between, on the one hand, rigid boundaries and, on the other, challenging frontiers raises the question of the certainty of scientific knowledge, in particular in relation to the action that it may provoke (to be addressed in chapter 8).

A third view manages to stay rather indifferent about the firmness or malleability of the boundary/frontier by insisting that the main issue is global social hierarchy, in more than one sense. In terms of limits, first, the risk of reaching or breaching a boundary would be much lower if resources were more equally shared. Second, existing hierarchy also entails that some groups in society are more able to impose their views on social problems and their solutions on others. Therefore, third, social hierarchy can also turn into a main cause of climate change, as the dominant classes avert calls for greater equality by enabling widespread material well-being provided through resource use (a nuanced version of this argument stands in the background of much of the analysis in part III below). And despite the global nature of the issue, fourth, the consequences of climate change will hit some world regions much harder than others, one of the reasons being the limited capacity to protect oneself from dangers (Leichenko and O'Brien 2008).

The three approaches to climate change (see Huff and Mehta 2019 and Jonsson 2019 for rather similar readings) are not entirely incompatible with each other; in many statements they are indeed combined in one way or another. But the different emphases lead to different inclinations towards action, an issue to which we shall come at the end of this analysis. Moreover, they are often also supported by different socio-theoretical approaches to climate change, thus increasing the difference of perspective between them.

Modernity, capitalism, power

The proposal by earth scientists to call the current planetary age the Anthropocene was motivated by the insight that humankind itself had become a geological force, altering the state of the planet by its actions (Crutzen 2002; Crutzen and Stoermer 2000). Climate change is one key outcome of this force. Within the intense debate triggered in the humanities and social sciences, as already mentioned above, one key question has been the precise role attributed to humankind when using this new epochal designation. Clearly, a large part of the current global population contributes little to almost nothing to climate change in terms of CO_2 emissions – while many of them suffer over-proportionally. Historically, there have been negligible CO_2 emissions from outside Western Europe and

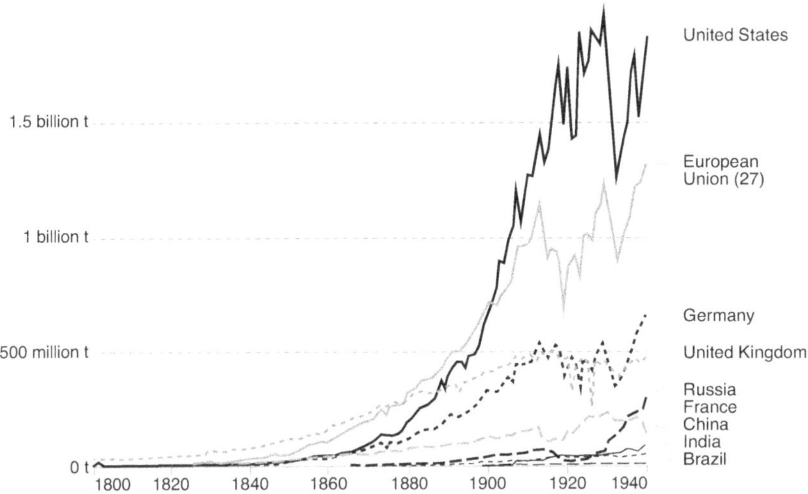

Figure 1.2 CO_2 emissions, selected countries, 1800–1940 ('European Union (27)' refers to the current territory of the EU)

Source: Hannah Ritchie, Max Roser and Pablo Rosado, 2020, *CO_2 and Greenhouse Gas Emissions*. Published online at OurWorldInData.org. at https://ourworldindata.org/co2-and-greenhouse-gas-emissions

North America (except the Soviet Union from the 1930s) until the middle of the twentieth century (Figure 1.2).

While it is doubtful whether the mere reference to the human being (*anthropos*) already implies that *all* human beings contribute to altering the state of the planet, or even that they do so in *equal* measure, the debate has at least had the merit of raising the question of the impact of different people and world regions on the planet and its atmosphere, now legally loosely defined as a case of 'common but differentiated responsibilities' (the principle was developed in the 1970s; from the 1990s, it has appeared in many international documents, including the Paris Agreement on climate change of 2015; see below, chapters 6 and 8).

As we have seen before, climate change is closely associated with fossil fuel use, and the use of fossil fuels reached new dimensions with the deep mining and industrial employment of coal from the early nineteenth century onwards. This observation coincides neatly with theorems about the origins of 'modern society' or 'modern capitalism', as elaborated in the historical social sciences. From this angle, theorists of modernity and capitalism have intervened in the debate about the Anthropocene, not least aiming to identify the sources and dynamics of the new geological force, with the former tending to accept that the human species is at the root of the issue and the latter seeing only the capitalist class in this position.

For our purposes, this dispute translates into the question of which kinds of problem were meant to be solved by increasing the use of fossil fuels – and thus generating climate change – and whose problems these were. The mainstream thinking about modernity, crudely summarized, holds that pre-modern societies tied their members into prescribed customs and ascriptive hierarchies and showed only limited material development. Modernity addressed both problems by, first, promising and, later, largely achieving 'abundance and freedom', to use Pierre Charbonnier's (2020) recent formula (the historical promises of modernity and capitalism before their triumph are analysed in chapter 3 and reviewed as possible driving forces of climate change in chapter 10). Current critical reviews of the history of modernity in the light of climate change, however, point to the way in which these problems were solved. In Dipesh Chakrabarty's (2021: 32) striking expression, 'The mansion of modern freedoms stands on an ever-expanding base of fossil fuel use.' This reasoning suggests that the problems are indeed those of the human species. Even if not all human beings benefited from their solution at the same time, or some human beings not at all until now, the trajectory is clearly outlined: the increase of freedom and material well-being goes along with the increasing use of fossil fuel and, thus, climate change.

In turn, critical theorists of capitalism would mostly not entirely deny the achievement of (some kind of) freedom and functionality due to the combined political and economic revolution towards modernity. However, they underline the existing social hierarchy at the origins of modernity and capitalism, which entails an asymmetric capacity for agency or, in short, an asymmetry of power. Social problems may be very widely defined as freedom and material well-being, but they will tend to be addressed as the problems of the dominating class, which are capital accumulation and control of workers, entailing exploitation and oppression of the dominated class. In this view, as updated for our times, the resort to fossil fuels leads onto that way of politico-economic development that serves the dominating class (this is, in short, Malm's [2016] reasoning). The approach implies that other ways may have been possible, which would not have had climate change as a consequence, but that they were not adopted for reasons of domination and hierarchy.

Undeniably, most human societies are marked by social hierarchies, and this was very pronouncedly the case for those West European societies that were the site of the supposed origins of modernity and capitalism. Ahead of more detailed investigation (in chapter 4 below), it is less evident that the dominant class at the time was a capitalist class and that using fossil fuels solved its problems, disregarding the social problems of the rest of society or even at the expense of those. In a long-term perspective covering several socio-ecological transformations, it is advisable to take a broader approach: social hierarchies entail an asymmetric distribution of power – not only within but also between societies. From positions of higher power, the chances of defining the problems that are going to be addressed and solved is greater than from lower positions. But, moreover, it is useful to distinguish different sources of power, such as political, economic and ideological power (broadly following Mann 1986 who in turn draws on Giddens 1984), and to allow for the possibility that the powers are variably distributed. In other words, the power of specific social groups needs to be identified and the potential of power struggle with other groups explored (this conceptual reasoning is further developed in chapter 9).

This approach still leaves open the possible conclusion that the combined political and economic power of a capitalist class was overarchingly dominant and set modern societies on the trajectory of climate change. However, this is no longer the starting assumption. Rather, this approach would introduce the ideological power that comes with the 'promissory notes' (Wittrock 2000) of modernity from the beginning. And, as indeed the following analyses will show, the picture has subsequently become much more complicated, in particular since the middle of the twentieth century.

Problems, resources and interpretations: the approach

To further explicate the approach to climate change that will be taken in what follows, these two socio-theoretical explanations of long-term social change serve as a backdrop. Systematically investigating resource constraints, as well as the sociopolitical opportunities that the exploration of resource frontiers offered, a step towards an 'alternative history of modernity', which Dipesh Chakrabarty (2021: 183) saw as urgently needed in his writings on climate change, is taken. Such an alternative history of modernity develops a new angle on human history in two main respects: First, it connects the history and sociology of modernity and capitalism to the 'long' history of humankind by focusing on continuities and ruptures in the human use of biophysical resources. Second, it provides a larger frame for understanding human social organization, emphasizing biophysical resources, on the one hand, and societal self-understandings, on the other. 'Material' and 'ideational' elements, in Max Weber's sense, are thus joined in a more fundamental way, turning the available theories of modernity and capitalism into specifications, as well as indicating what they are specifics of.

The two main approaches, namely, share two characteristics, one of a general, the other of a more specific kind, which are problematic and in need of revision. First, they operate with some notion of a determining, or at least hegemonic, logic. Thus they leave only a very limited space for human agency and historical contingency. It would be wrong to say that they do not leave such space at all; some analyses go deeply into what is seen as decisive actions. However, the point of such analysis mostly is to show that such action made sense and could hardly be otherwise because of a functional requirement or the state of competition and class relations. While there is detail and nuance in the more sophisticated historical reconstructions from either side, one will be hard pressed to find 'events', understood as structure-transforming occurrences (Sewell 2005), other than those that confirm the presupposed logic.

Second, both approaches show only limited openness to the questions as to how a problem and the need for action are defined and who does the defining and the acting. For functionally oriented social theories, there is an obvious answer. (Mainstream political theories, it may just be said in passing, link freedom to reason to determine the superior solution by theoretical fiat.) Functionally superior decisions and actions tend to be rewarded, and inferior ones penalized. Over the long run, inferior social arrangements will be abandoned and will collapse and disappear, as was recently argued with regard to Soviet socialism. From this linear-evolutionist perspective, which has certainly not disappeared from social theorizing, though, it is a problem, and not a minor one, that the apparently superior trajectory of increasing fossil fuel intensity has run into a dead end. Theories of capitalism are somewhat more open because of their less monolithic assumptions. There are two key collective actors that are in conflict with each other, the capitalists and the working class, even though one of them is hegemonic. And the hegemonic class is exposed to two key issues: the competition among enterprises, and the resistance of the working class. These more complex, as well as more conflicting, assumptions encourage the painting of a more nuanced picture. Most importantly, they locate the dynamic of resource expansion directly in social conflict.

Nevertheless, the range of problem definitions and of interest of actors remains reduced, and to a considerable degree predetermined, in theories of capitalism. There are conceptually preconstituted groups – social classes – whose interests are basically known beforehand. These classes confront each other in different historical constellations, and the chances of asserting their interests vary, but the greatest advantage always resides with the capitalist class. The possibility that a changing constellation may require collective interpretative work to define what problems have arisen and what action may be demanded by whom and for what purpose remains underestimated. Such an approach falls short if the histories of capitalism and modernity are to be more adequately understood as sequences of major social transformations, the experience of which mobilized collective creativity to interpret these experiences and act in the light of those interpretations, always granting that such interpretative work is undertaken in hierarchical contexts with an asymmetric distribution of interpretative agency and power (Wagner 2008).

Therefore, the following analysis will focus on such reinterpretations of key societal problems, given the changing foundations of societies in biophysical resources. In doing so, the two approaches to social theory just described will be drawn upon, but they will be placed in a broader conceptual frame. More concretely, chapter by chapter, social transformations will be characterized, first, in terms of the changes in the use of biophysical resources and, second, in terms of the societal reinterpretations of their situations and the main problems they face, or what I have called elsewhere their societal self-understanding (Wagner 2012). Functional achievement, social conflicts and hierarchies, and institutional transformations, all of which are the focus of standard historical sociologies of modernity and capitalism, will be 'sandwiched' in between and, as a consequence, often take on a different meaning and significance.

This broad approach translates into a sequence of research questions. First, it needs to be explored whether any prevailing logic of social interaction shapes the path of increasing fossil fuel intensity, and, if so, from when. Second, assuming that no single logic prevails globally across long stretches of history, there may be changing constellations of plural logics, which need to be identified in their historical contexts. Third, as just outlined, not even a plural constellation of logics will fully determine the path of human use of biophysical resources. Thus we need to get a sense of to what degree regularities impose themselves under certain conditions and to what degree creative reinterpretation of problems alters the course of history. Towards this end, I postulate that there may be critical junctures at which a social configuration encounters limits and is more open to creative change than at others. At the same time, a path of development may also lead to social tipping points, after which change is difficult, if not impossible, to reverse. (These historico-conceptual reflections are pushed one step further in chapter 2, and the findings of the historico-sociological analysis in this light will be summarized in chapter 10.)

On method

One straightforward objection to this approach is that it is quite simply not feasible. At first sight, it appears as if the ambition were to provide a comprehensive analysis of global history over several millennia, adopting a perspective from which it has not yet been studied. Some recent works in global history have indeed been very ambitious. But those authors who aimed at developing a comprehensive perspective on all – or at least most – aspects of social life limited themselves to periods of a century or little more, and furthermore they focused on the more recent past for which more sources are available (e.g., Bayly 2004; Osterhammel 2009). Others who dared to consider longer time spans scrutinized more specific questions, such as empires (Burbank and Cooper 2010; Darwin 2007), migration (Belich 2009), economic transformations (Parthasarathi 2011; Pomeranz 2000), even single commodities (Beckert 2014), and more recently also climate impacts (Brooke

2014; Leroy Ladurie 2004–9). To try to do all of this at the same time would appear to be mere folly.

But, on a closer look, the task seems less daunting because it can build on foundations that are already in place. First of all, works in global history, like those just mentioned, are being drawn on. They do not only offer synthetic overviews over periods and questions; at least as importantly, they provide a truly global way of observing and reflecting, in symmetric terms, on world regions that hardly existed a few decades ago. Similarly, second, established ways of viewing human history have been challenged across the last few decades due to new research findings as well as different conceptualizations. For early history, say, roughly before 1500 CE, intersecting debates in archaeology, anthropology and history have questioned a prevailing view of a largely linear evolution of human history (e.g., Graeber and Wengrow 2021; see chapter 2 below). For early modern and modern history, that is, later than 1500 CE, these have been debates that questioned the binary of viewing the last half-millennium either in terms of the unfolding global debates originating in Europe or in terms of the rise of capitalism as shaping an emerging world economy. For both of these macro periods, these are ongoing debates, which keep raising new issues and refocusing questions. Thus, while the analysis proposed here cannot rest on firm conclusions, the debates serve as frames of reference against which to develop the new perspective as suggested here (see, in particular, chapters 3 and 4 below). Third, stimulated not least by rising public concern about resource exhaustion and environmental degradation since the 1960s and about global warming since the 1980s, research activity in environmental history has intensified (surprisingly, Jürgen Osterhammel [2009: 541] still claimed there was little such research on the nineteenth century that he could draw on). In parallel, research in intellectual and conceptual history, which is a lively area of study in the works of Reinhart Koselleck, Quentin Skinner and Michel Foucault, has turned to connecting political ideas with resource availability (key recent examples being Charbonnier 2020 and Jonsson and Wennerlind 2023). Bringing findings from these two areas of historical research together permitted me to connect resource regimes with societal self-understandings.

Fourth, I need to comment on some differences in approach and sources between the long-term perspective (in part II), here called an alternative historical sociology of modernity and capitalism, and the more fine-grained – even though necessarily still somewhat sweeping – approach to the period after the middle of the twentieth century (in part III). The former leads the historical analysis up to the middle of the twentieth century and draws on the kind of sources mentioned above while reading them from the contextual angle of identifying problems and the search for their solutions, thus enlarging the existing conceptual frame. In turn, the analyses of the more recent period, during which the 'Great Acceleration' generated global climate change, draw on political and economic sociology, environmental sociology and politics, sociology of scientific knowledge and science and technology studies, as well as contemporary history, which now throws light on events until the 1970s and 1980s, crucial both in terms of resource regimes and of a changing global constellation due to decolonization. Specialists in any of the just mentioned fields may find that the coverage of the findings is insufficient or even inadequate, maybe in particular for environmental sociology and politics, which are of core concern here. I would ask them to bear with me and consider whether my approach opens up a new perspective on the issues they are dealing with. At various points, I will try to show exemplarily why I think this to be the case.

Throughout, the focus on self-understanding and interpretations of problems requires the consultation of contemporary sources. For earlier periods, this can be done through using up-to-date historical analyses, as well as reviewing classical sources in a new light. For the more recent period, selected contemporary diagnoses will be analysed in greater detail. Still, no claim can be made that the selected interpretations are representative, which would require analysing entire interpretative fields with their various positions. Rather, the claim is that these diagnoses are exemplary in the sense of revealing something about the societal (often: elite) self-understanding of the time. Read from the current moment, furthermore, fresh insight is provided into what was known and focused upon and what neglected. The selection of texts can obviously be questioned, as no detailed reasoning can be provided here supporting their exemplariness. Even so, I hope such questioning would further the debate, rather than merely rejecting my conclusions.

Having thus set out something like a method, let me come back to the notion that this may be an impossible enterprise. As the reflections above should have made clear, climate change is a highly complex social phenomenon of large scale and long duration that defies analysis in many respects. To make it amenable to analysis, I made a few assumptions, partly for reasons of concise presentation, but partly also to keep focus in my analysis. Thus I narrowed the argument by focusing on fossil fuels as the main cause of climate change and, in a second step, by using carbon dioxide emissions and carbon dioxide concentration in the atmosphere as the main indicators of climate change – broadly following the IPCC mode of reporting. This is clearly a simplification, which can be subjected to valid questioning, but it seems to be a defendable one given the significance of fossil fuels and carbon dioxide. To elaborate the reasoning and guide the presentation, I will repeatedly use figures representing CO_2 emissions (as above in Figures 1.1 and 1.2) not as conclusive evidence but to open up the questions that need to be asked.[1]

Clearly, there is much more knowledge available on issues of interest here than I have been able to consult. In general, I have followed the maxim of marginal utility: when consulting a further source on a specific topic and finding that little or no additional insight was gained, I concluded that I might have explored this topic in sufficient depth. This may often have been true, but certainly not always. Furthermore, I am aware of the fact that there are some issues of relevance where my research should have gone further, but I decided against it for the simple reason that I might never finish this book if I did so in all those situations. Thus there are cases in which further exploration is necessary, but I hope and trust that what I say on those issues reflects a depth of knowledge that is sufficient for the argument I am trying to make. Or, in other

[1] There are several publicly available sources on carbon dioxide emissions and concentration in the atmosphere. All the figures in this volume are taken from *Our World in Data* (https://ourworldindata.org/), which includes long-term historical timelines and world-regional differentiation. The data on carbon dioxide emissions have been prepared and presented by Hannah Ritchie, Max Roser and Pablo Rosado, including indications about the sources of their data and their construction (https://ourworldindata.org/co2-emissions). Unless otherwise noted, the figures refer to annual CO_2 emissions from fossil fuels and industry. The website is interactive, and readers may want to use it to look at countries other than those selected or to focus on other periods.

words, that it is sufficient to spark a discussion and further research in order to improve on the analysis.

On terminology

A note on the terminology used for energy sources is required to avoid misunderstandings. Much current debate works with a straight distinction between fossil energy sources and renewable energy sources, the main assumption being that we have to phase out the former and increase the use of the latter. For public debate, this may be a useful distinction, but it is, strictly speaking, incorrect and can be misleading. By fossil fuels, we mostly mean coal, oil and gas. When burnt, these normally release carbon dioxide into the atmosphere; that is why they are a main cause of global warming. They are sometimes also referred to as paleo-organic sources of energy, as they originated in plant residues stored in the earth over millions of years. In principle, therefore, they are renewable, only this is a biogeological process that takes too long for human purposes. By renewable sources, in turn, we today mostly mean wind and sun, as these are the sources in the exploitation of which recent progress has been made with a view to electricity production. At the same time, though, these are also the most time-honoured sources, allowing the growth of plants and animals (as well as human beings) upon which we feed, as well as providing energy for grinding grains and for movement across water.

Wood and water are renewable sources of energy, too, with water sources being reproduced through rain, and wood sources through forest growth and human forestation. But they do not play a major role in current debates for two main reasons. On the one hand, they are not seen as a major problem contributing to climate change. Hydro energy does not emit carbon dioxide, and, though the burning of wood does, it is not a major source of CO_2 emissions today. On the other hand, they are not seen as a major part of the answer to climate change either. Combatting climate change, however, requires reforestation, which limits the use of wood as an energy source. The possibilities for hydro energy are mostly already being exploited, and further building of dams meets strong local resistance on both social and ecological grounds. The use of wood and water as energy sources, though, was crucial at certain historical moments, and these will be explored in chapters 4 and 7 respectively.

Nuclear fission was considered a key source of energy between the 1950s and the 1980s, and to some extent this is still the case today. We will explore the particular place of nuclear energy with regard to climate change in chapter 7 (and subsequently in socio-political terms, too). Because of its ambiguous location in recent debates, it should just be underlined here that nuclear energy comes neither from a fossil source, as uranium is a mineral, nor is it renewable. However, only small quantities are needed to generate a large amount of electricity, and no carbon dioxide is emitted in the process. Therefore, even though non-renewable, nuclear energy can discursively be referred to as a (partial) answer in combatting climate change. (So-called breeder reactors are supposed to generate more fuel than they consume, which would turn nuclear energy into renewable energy. But, for a number of very different reasons, their development has largely been halted.)

The variety of energy sources makes it impossible today to consistently operate with a few summary categories, such as the terms 'fossil fuels' and 'renewable' sources. In a historical perspective, though, one can delineate long-lasting energy regimes with approximate categories. Thus human history during most of the Holocene until the late eighteenth century was marked by the use of organic sources of energy, derived from solar energy, as the basis of plant and animal life, as well as by the specific occurrence and – from the human point of view – availability of water and wind. As this is terminologically counter-intuitive, it needs to be noted that the term 'organic' as used here excludes 'paleo-organic' sources. Although having been used for a much longer time, these latter sources begin to regionally rise in significance from the seventeenth century onwards. In line with current usage, they will be referred to as 'fossil' energy sources. The period of the original transformation during the decades around 1800, normally called the 'Industrial Revolution', is often also described as a shift from animate to inanimate sources of energy. This expression, in turn, is understood as increasingly replacing animal and human labour with machine labour. Such terminology lends itself to emphasizing technological progress, but at the same time the need for the new machines to be powered by fossil fuels is de-emphasized. Confusion resulting from this distinction will be encountered in the debate about the sources of economic growth in the middle of the twentieth century, analysed in chapter 6.

Currently, human societies supposedly undergo a new 'energy transition', away from fossil fuels towards renewable energy sources, specifically wind and solar energy, as current rhetoric and jargon has it. However, there is more than one reason to be sceptical. First, the persistence of hydro energy and the – maybe passing – emergence of nuclear energy complicate the binary image. Second, the call for this transition emerges from a multiple challenge: mitigating climate change; staying within the limits of available resources; avoiding further environmental degradation; and achieving all this within a short time span. While some measures may work in parallel towards meeting these requirements, not all of them do. Third, and arguably most importantly, it is uncertain whether the transition as it is imagined continues to provide an adequate answer to the problems that supposedly had been addressed by the resort to fossil fuels. While the first two issues can largely be explored by drawing on research on energy and the environment, the third one needs a thorough understanding of the social logic of fossil fuels. I hope to have offered at least some elements for such an understanding by the end of this book.

A sequence of socio-ecological transformations: overview of the reasoning

The following presentation emphasizes moments of transformation, both of resource use and of self-understanding, because these are moments in which social phenomena become visible and interpretations explicit. I will call these periods of change socio-ecological transformations because a change in resource regime goes in parallel with a change in societal self-understanding, often also of political and economic institutions. Most of the known major transformations in the history of humankind remain significant within the larger frame adopted here, compared to more standard historical sociologies, but they appear in a different light. In anticipation of the later detailed analysis, these differences shall be briefly highlighted.

The 'neolithic' or 'first agricultural revolution' (from *c.* 10,000 BCE) is often seen as an evolutionary transition from nomadic hunter and gatherer societies to settled agriculture-based societies. While it certainly entailed a shift in resource use, it is uncertain whether such shift made societies more 'affluent' or even resource supply more stable. In the light of recent evidence, it is also doubtful whether any such 'revolution' occurred with expectations or intentions of this kind.

Some of the emerging settled agricultural societies expanded widely in space and developed strong social hierarchies, creating imperial formations (*c.* 3000 BCE – 1500 CE). With limited changes in technology, though, they did not achieve significant higher resource use per capita; they are, rather, marked by a more accentuated division of social labour and by more pronounced social hierarchies (the early history of human societies is briefly treated in chapter 2, less in terms of a comprehensive account than in terms of opening up questions for subsequent analysis).

The next major revolution in the human use of biophysical resources occurred with the development of the 'trilateral Atlantic trade' regime after 1500. It took place in parallel with a major rethinking of the conceptual bases of human social organization. The reference to the period between 1500 and 1800 as 'early modernity' or 'trade capitalism' that precedes 'industrial capitalism' is misleading, as it sees the era only as a forerunner of later developments (chapter 3).

The close coincidence of the Industrial Revolution and the French Revolution has made the decades around 1800 a key reference point for conceptualizing both modernity and capitalism. To understand better the – historical as well as conceptual – relation between the two, one needs to analyse if and how the expectational connection between 'abundance and freedom' was based on the exploitation of the 'first vertical frontier' of resource use, namely the deep mining of coal and iron ore (chapter 4).

The exploration of the 'second vertical frontier' of crude oil and gas, from the late nineteenth century onwards, is often seen in the developmental continuity of 'industrial society' or 'industrial capitalism'. It is overlooked that the new resources supported bringing about a major and crisis-driven transformation of western, early industrializing societies (chapter 5). One can identify the origins of this transformation as around 1900, but it was fully and consciously brought about after the end of the Second World War and the defeat of Nazism, generating the current resource-intensive form of social organization in the West against the background of the political crises of the interwar period.

With this insight, the analysis moves from a historical, broadly chronological and rather sweeping presentation (in part II) to a more fine-grained one, identifying the different aspects and components of social problem solving based on biophysical resources (in part III). The origins of the move towards high fossil-fuel intensity lie in the middle of the twentieth century, when the purpose was to consolidate democracy without relinquishing the power and privileges of the elites in one world region, the West (chapter 6). Once this has been ascertained, the question arises as to what are the characteristics of fossil fuels that lent themselves to such endeavour and whether alternatives to fossil fuels were explored during the early post-Second World War decades (chapter 7). Given that knowledge about the negative consequences of the fossil fuel path existed, furthermore, one needs to ask what knowledge attitudes prevailed over the increasingly substantiated ecological concerns (chapter 8). These insights are subsequently brought together (in chapter 9) to identify problem displacement as the key component of the social logic of fossil fuels.

These analyses lead in parallel towards the 1970s, a period that is identified as a crisis moment for the fossil fuel trajectory in the West and as a critical juncture in world-historical developments. A 'problem squeeze' in western societies had the effect that fossil fuel intensity did not increase in the West from the late twentieth century onwards, but did globally, in particular in East and South Asia, exacerbating the climate crisis. While this change could be read as the mere diffusion of the resource-intensive trajectory from the West to the East, it signals a major transformation of the global political constellation, as well as a further acceleration of human-made climate change (part IV). This insight forces us, but it also enables us, to critically review ideas of the logics of expansion driven by population growth and/or the striving for profit, comfort or freedom and to envisage possible futures (chapter 10). On this basis, too, the key components can be identified that are necessary to break with the social logic of fossil fuels (chapter 11).

Part II

An Alternative Historical Sociology of Modernity and Capitalism

2
Logics of History

Thus far, I have set the current and global phenomenon of human-made climate change into the broader historical context of the human use of fossil fuels and, still broader, of biophysical resources in general. This step entails an enormous widening of the angle and the need to gather and interpret information from a broad range of fields of knowledge. In turn, it makes it possible, in principle, to distinguish different relations of human beings to biophysical resources and to identify the major historical transformations of those relations. We borrow from William H. Sewell, Jr. (2005) the notion of 'logics of history' to explore the questions of whether human history moves in any identifiable direction and what the driving forces for historical change are.

When analysing anthropogenic climate change, an underlying empirical assumption is, as it cannot be otherwise, that the human use of biophysical resources, and of fossil fuels in particular, has historically been increasing. If this were not the case, we would not face climate change today. The historical data about carbon dioxide emissions serve to sustain this view. In a standard representation (see Figure 2.1), they show steadily rising emissions from the middle of the nineteenth century onwards – the world economic crisis and the Second World War are visible as dips – as well as the apparently exponential growth after the middle of the twentieth century, now known as the Great Acceleration.

But graphic representations are treacherous. Had we only selected the period from 1850 to 1914, we could detect something like exponential growth between 1890 and 1914 (see Bonneuil and Fressoz 2016 [2013]: 70), the period sometimes called the first era

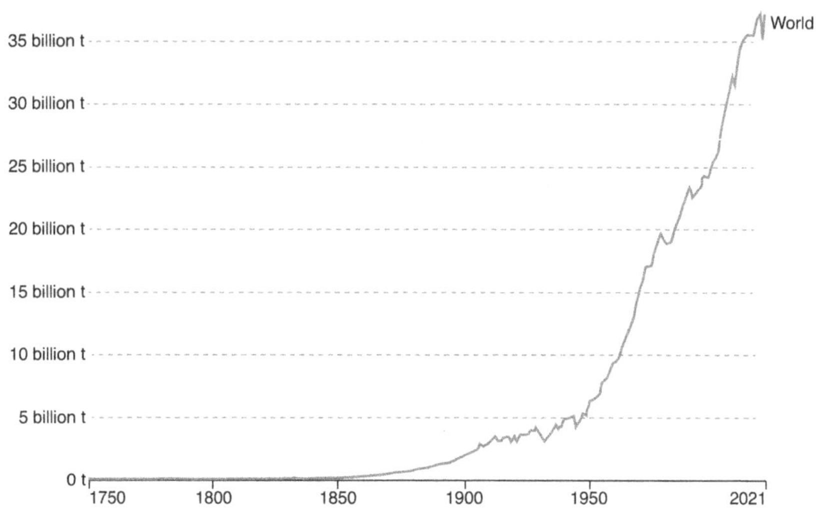

Figure 2.1 Global CO_2 emissions, 1750–present

Source: Hannah Ritchie, Max Roser and Pablo Rosado, 2020, *CO_2 and Greenhouse Gas Emissions*. Published online at OurWorldInData.org. at https://ourworldindata.org/co2-and-greenhouse-gas-emissions

of globalization (e.g., Baldwin and Martin 1999), which some may want to rebaptize the First Great Acceleration. More importantly, data curves of this kind tend to be read prematurely as indicating steady and linear evolution, in this case as confirming a connection between the beginnings of modernity and/or modern capitalism and climate change. Without further analysis, though, we could equally well be looking at a series of historical transformations rather than a linear development. And rather than assuming the reign of a single logic as cause of the development, we may have to grasp the interrelation of plural logics, if any, at work in those transformations to understand how humankind has arrived at the point where we are now. This is the task of this book, and I will start it with some conceptual explorations and a look at the question of socio-ecological transformations in early human history.

Scarcity and frontiers

Human beings need food and shelter. Non-human nature provides the potential for food and shelter, but it does not offer it. Human beings have to avail themselves of the possibilities that non-human nature provides, and this is not without effort or danger. In some broad sense, human beings have necessarily an instrumental relationship to non-human nature, namely as using nature to satisfy human needs. We may call this the 'relationship between nature and economy' (Jonsson and Wennerlind 2023), using the latter term for the way human beings approach the question of satisfying their material needs (see also Jonsson et al. 2019).

Once this is acknowledged, there remain a large variety and diversity of ways in which the relation of human beings to non-human nature can be represented. One of them is through the concept of scarcity, indeed a central concept in the economic sciences. Insisting that there is not simply one economic concept, Fredrik Albritton Jonsson and Carl Wennerlind (2023) have recently tried to map the 'varieties of scarcity' across the past half-millennium in the – mostly European – history of ideas, identifying two basic ways of interpreting the relation between nature and economy, one which emphasizes 'the bounty of natural resources, the power of human ingenuity, and the insatiability of desires', whereas the other underlines 'limits, unintended consequences', and the importance of 'moderation and constraint' in the satisfaction of needs that indeed are simple and not unlimited. They refer to the former as the 'cornucopian' concept of scarcity, from ancient Greek for 'horn of plenty', and to the latter as the 'finitarian' concept. Their approach succeeds in demonstrating this persistent variety of interpretations of the problem of scarcity. Based in intellectual history, though, it only loosely relates the changing conceptions of scarcity – partly alternating, partly competing – to changes in the actual satisfaction of material needs. For our purposes, we need to more closely connect societal self-understandings, among which are conceptions of scarcity, to ecological regimes of resource use.

The basic meaning and significance of scarcity seem to be self-evident. People starve because they do not have enough food. They freeze to death because they lack shelter or, increasingly due to climate change, they die because they cannot protect themselves from heat. The lack of sufficient food and shelter to go on living may be called absolute scarcity. Absolute scarcity was and remains a significant phenomenon; possibly, it becomes even more significant (again) in our time. For better or worse, however, scholarly and public discussion of scarcity has strongly shifted to other aspects. Traditionally, to speak loosely, economics has dealt with the satisfaction of material needs, as the ancient Greek term referred to the knowledge of running a household. Thus biophysical resources always stood at its centre, and absolute scarcity was a constant possibility. This remained the case until the early nineteenth century. Thomas Robert Malthus, whose focus on scarcity of natural resources has already been mentioned, was a contributor to the field of political economy. The 'modern' economic sciences, though, focus on the allocation of resources, rather than on their availability. Therefore, they tend to make scarcity relative, namely a situation in which a group has less of a good than it desires to have. Mainstream economics also has a solution to scarcity thus defined, namely market exchange regulated via prices. If the demand for a good is higher than its availability, then prices will rise, which in turn will create an incentive to produce more of this good. Note that material resources disappear in the background in this reasoning (we will come back to this issue in later chapters). In this perspective, more precisely, the allocation of scarce goods will be determined by 'effective demand', which connects the wish to have a good with the ability and willingness to pay for it at market prices. Useful at it is under some assumptions, this concept neglects what one can call cultural and social scarcity. The cultural value of a good refers to the way it is prized – in contrast to priced – in a given cultural context, and it can be scarce or abundant with no relation to its actual price or the production cost in the background. Social scarcity refers to goods that are generally sufficiently available but cannot be accessed by certain social groups.

Despite this widening of its understanding, scarcity remains in some broad way related to supply or availability, and in most cases ultimately to some lack in supply or availability of biophysical resources, however mediated (one may consider that there are also 'social limits to growth' [Hirsch 1976], but this question will not be discussed here). Beyond the economic expression 'supply' and the apparently technical-managerial term 'availability', the expressions 'boundaries', 'limits' and 'frontiers' have been widely used in relation to biophysical resources. At first sight, all three terms have the same meaning. They all refer to space, be it literally or metaphorically, and they all appear to refer to the point up to which resources are available. As briefly mentioned earlier, though, this is not at all the case today. Looking impressionistically at current usage, the term 'limits' refers to a point beyond which one cannot go. It has some rigidity to it, as used in the title of the report *Limits to Growth*. As an expression in ecological debate, the word 'limit' seems to have increasingly been replaced by 'boundaries', most prominently in the term 'planetary boundaries'. Both words are predominantly being used as a warning signal, but there may be a significantly different connotation: 'boundaries' are not a point beyond which one cannot go; they are a point beyond which one should not go because of the dangers that such transgression will entail. A 'boundary' is less rigid than a 'limit', but the possibility for humankind to transgress it makes it an even stronger signal. Unlike 'limit', it does not point to incapacity; it points to the hubris of being capable of transgressing but incapable of mastering, or even understanding, the consequences. Despite the originally almost synonymous use, in contrast, the term 'frontier' has taken on a very different meaning since it was used by Frederick Jackson Turner (2014 [1893]) to characterize the westward expansion of the United States during the nineteenth century. The concept of frontier now came to refer to an existing limit or boundary, but one the transgressing of which was not only possible but would bring benefits, even in terms of major social change. (We will come back to the US 'frontier' in chapters 4 and 5.)

Using – cautiously – this terminology, one may want to say that human societies try to transgress existing resource frontiers when and because they are driven by scarcity, a fruitful hypothesis pursued in detail by Edward Barbier (2011) that expresses in very general terms the approach taken here. It is with a view to solving topical problems that human societies expand their use of biophysical resources and, from a certain level and type of resource use onwards, generate climate change. The general statement, though, needs considerable context-specific elaboration.

Considering first the scarcity aspect, we need to ask whether scarcity was recognized as such, and whether it was seen as a problem that can and should be solved. Moreover, for each situation, we need to understand whether scarcity was absolute and the survival of (parts of) the population was at stake for frontiers to be explored and transgressed, or whether it was relative. Problems of relative scarcity, in turn, may have tended to be addressed through different kinds of solutions: cultural and social scarcity may be created for certain goods and certain sociocultural groups with a multiple purpose and/or effect, namely to generate cultural distinction, to entrench social domination, and to avoid exploring new resource frontiers. The assumption here is that a certain social hierarchy and power differential must exist for scarcity to become socioculturally differentiated. But this hierarchy may exist within a society or also between societies (bearing in mind that social configurations are not always as closed and coherent as the term 'society' tends to suggest).

Second, coming to the frontier aspect, the general question is when and how what appears as a limit or boundary can come to be interpreted as a frontier to be explored and transgressed with a view to solving a scarcity problem. The currently used term 'planetary boundaries' is meant to suggest that there is no space for interpretation any longer; we will come back to that implication. Inadvertently, though, the term directs attention to the repeated transformation of spatial boundaries into frontiers by human beings in the recent history of the planet. Inspired by Barbier, historical socio-ecological transformations will subsequently be discussed as the transgression of horizontal and vertical terrestrial and maritime frontiers. Moreover, the increasing figurative use of the term 'frontier' points to another tool of reinterpretation of the relation between scarcity and frontiers, namely overcoming scarcity through new knowledge. The formula leaves it open whether a frontier will be transgressed through innovation, through expansion of the space from which resources are drawn, or whether a frontier is rather confirmed by creating social scarcity due to increased prices that only some social groups can afford to pay.

Logics of history (1): unstoppable expansion

The conceptual couple of scarcity and frontiers provides a general tool for analysing human history in the light of the expanding use of biophysical resources. In the brief preceding characterization, I have suggested that historico-contextual analysis is required to see how human frontier expansion can be understood through the prism of the numerous conceptual possibilities that this coupling opens up. Beyond emphasizing such variety, though, scholars have also tried to identify an underlying logic of expansion, which would explain the long-term trajectory on which human societies have embarked with regard to the use of biophysical resources.

Three main arguments for such logic have been evoked, and each of them can itself be placed in the historical context within which it was originally elaborated and within the intellectual trajectory that it pursued in the light of further socio-ecological transformations.

The first one is *biological-demographic*. Like other living beings, humans are driven by a quest for self-preservation, both as individuals and as a species. They have become the most successful species, having spread across the globe and increased their number from something like a few million at the beginning of the Holocene to eight billion today. There is no need here to explore the specific capacities of human beings – such as language, tool making – that have made this domination possible. For current purposes, we are only interested in the impact of the use of those capacities that leads to expansion. From early on in Holocene human history, one can distinguish two kinds of such impact, one leading to crisis and the other one stemming from success.

On the one hand, human societies have at times used biophysical resources to the point of depletion, such as cutting forests for firewood and timber, or to the point of degradation of the environment, such as overusing fertile soil. Hunting may also have already led to the extinction of some species of large mammals. Such consequences were territorially circumscribed, and, whenever possible, the reaction of human societies was to move or to expand across space. (We recognize here the good historical reason for the spatial reference or metaphor in our current concepts.) Under viable environmental conditions, on the other hand, the population of human societies has tended to grow. As a consequence, the available resources on the territory they inhabit may become insufficient to feed the growing population. Again, the response often was to inhabit larger spaces. One may be tempted to merge these two kinds of impact into one, as the common problem is the lack of sufficient resources, and the common answer is expansion in space. However, in the first case the problem emerges from decreasing supply, and in the latter from growing demand.

A further remark is in order about the relation between the local and the global. During much of the Holocene, the resource problems that human societies encountered or created were local, and they could be solved by movement in space, unless obstacles stood in the way of such a solution. I will argue later that systematic 'displacement' has become the dominant way for human societies to try to overcome ecological limits in more recent history. But here we see that, in a broad sense, such problem-solving strategy was learned early on in human history.

Despite his reputation, we will need to reconsider Thomas Robert Malthus's views at various points of our reasoning. It is useful to mention him here again. Malthus (1798) had assumed as a general law that the population of human societies tends to increase much more quickly than the possible growth of food production on available soil, the soil thus posing a limit to social development. Up to the present day, economic historians speak of 'Malthusian stagnation' for situations in which natural resource limits prevent an economy from growing (Barbier 2011: 84–91). For the argument to hold under its own assumptions, expansion in space needs to be ruled out. And indeed, Malthus had already explicitly assumed that all space on the earth is 'already possessed'. In this sense, Malthus had inadvertently theorized 'planetary boundaries', with the main boundary being the surface soil and the resources it provides. (We shall see in chapter 4 what proved him wrong, and in chapter 9 in which sense he may still be right.)

Right or wrong, Malthus had provided a biological-demographic explanation for the tendency of human societies to expand, while at the same time implying that such expansion would come to a halt whenever the biophysical resources available to a given society turned insufficient to secure survival. Roughly at the time of Malthus's writings, two *social* theories were elaborated that similarly diagnosed a tendency of human societies to expand but offered different understandings for such tendencies. Both of these theories emerged from the Enlightenment context, as did Malthus's, but in contrast to Malthus they both assumed that recent social change had decisively altered the human condition, or at least had the potential for doing so. In the brief discussion that follows, we will re-encounter the theories of modernity and capitalism, which were introduced in the preceding chapter in terms of the general approach they take to social change. Here we focus more specifically on their identification of a logic of expansion, of driving forces for social change, that they saw as having emerged in recent history (and we will meet these theories at later points again; a concluding discussion will be found in chapter 10).

A *sociopolitical* approach combines a view of history as the realization of freedom with an account of social transformations as a path towards higher functional achievement. The idea of the realization of freedom in the course of history was proposed by scholars such as Condorcet and Hegel, but it remains pervasive today – surprisingly, many might say. Three recent examples may suffice: neo-modernization theorists point to empirical evidence, mostly based on surveys and statistical indicators, that suggests steady, if uneven, progress in this direction. A forceful recent example is *Freedom Rising* by Christian Welzel (2013), a close collaborator of world values researcher Ronald Inglehart. Social philosophers, in turn, hold a somewhat similar view, though they maintain it by quite different means. In a post-Hegelian perspective, Axel Honneth, for instance, suggests that historical sequences of claims for recognition and the struggles to achieve them enhance the conditions for human autonomy, recently in *Das Recht der Freiheit* (2011). This approach is open to considerations of historical contingencies as well as to paradoxes in the realization of normative claims, but it is firm on the notion of freedom as the core principle of recent history. Merging elements of the Christian theology of liberation with a decolonial perspective, Enrique Dussel, in turn, sees world history as being shaped by struggles for liberation (*Política de la liberación*, 2007).

At first sight, it is not at all evident why the growth of freedom should go along with increasing human use of biophysical resources. In this thinking, however, it was assumed that free societies would adopt institutional arrangements that increased the capacity of solving social problems. Present in political economy and in Hegel, but fully elaborated by Talcott Parsons in the twentieth century, the core idea was that 'modern societies' are based on the differentiation of social institutions according to the functions that they are meant to fulfil. The key example is the principle of market self-regulation in organizing for the satisfaction of human material needs. Liberating economic actors from oversight and regulation by the state would not only enhance freedom but, due to functional differentiation, would also increase the 'wealth of nations'. Thus it may be legitimate to also assume that such increase in wealth would go along with greater use of biophysical resources. (The connection, though, is not always explicit, and we will explore it further in chapter 3.) In this light, the conjoined commitment to enhance wealth and freedom can be said to be at the basis of a sociopolitical logic of expansion in the use of biophysical resources.

There are two variants of the sociopolitical approach that should be mentioned at this point because they will become relevant in the later detailed investigation. The institutionalist approach suggests that stability of institutional frameworks in which free human action can unfold is a key determinant of social development (Daron Acemoglu and James A. Robinson are current key proponents). In turn, what we may call the techno-epistemic approach emphasizes the human capacity to develop innovative solutions for problems to overcome existing constraints (Joel Mokyr is a current key proponent). Current versions of both approaches make strong claims to provide valid interpretations of long-term historical change, including an understanding of world-regional differentiation, and as such they are of relevance for our reasoning. They are variants of the sociopolitical approach because they both similarly connect freedom with creation of wealth. However, they do not start out from basic assumptions about human behaviour such as the striving for freedom or for greater wealth – or maybe better: they take such assumptions for granted – but look either at the conditions under which human strivings can play themselves out most fully or at the means through which such strivings are most successful. As such, they focus more on historical junctures than on overarching explanations of human history, and it is in this light that I need to address them at later points of my reasoning (in particular, chapter 4, for the institutionalist approach, and chapters 8 and 10 for the techno-epistemic approach).

By and large, the sociopolitical approach, including these two variants, evaluates positively the socio-historical transformation and the new trajectory of 'modern' societies that it diagnoses. Devoted to explaining the same transformation, the *politico-economic* approach makes a more critical assessment. In turn, it arrives at a much more clear-cut identification of the expansionist dynamics of these modern societies, here called capitalist. With economic activity organized in competitive markets and society divided between the owners of the means of production and those who only have their labour power to sell, there are two sources of conflict that push for expansion. First, the competition between companies forced capitalists to persistently search for new ways of making profit, at the risk of otherwise falling behind. Similarly, and second, the class struggle between bourgeoisie and proletariat limited profit opportunities whenever the workers made gains, and thus forced capitalists to search for new such opportunities. Both these struggles led to the 'tendency of the rate of profit to fall', unless countervailing tendencies could be unleashed. Against this background, Rosa Luxemburg (1951 [1913]) arrived at the conclusion that the reproduction of capitalism depended on the steady expansion into hitherto 'non-capitalist' spheres of social life. She developed this theorem in the context of the imperialist expansion of the late nineteenth century, but her notion of 'land seizure' (*Landnahme*) should be understood both literally and figuratively. Given that intensified exploitation of nature, be it directly as 'land-grabbing' or through new extraction techniques, certainly can be considered as *Landnahme*, this concept figures strongly in the recent integration of ecological concerns into Marxist thought.

At this early stage of our reasoning, one can plausibly assert that there is some validity to all three explanations for the tendency of humankind to historically increase its use of biophysical resources. Given that the proposals are not entirely incompatible with each other and could rather be considered as somewhat complementary, moreover, one might even say that, taken together rather than as monocausal explanations, they provide sufficient reasoning for understanding the long-term background to our fossil fuel-intensive societies and climate change. (York and colleagues [2003] take a different, namely indicator-based rather than historico-interpretative, approach to empirically testing 'environmental impact theories'.) Nevertheless, this constellation of explanatory approaches also raises further questions for the following, more detailed investigation.

The biological-demographic approach points to the 'success' of the human species in populating the earth, but it postulates a constant driving force over thousands of years and, thus, has little to say about why this constant force has impacted on the climate of the earth only during the past two centuries or little more. In contrast, the sociopolitical and the politico-economic approach have the advantage of indeed focusing on more recent historical transformations. To some extent, furthermore, their analyses align well with data about fossil fuel use and CO_2 accumulation in the atmosphere (as seen in Figure 2.1 above). As we shall see later, though, this is the case only to some extent, for two different reasons.

First, both the theories of modernity and capitalism remain ambiguous about dating the origins of these phenomena to the period around 1500 or around 1800, but only the latter stand aligns with resource and climate data (a question to be further explored in the next chapter). Second, neither of the two theories takes good account of transformations of the phenomena they are focused on. They tend to treat modernity and capitalism as persistent social phenomena with a fundamentally unchanging dynamic (except for some theories of capitalism to which I will refer below). Thus they show little interest in understanding the considerable increase of fossil fuel use and CO_2 accumulation during the twentieth century, even compared to the nineteenth century, nor in the further Great Acceleration since the middle of the twentieth century. These deficiencies show that, rather than a general theory of modernity and/or capitalism, we need an analysis of the transformations of modernity and/or capitalism to understand the increased human use of biophysical resources and its consequences.

Finally, we also need to deal with the differences between the sociopolitical and the politico-economic approach to the historical sociology of climate change. Maybe one can argue that the search for freedom, material abundance and profit are not utterly incompatible objectives. Maybe they can be combined in a specific societal arrangement, which would make the two approaches indeed fully complementary. As we shall see later (chapter 6), the post-Second World War period of 'democratic capitalism' in the West is sometimes seen as such a viable combination of different driving forces, although conveniently overlooking that this compromise was based on the acceleration in the use of biophysical resources. Even if this could be ascertained for our societies, though, this would still neglect the fact that members and groups within our societies are variably interested in pursuing any of the three objectives and that different kinds of power are used to reach the different objectives. Thus the question of whether the sociopolitical or the politico-economic approach is more adequate for analysing climate change remains open, and it has to be answered by a comparative analysis of socio-ecological transformations, comparative both over time and across world regions. Only historico-contextual analysis can show which problem-solving strategy will be embarked upon and which social groups lead the work of reinterpreting the problem.

The remainder of this chapter will make a first step into such historico-contextual analysis. Not a historiographical study in its own right, the chapter draws on existing work, in particular those comprehensive studies that look at world-regional connections and those studies of longer periods that aim to understand social transformations, in both cases with special interest in planetary events and in transformations of resource use. My reflections will extend to the so-called early modern period, the latter to be analysed in more detail in the subsequent chapter. The core objective is to grasp whatever logics there may have been at work in the course of early human history, given the available knowledge, and rather than any unequivocal logic of expansion, as in the above-mentioned approaches, I will conclude with only a few such elements: contingency of outcomes, given highly varied circumstances; social hierarchy as a significant 'driver' of change; and an experience-based problem-solving attitude, given the lack of broader orientation and only weak control over the outcome of action.

Logics of history (2): contingency and hierarchy

The history we are referring to here is the history of human life during the Holocene, that is, roughly the last 12,000 years. The Holocene was marked by relative climate stability – not really stable in the strict sense, as we shall see, but stable in comparison to the earlier Pleistocene and, as it seems, to the successive era of human-made climate change in which we now live. The climate stability of the Holocene is widely seen as having been the condition for the domestication of plants and animals by human beings, in other words the beginning of agriculture and cattle breeding. The ensuing firmer territorialization of human social life meant a major transformation in the relation of human beings to biophysical resources, not least permitting an intensified resource use.

Against this background, the 'early Anthropocene hypothesis' (or 'Ruddiman hypothesis', after the scholar who first formulated it; Ruddiman 2003) holds that humankind had already become a geological force several thousand years ago. More precisely, large-scale deforestation to make land available for agriculture had led to increases in the temperature of the atmosphere. The available climate data do not show this temperature increase; they rather demonstrate the climate stability of the Holocene. However, the hypothesis suggests that the climate effects of deforestation offset a temperature decrease that would have happened in the beginning of a new glacial period. Thus human action is supposed to have inadvertently generated climate stability. The hypothesis is based on two pillars: comparative analysis of ice ages, on the one hand, and on the other, modelling of the climate effect of deforestation. Each of the pillars is somewhat shaky, and whether they together sustain the hypothesis is rather doubtful. The available data and theories are insufficient to either confirm or refute the hypothesis (Brooke 2014: 286–7; see now Ruddiman et al. 2020). For our discussion, it sensitizes to the possibility, long absolutely discarded, that human aggregate action can impact on planetary conditions. Given the state of our knowledge about human societies at that time, there are few conclusions to be drawn from the debate, except that the rise of agriculture marks the beginning of the possibility of potentially problematic increases in the human use of biophysical resources.

The history of humankind during the Holocene has often been written as the history of the rise of human civilization. Humanity, so the argument starts, first advanced from the stage of societies of hunters and gatherers to one of agricultural societies. The more settled character of agricultural societies then enabled the formation of cities, with a more differentiated division of labour. From then on, there was an increasing number of human beings who devoted their time to other tasks than providing food and care for offspring. The specialization of work, in turn, permitted the development of new forms of knowledge. A further step was reached when this knowledge enabled the use of inanimate sources of energy, the main step towards the next stage: industrial societies. This time-honoured account, here reproduced in ultra-brief and stereotypical form, has been refined with new sources of historical knowledge but keeps informing much research in the historical social sciences, as well as public debate in the supposedly 'advanced' societies. More recently, this stage conception of history has been enriched with explicit consideration of the transformation in the use of biophysical resources, distinguishing different regimes of 'social metabolism' (e.g., Fischer-Kowalski, Krausmann and Pallua 2014). As such, it has also acquired a critical edge, by pointing to the fact that later stages, and in particular the industrial one, went along with the multiplication of the per capita use of biophysical resources.

Despite the recent critical ecological turn, this view of history is informed by some notion – if not of progress, then – of ineluctability. Each successive stage was seen as marked by advantages over the preceding one in terms of the biological objective of reproduction of the species, but also in terms of the improved living conditions of the actual human beings. However, there are strong reasons – both conceptual and empirical – for thinking that this account of linear evolution in human history is built on very thin ice. A main problem of any such account is that it stretches over a very long time span – more than 10,000 years – on the basis of extremely patchy knowledge. Aiming to express the general law of human social evolution, furthermore, it claims to cover the whole globe but tends to emphasize similarities between societies over differences.

While the desire to have some such account is understandable, conceptual caution is required in the face of such large-scale and long duration. If we assume – with William Sewell, Jr. (2005), for instance – that social change is marked by collective creativity as one of its sources, and by contingency of its outcomes, then it becomes hazardous to judge the emergence of a social phenomenon – such as agriculture or cities – by its apparent functional effects rather than by its causes. In the alternative view, espoused here, those causes will ultimately be found in human actions and chains of interactions, but those actions and interactions are clearly difficult, not to say impossible, to trace for events that occurred thousands of years ago. This dilemma can be resolved by conceptual fiat or by conceptual caution. The latter option is taken here because of the inclination towards judging the past from the angle of the situation in the present when stretching the work of concepts across long time spans and large spaces.

For current purposes, such conceptual caution has recently been applied by David Graeber and David Wengrow (2021) in their reading of the history of humankind. Based, in particular, on recent advances in archaeological knowledge, they argue that there is no sufficient evidence for claiming that agriculture was functionally superior to hunting and gathering, nor that it became the dominant form of economy quickly. Rather, farming was at times adopted 'as an economy of deprivation' (Graeber and Wengrow 2021: 274), and a nomadic economy of hunting and gathering coexisted over long periods with agricultural societies, even in the vicinity and with considerable relations of exchange. Similarly, not all early cities developed a division of labour with an agricultural hinterland, nor did they inevitably increase the ecological footprint of their citizens compared to farmers (Graeber and Wengrow 2021: 283).

This cautious reading convincingly dismantles the account of history as functionally driven evolution. As a side effect, it also refutes the implication of the earlier account that increasing use of biophysical resources occurred with some degree of inevitability. The available evidence, though, does not support the elaboration of a counter-narrative in which functional achievements and resource use for such purpose play only a minor role. The course of human history was not predetermined; it was contingent, but this does not mean that there were no causes for the course that was taken, including functional ones. Moreover, the actual course that human history has taken over the past 12,000 years has formed a trajectory and, with it, has shaped human beings and the earth. As humankind made this trajectory while advancing on it, some effects of the past may have become irreversible, and the possibilities for the future were altered with the shape of the trajectory.

Discarding the a priori assumption of linear functional evolution, the task is to reconstruct the contingent transformations of human social organization that, up to the current moment, have led to increasing the human use of biophysical resources. As mentioned above, Edward Barbier's (2011) work on *Scarcity and Frontiers* is a useful guide for this task, its roots in economic theories of development notwithstanding. In contrast to evolutionary historiographies, for which location in time is central, Barbier adopts a systematic comparative perspective across world regions and asks how and with which effects different societies employed biophysical resources. He (2011: 71–2) does see 'an irrevocable link between increased food production, sustained population and economic growth, and obtaining abundant sources of natural resources and land to avoid problems of environmental degradation and scarcity' as a consequence of the agricultural transition. Nevertheless, similar to Graeber and Wengrow, most of Holocene human history demonstrates to Barbier a great variety of forms of social organization. He is inclined to explain this variety through geography and regional climate and, as historical time goes on, also through the kind of contact with neighbouring societies, all of which can have enabling as well as constraining effects on resource availability and use. Thus, even though functional – in his terminology, 'developmental' – concerns matter, there is considerable space for contingency in his account, in particular for the period until the third millennium BCE.

When we arrive at that moment in human history, the account becomes more complicated. Graeber and Wengrow are certainly right when they argue that cities have existed without the whole set of features that, in the standard account, provide them with an evolutionary advantage. As they mockingly describe that account: 'If you put enough people in one place [. . .], they would almost inevitably develop writing or something like it, together with administrators, storage and redistribution facilities, workshops and overseers. Before long, they would also start dividing themselves into social classes. "Civilization" came as a package [including] the possibility of philosophy, art and the accumulation of scientific knowledge' (Graeber and Wengrow 2021: 277).

Their discussion of recent counter-evidence is indeed illuminating and confirms the principle of conceptual caution. However, in contrast to their reasoning about the long-lasting coexistence of agricultural societies with nomadic hunter-gatherer societies, it is more difficult to deny that city-based empires had a lasting and significant impact on world history. For our purposes, we need to briefly explore whether this was due to the intensity of their resource use or for other reasons, among them maybe their elaboration of comprehensive interpretations of human life on earth, usually indeed referred to as human civilization.

Even those scholars who, like Barbier, focus on the rise of cities and their relation to the agricultural hinterland and emphasize the enabling aspects of the division of labour do not always fall in line with a linear-evolutionist account. Barbier (2011: 126–8) underlines that this economic-ecological constellation keeps suffering from 'Malthusian stagnation'. Agriculture-based settlement in environmentally conducive regions enables population growth and, in early phases, increases in 'affluence', understood as rising use of biophysical resources in terms of the theory of social metabolism (Fischer-Kowalski, Krausmann and Pallua 2014: 13–14). However, the increasing population needs to be fed, and land becomes a constraint. This constraint could be overcome by spatial expansion, by extension of trade to acquire further resources, or by technical innovation. The latter two options were also pursued, for example by creating the Silk Roads or by building waterways or irrigation systems, depending on geography. But the most characteristic option was solving the scarcity problem by frontier expansion through incorporating further territory. Arguably, each of the options favoured a more hierarchical form of government capable of pursuing the strategies and mobilizing the population in these pursuits. In some settings, the cities extended their power and became the nucleus of empires. Thus the period from 3000 BCE to 1500 CE is marked by the rise – and later decline – of land-based empires created through frontier expansion.

In contrast to Malthus's later view, the ruling urban elites did not consider the adjacent territory as 'already possessed' or, if so, they considered themselves capable of seizing it from its current occupiers. Importantly, the significant change here is not functional improvement, as the per capita resource use did not increase, and general living conditions did not improve, even though more land resources were mobilized for agriculture. That is why 'Malthusian stagnation' persists, but the term takes a very particular perspective and does not seem quite adequate for imperial formations that extended their power. It is not at all evident that the ruling elites defined their core problem as improving living conditions or increasing population and designed their main actions towards these ends. Rather, the long-term significance of this transformation is the concentration of power in small groups at the centre of an empire with enhanced command over a population and increased power of mobilization of biophysical resources.

Viewed from the perspective of linear evolution, it is difficult to see the formation of such empires as an advance. Rather, the large-scale agriculture-based empires were a dead end in politico-economic terms, despite the 'civilizational' achievements that they created. Given that some of them stabilized over extended periods, their rise may be better understood in terms of a 'punctuated equilibrium' (Brooke 2014) than as a step on a single trajectory of evolution. There were reasons for their emergence, including importantly those relating to climate and biophysical resources, and conditions for their stabilization. But neither the emergence nor the stabilization can fruitfully be understood in terms of functional advances in resource use. And neither can their 'decline', which, rather, showed functional limits. Some of these empires suffered from what has been called overreach, neither able to halt expansion nor to consolidate, which made them vulnerable to external aggression to which they succumbed at some point (for recent long-term comparative studies of empires see, e.g., Beckwith 2009; Burbank and Cooper 2010).

Let us take a brief look at Greek antiquity in the historical context of the rise of land-based empires. This may appear as a digression but will acquire some relevance later on. The Greek *poleis*, city-states, of the period after 800 BCE were atypical of the grand frame set out before. Rather than having an urban power hub at their centre, they were a kind of confederation, or several, with Athens for some time being hegemonic but also militarily contested in that role. While the individual cities had some hinterland, this was small, and neither cities nor alliances of cities were striving for land expansion. Rather, they expanded across the Mediterranean Sea and developed maritime trade with what one can call a core–periphery structure, based on new settlements but without systematically occupying and controlling territory. Finally, power was not concentrated in hereditary or religiously justified form but contested and, for some period, organized in democratic form. 'Problems' – often whether the city should go to war or not – were publicly discussed and 'solutions' voted upon in an assembly. Nevertheless, one can call ancient Athenian democracy imperial, and the link between democracy and empire is a theme we will return to at a later point.

The Little Ice Age as a case in point

Before the recent development of 'global history', the common historiographies written in Europe used to make at this point in time not only a European turn but also a jump across an extended period of time that was not considered to be well intelligible in the desired evolutionary perspective, the aptly called Middle Ages, sometimes even referred to as the Dark Ages (but see recently Arnason and Raaflaub 2011; Arnason and Wittrock 2004; Smith 2005). The intention here is not to close the gap and re-weave the thread that connects antiquity to modernity but rather to show how this period helps to see historical change from a problem-solving perspective and how resource use and climate change enter into such a perspective. This will be done by a brief, exemplary look at how climate change interferes with the course of human history.

Let us take a closer look at the climate of history in what Europeans call the late medieval and early modern period. When at school in Germany, I was at some point confronted with the following lines: *Vom Eise befreit sind Strom und Bäche, durch des Frühlings holden, belebenden Blick* ('From the ice they are freed, the stream and brook, by the Spring's enlivening, lovely look'). They are from Johann Wolfgang Goethe's drama *Faust*, first published in 1808, the section they are taken from being commonly known as 'An Easter Walk'. As beautiful as the lines are, they did not seem to match the title. My experience was that any ice there may have been on streams and brooks in winter – and often there was, in contrast to now – would have disappeared by the end of February at the latest, way before Easter, even in years when Easter came early. I was not aware then that Goethe was writing during what became known as the Little Ice Age, an extended period of lower-than-average temperatures breaking the relative climate stability of the Holocene.

The Little Ice Age was a global phenomenon, even though it showed considerable regional variations. Overall, it may have been more pronounced in the northern hemisphere, but this impression may also be due to the greater amount of data available for the North. The dating also varies. One can speak of a global cooling period that lasted from the late fourteenth century to the middle of the nineteenth. However, the cooling was considerably more pronounced from the late sixteenth to the late seventeenth centuries. While the phenomenon has been known for some time, it is by far not comprehensively understood. Over the past two decades, research on the Little Ice Age has intensified, partly because of improved methods and enlarged sources in climatology, archaeology and history, partly due to the generally enhanced interest in climate change. (The IPCC avoids employing the term 'Little Ice Age' for lack of precision, but its latest report, the Sixth Assessment, confirms more clearly than earlier assessments that the period between 1450 and 1850 was the 'coldest multi-century interval of the post-glacial period'; IPCC 2021: 295 and 318). In the present state of knowledge, some key issues are important for our current purposes.

It is widely shared common-sense knowledge that climate has an impact on social life and social organization, even though most of this is rather speculative for lack of adequate methodological tools. In turn, relatively little attention has been devoted to the question of how climate change may provoke social change, even though this question is much more researchable because it permits a comparison between the social constellation before and after climate change and, whenever such evidence is available, can draw on human observations and interpretations of climate experiences. The Little Ice Age is an occurrence of this kind, as it is sufficiently recent for abundant evidence to be at hand, once one starts looking for it.

The core period of the Little Ice Age coincides in Europe with the religious wars, the formation of 'modern' state apparatuses, the Glorious Revolution in England, and in China with the fall of the Ming Empire. Going beyond the core, it includes the Great Plague at one end and the French Revolution and the Napoleonic wars at the other. There are numerous reports about droughts, bad harvests, famines and rebellions. True, the rising price of bread is regularly mentioned in analyses of the French Revolution. But, surprisingly, most of the mentioned events have usually been analysed in political, economic and cultural terms, largely without considering the planetary changes that may have played a significant role in provoking them. But more recent work has changed focus (see, e.g., Blom 2017; Brooke 2014; Fagan 2001; Parker 2013), and by now we can convincingly assert that climate change causes – in the broad sense of causation – social change (for an overview, see Degroot et al. 2022). And we are well advised to keep this focus, as we are already gathering further evidence in the present and will find more in the very near future.

In turn, it remains the predominant assumption that the more remote past can tell us very little about the ways in which social change causes climate change. An exception is the early Anthropocene hypothesis, first advanced by William Ruddiman, as briefly mentioned above. Human impact on the Little Ice Age is far from being confirmed either, but the case for it is stronger than for the Ruddiman hypothesis (e.g., Brooke 2014: 441; Ruddiman also supports the following Little Ice Age hypothesis.). While the CO_2 concentration in the atmosphere had basically remained constant before 1800, on a closer look it slightly decreased from the middle

Figure 2.2 Global atmospheric CO_2 concentration, 1530–present

Source: Hannah Ritchie, Max Roser and Pablo Rosado, 2020, *CO_2 and Greenhouse Gas Emissions*. Published online at OurWorldInData.org. at https://ourworldindata.org/co2-and-greenhouse-gas-emissions

of the sixteenth century to slowly pick up again from roughly the 1620s onwards until reaching a steady level again (see Figure 2.2). A decrease of CO_2 concentration is likely to go along with decreasing temperatures, as current climate policy supposedly is aiming at. Thus this indicator is compatible with the overall insight into the Little Ice Age. But it is much more specific, and it is not as such explained by broader hypotheses about volcanic activity or reduced solar impact as causes for the cooling.

This decline has recently been linked to the European colonization of America. More precisely, the indigenous American population decreased by 95 per cent between the early sixteenth and the early seventeenth centuries, mostly due to the spread of diseases, partly also directly to colonial violence. As a consequence, large areas of agricultural land were abandoned, and natural reforestation set in, turning those regions again into a carbon sink. One has to say that the evidence is not clear. While the population estimates can be considered fairly reliable, it is less evident that the amount of reforestation in this one world region can have had a strong impact on global CO_2 concentration and, thus, global climate. The most recent detailed analysis strongly supports the hypothesis

(Koch et al. 2019), but another also quite recent study, involving leading climate scientists, is more sceptical (Zalasiewicz et al. 2015; see also Cho 2014 for recent debate).

The hypothesis is highly relevant for our purposes, but it is also highly problematic. Starting with the latter, it is striking that literature in support of the hypothesis is cited – partly with qualifications, partly without – by scholars whose work includes critiques of colonization and of the main western narrative of human history (e.g., Ghosh 2021: 52–3; Graeber and Wengrow 2021: 258). The hypothesis fits just too well with ongoing debates about global environmental justice, as it seems to show that colonial domination had an impact on the planetary condition from early on. In such a context, however, it is employed regardless of the fact that the spreading of fatal diseases was mostly not intentional, even though sometimes it was. More generally, the early phase of the colonization of America hardly fits into a straight critical narrative of modernity, capitalism or instrumental domination of nature and others, as will be further discussed below.

The hypothesis is nevertheless highly relevant because it underlines global connections of planetary significance at a moment of major social transformations in several world regions. In particular, it emphasizes both the importance of change in the use of biophysical resources for the planetary climate and the potential for human intervention to alter the use of biophysical resources, even though unintentionally, so that the planetary climate changes as a consequence.

Returning to the broader picture of the late medieval and early modern period, it becomes now clearer why no strong thread of 'evolution' or 'development' can be woven, as supposedly 'natural' and 'social' phenomena intermingle and can be seen as mutually 'causing' rather sudden interruptions of climate and of social life. From the middle of the fourteenth century onwards, the epidemic called the Black Death or the Great Plague killed a significant share of the population of Eurasia. It was caused by the bacillus *Yersinia pestis*, and its rapid transmission was possibly due to the long-distance trade via the Eurasian continental connection of the Silk Roads. A century later, as social life recovered from the epidemic, Spanish and Portuguese seafaring expeditions used a planetary phenomenon, namely the regularity of winds and currents over the oceans, to sail both eastwards to South Asia and westwards to America, inaugurating new trade connections – and decimating the Native American population, as we have seen. Subsequently, food crises related to the cooling of the Little Ice Age may well have played a role in revolts and warfare that were frequent in the sixteenth and seventeenth centuries. Historians have increasingly attempted to draw these connections, often with an enormous amount and a great variety of source material. They have greatly enriched our knowledge, but at core they have made the situation more complex. To use Brooke's (2014) terminology, which has a strong theoretical underpinning of its own, events may have been 'punctuating' any trends or equilibria that may have existed otherwise and put both nature and society in different states.

Logics of history (3): problem solving

This may look like an unhelpful conclusion for students of human history, but perhaps some further insight can be derived from it. Human societies may sometimes find themselves in a situation where they know what they should be doing or at least are being nudged strongly in a certain direction. To move from hunting and gathering to agriculture, or to enlarge the available land base in the face of population growth, as we have seen above, were long considered to be steps in the right direction of history. And in some way or another, even though it may have taken a long time, humankind took those steps. With the help of recent scholarship, we have tried to cast some doubt about whether one can say that this was the right direction, or whether there was any right long-term direction at all. Now we can go one step further.

Our excursion into the Little Ice Age showed that human societies often were not in that kind of situation at all. The cooling, but also the preceding epidemic, were large-scale events that took societies by surprise. They had not seen them coming, and they did not expect them. They were largely external to them, and where they were not, as discussed above, human beings did not know about their own role in bringing them about. But these events had consequences: they brought death and famine; and they probably triggered violence in the form of revolt, repression and war. They were problems that needed to be addressed, but there was no model or recipe as to how one should address them.

The recent interdisciplinary scholarship that I have mentioned emphasizes that these events threw societies into disarray. But it also explores the responses and the ways of exiting from calamitous circumstances. It is fairly well known, for instance, that wages in Europe were rising at the end of the Great Plague because of the shortage of labour power, as one would now say, and that this rise possibly pointed a way to economic recovery. It is nevertheless daring to claim that 'the rise of Europe' was a consequence of the Great Plague, as James Belich (2022) does. More cautiously, Geoffrey Parker and also John Brooke point to the strengthening of state institutions in response to widespread crisis during the Little Ice Age and even consider differential commitment to knowledge generation as a different response to the epidemic in Europe and China. The main difference between the two expressions is that 'the rise of Europe' points to a *telos*, a goal, of which one can only know with hindsight that it came about (assuming that the expression is adequate for that which came about), whereas the strengthening of government and the encouragement of knowledge generation refer to actions and intentions in the present in response to problems.

This difference becomes crucial for our work of trying to identify logics of expansion in human history that drive the increasing use of biophysical resources and lead to the current situation of massive anthropogenic climate change. The former approach starts from the outcomes, delineates a historical trajectory in light of the outcomes, and then searches for the logic that led step by step steadily forward on this trajectory. The latter approach, in contrast, assumes that any trajectory only comes about through the actions of human beings and the chains of interaction between them. As Anthony Giddens (1984) has put it, society is constituted through such chains of interactions. As a consequence, any trajectory that emerges is likely to be 'crooked', to paraphrase Immanuel Kant, and the human ride creating it is 'rough', to use Brooke's expression. This approach may fail to confirm any logic at all. But it should be underlined that this result would not be determined by the opposite assumption that world history is a 'chaos of chance events – in its entirety like the swirling waters of a whirlpool' (Jaspers 1968 [1949], with a nature metaphor). If so, a likely reason would be that no such logic has been operating in a determinant way, or at least, there may have been a plurality of intersecting logics whose interplay both encountered and created unforeseen events.

At this point, we can end this brief scrutiny of most of Holocene history by concluding that no such logic could be identified. This is not surprising for the logic of capital and the logic of modernity, as these logics were not expected to be operating in world history before 1500. But we cannot confirm either that a logic of population growth had pushed human societies to the limits of available biophysical resources. When human societies experienced significant population growth under favourable ecological and social conditions, they tended to address the problem of feeding a larger number by either moving entirely in space or by extending their boundaries through horizontal terrestrial expansion. In the terminology explored above, we may say that societies experience scarcity in moments of crisis, more often than not externally generated, and try to solve the problem by moving across frontiers.

The latter solution was more likely to be embarked on in hierarchically organized societies in which the ruling group could develop and impose such an answer to the problem – an observation that returns us to the question of the power of authoritatively identifying and interpreting a problem. Rulers or ruling elites, specifically, have resorted to expansion in horizontal space to extend their control over resources, creating imperial polities as a consequence. The longer historical perspective makes visible that spatial expansion is not specific to capitalism and its supposed expansionary logic of commodification. It is better understood, more generally, as a means of control over resources by power holders of various kinds.

Obviously, this is no more than an interim conclusion. It is not only very possible that major social transformations after 1500 created logics of expansion that did not exist before; this is even the core argument of theories of capitalism and modernity. Moreover, even if Malthus proposed a general 'principle' of population development, he formulated it at the end of the eighteenth century, thus arguably with recent changes more strongly on his mind than earlier human history. It is to this question that we now turn.

3

The Advanced Organic Economy of 'Early Modernity'

The period between 1500 and 1800 has long been referred to by historians of Europe as 'early modernity', suggesting an extended era of social transformation that leads up to the present time, or even a long process of gestation that could not but lead to the superior social arrangements of modernity. In contrast, critical analysts of capitalism have focused on the transformative dynamics created by the enlarging maritime trade connections bringing about a 'capitalist world economy' in the form of merchant and plantation capitalism, which is seen as the forerunner to the industrial production capitalism that emerged in the nineteenth century. In both cases, these three centuries are considered to be preparatory for the present, even though the different emphases in the two approaches gave rise to long-lasting controversies.

Two of those disputes need to be briefly mentioned. First, there has been a controversy between supposed European and global approaches. While Europe-based interpretations clearly dominated the field of historiography during the nineteenth and much of the twentieth centuries, the disputed question is whether world-historical transformations across the past half-millennium have their core spatial location in Europe and spread from there or whether they emerged from new forms of global connectedness after the late fifteenth century. Second, the approaches can also be distinguished by the respective emphasis they give to political or economic aspects, either signalling the emergence of new state forms and interstate relations, identified in the so-called Westphalian system of sovereign states, or alternatively pointing to commercial relations acquiring global extensions. This is much more than a difference in empirical emphasis, as significantly different conclusions about the dynamics of world history would be derived from each approach. The focus on new state forms often – not always – goes along with the notion that the state is the container and organizer of social life, including economic activities. In contrast, the focus on extended commerce tends to suggest that economic practices break out of the boundaries of political institutions.

There is a third difference of emphasis between the two approaches, less often noted and less clear-cut, but central for our purposes. In the 'early modernity' approaches, the creation of new forms of state goes along with the elaboration of a new understanding of the foundations of sociopolitical organization. Thus the institutional transformation in the aftermath of long-lasting warfare is related to a reinterpretation of social life. In the world-economy approaches, in turn, the global extension of commercial relations is connected to the provision of biophysical resources. This occurs in two ways: first, as the diagnosis of resource scarcity in Europe after the Great Plague and the onset of the Little Ice Age; second, in terms of the availability of resources on extra-European soil that could be extracted by use of power more than by conventional trade. In both approaches, these aspects tended to be subordinated to the dominant political or economic reasoning, even though they are identifiably central. In the past few decades, research in intellectual history and in environmental history has increasingly focused on these aspects, and they have gradually entered the dominant reasonings, more in the world economy than in the early-modernity approaches. However, they still remain in a conceptually supportive role and, furthermore, they are only rarely connected to each other (a very recent exception is Charbonnier 2020, which will be discussed in detail on pp. 81–2).

The great historical divide: 1500 or 1800?

A useful way of framing the interpretation of these three centuries of global history is to review the ongoing – maybe one should say simmering – dispute about the relative significance of the transformations after 1492 compared to those during the late eighteenth and early nineteenth centuries. The co-occurrence of the French

Revolution and related political events, on the one hand, and the Industrial Revolution, on the other, mark this latter period as the one of the origins of 'the modern world' (Bayly 2004) and the beginning of an unprecedented overall 'transformation of the world' (Osterhammel 2009), and these claims move the three preceding centuries into the background. Furthermore, many of those who hold this view would tend to suggest that the seeds of those modern configurations can be found within Europe during the centuries before 1800, rather than in the relations between Europe and other world regions. The plurality of sites of political power, the rise of cities and of universities, the establishment of property rights, the scientific revolution and the Enlightenment would regularly be named as elements that contributed to putting European societies on the track to modernity and capitalism.

Marx and Engels (1848) mention the 'discovery of America, the rounding of the Cape', as background for the rise of the bourgeoisie. Later, Marx developed the concept of 'primitive accumulation' to capture the necessarily non-capitalist origins of the rise of capital. Arguably, he remained ambivalent about locating this process primarily in the land enclosures in England, thus as an intra-European phenomenon, or alternatively in the exploitation of people and resources outside Europe after the maritime expansion. Be that as it may, partly inspired by Marx's thinking, Immanuel Wallerstein (1974–1989) has – empirically and conceptually – widened this perspective with his world-systems approach. In his terms, the crossing of the Atlantic Ocean and the subsequent growth of long-distance maritime trade and European settlement in America and Southern Africa mark the emergence of a capitalist world economy as well as the beginnings of European colonization and, subsequently, world domination. Indeed, it seems it is hard to overstate the significance of these occurrences for world history. Prima facie, therefore, those who assign greater significance to the events after 1492 than to those after 1789 have a more promising perspective.

Again, however, it is not sufficient to claim that these transformations have had a lasting impact, up to the present, according to the same logic of domination and exchange that was in place at that moment (e.g., Moore 2015 and elsewhere). While the significance of the historical moment is beyond doubt, it is much less certain that it has set world history on a linear trajectory up to the present. Rather than reading from the future backwards, as is often done in the two main accounts, one needs to look at the past as if it were a present in which the intentions and interests of the actors need to be identified to understand the way they acted. For current purposes, we will do this by placing the emphasis on changes in resource use, in a first step, and in the societal self-understandings, in a second, to subsequently reflect on the interconnections between the two changes. Before moving to resources and interpretations, for clarity, we need to briefly state from this perspective what this transformation was largely not, despite contrary opinions.

First, this period may have marked the beginning – as widely understood – of European world domination, but it did not mark the moment of the Great Divergence (Pomeranz 2000; for an early comprehensive critique see Vries 2001; for an overview over the ensuing debate, see O'Brien 2010), which indeed Pomeranz located at around 1800, when 'Europe grew rich and Asia did not' (Parthasarathi 2011; for an early comprehensive critique, see Vries 2012). During the fifteenth and sixteenth centuries, the Atlantic voyages were occurrences at the south-western extreme of Eurasia, which were not assigned great significance in other parts of the region. Territorial empires were forming, such as the Russian territorial expansion towards the East, the Ottoman Empire's expansion into south-eastern Europe and North Africa, and the Safavid Empire, or reforming, such as the Ming Empire. Portugal and Spain were comparatively weak powers. Indeed, their maritime expansion can be seen as a response to an unforeseen problem that weakened their position: the rise of the Islamic Ottoman Empire in the Eastern Mediterranean and the weakening of the Silk Roads after Tamerlane endangered the established trade routes on which Portugal and Spain had also relied.

Second, this period is not fruitfully seen as the starting point of European colonialism, if by the latter we understand the occupation of a territory, domination of its population and the imposition of a government by the occupying power, in contrast to settlement or network extension (see, e.g., Belich 2009: 21). True, already in 1494 Spain and Portugal had asked the Pope to draw up the Treaty of Tordesillas, which was supposed to divide up the newly 'discovered' America between these two monarchies. Subsequently, both Spain and Portugal did consider themselves masters of the territory, but as a matter of fact they had seen very little of it and controlled even less. The crossing of the Atlantic provided for a first time an idea of the limits of the earth, which is of obvious importance for our argument. But the main consequence of this event was not territorial expansion along a horizontal frontier following the practice of the terrestrial empires. The shift to maritime expansion along new horizontal frontiers also entailed a transformation in the relations of exchange and domination, giving asymmetric trade and appropriation an increasing significance compared to occupation and extraction – even though the latter persisted and later regained relevance. The Portuguese, and later Dutch and British, practice of setting up trading posts on the coasts of Southern Africa, South Asia and East Asia without making claims to the inland territory was a key characteristic of the ongoing transformation.

Third, the period witnessed settlement of Europeans in the territories where their ships landed, but of rather small numbers compared to the nineteenth century (see chapter 4 below). Migration varied strongly by condition, region and timing. Of the estimated 2.5 million Europeans who migrated to America between 1500 and 1800, more than half migrated after 1700. The majority of the latter were British and settled in the Caribbean and North America. Before 1700, in turn, the majority was Portuguese or Spanish and settled in South and Central America. Up to the seventeenth century, a considerable number of European migrants were unfree labourers of different kinds. While descendants of Europeans quickly did become the largest part of the population in most regions of America, this was not due to settlement in large numbers but was a consequence of the diminishing indigenous population, due to inflicted 'European' diseases, to warfare and to the imposition of deadly exploitative and oppressive living conditions. In Africa and Asia, Europeans did not outnumber the indigenous population at all, and in many situations they were also far from dominating them, despite their military superiority. The major population movement during this period, mostly during the seventeenth and eighteenth century, more than eight million people, was from Africa to America in the slave trade (e.g., de Zwart and van Zanden 2018; McKeown 2004: 164).

All three assertions project into the entire period between 1500 and 1800, transformations that mostly happened only during the latter parts of the three centuries, but arose at full scale later on during the nineteenth century. Thus they are examples of trying to identify a logic of evolution by reasoning from the endpoint and searching only for elements that confirm the existence of such a logic. This procedure may at times be legitimate, as I shall argue below, for some features of the nineteenth century, in particular. However, its use is conditional on at least one of two features: either it must be possible to see the logic pronounced by actors during the period in question, thus as an interpretation of their own time with regard to tendencies that are observable, often accompanied by calls to either promote or resist such tendencies. Or it must be possible to analyse occurrences as consequences of human actions, either as the aggregate or as a concatenation of actions, thus as constituting a logic or trend, despite human beings not intending to generate these consequences and logic. Coming back to this kind of analysis later (in the next chapter and in chapter 10), I shall for now just state that this cannot be convincingly done for the three allegedly most significant features of the period in question: the Great Divergence; colonialism; and large-scale European settlement.

The maritime frontier and new parameters for resource-based interaction

Having said this, we can move on to explore in more detail that which we consider as the more plausible hypotheses about the dynamics of global social change from the sixteenth century onwards, looking first at the changes in resource use after the transgressing of the long-distance maritime frontier. To recap (see chapter 1), the agriculture-based empires mostly grew by expansion on land and predominantly traded 'internally' or 'domestically', as one would say today, between the cities and their hinterland. While an extreme, the case of China is telling. Long-distance trade was important for highly valuable goods, the Silk Roads being the outstanding example, and coastal expansion also happened. But probably in the face of overreach, the Ming Dynasty decided to stop maritime trade expansion and instead enhance internal trade by building canals and to fortify land boundaries by starting to build the Great Wall, thus opting for a form of imperial expansion and consolidation that had proven successful before (Darwin 2007: 88). In contrast, the West European expansion from the late fifteenth century onwards proceeded by pushing maritime frontiers and expanding long-distance trade much more strongly than the existing base of trade between the numerous cities and their agricultural surroundings. This style of expansion can be considered as having been preceded by the Hanseatic League operating in the North and Baltic Seas and the network of Mediterranean cities around Venice and Genoa, but it took on a new dimension and extension from about 1500 onwards, after Africa had been circumnavigated and the Atlantic crossed. 'The discovery of the sea as a global commons offering maritime access to every part of the world transformed the economics and geopolitics of empire' (Darwin 2007: 6). This is, arguably, the main novelty of the age that begins around 1500: new resources are made accessible owing to the maritime frontier expansion onto hitherto unknown territories and their resources; and these resources are brought into the seafaring societies from the outside without the compensation that 'ordinary' trade demanded. The question is what the significance of this novelty is for subsequent world history, and to answer it we need to first explore in more detail what the key characteristics of the European Atlantic expansion in terms of resource extraction and exchange were.

Key features of the West European maritime frontier expansion

First, from the landing on the Caribbean islands onwards, the Spaniards appropriated gold and – increasingly – silver, which they subsequently traded with China, in need of bullion for its extended monetary economy, in exchange for specialized manufactured products. This appropriation meant a 'windfall' benefit (Darwin 2007: 97; Pomeranz 2000: 269), highly important for the monarchical finance, not least for leading wars. Over the medium term, it acquired greater significance as the increase in wealth in Western Europe supported the rise of 'commercial societies' with a certain level of 'luxury', in particular in the Netherlands and Britain (see below).

Second, beyond the appropriation of gold and silver, long-distance trade acquired a greater significance than ever before. Sailing around Africa, the Portuguese became the new middlemen in the trade between South and East Asia, on the one side, and Europe, on the other, benefiting also from the Chinese maritime retreat. They were followed and outdone by the Dutch and the British trading companies, which imported spices as well as manufactured products to Europe, operating as state-authorized monopolies, including the right to violence and warfare.

Third, a new form of work organization was created, in particular in America, with the large-scale agricultural plantations mostly operated by unfree labour. Starting in the Atlantic islands, the most extensive use of plantations was made for sugar and later coffee in Brazil and for cotton in the South of the United States (Mintz 1985 is the classic reference for sugar; see Beckert 2014 for cotton).

Fourth, the plantation was a key component, but not the only one, of resource appropriation by European powers. With the closely connected rise of the Atlantic slave trade and the increase of plantations, African labour was working on American soil for European material needs. Thus both human energy and biophysical resources were appropriated, and this diminished the amount of land in Europe that was required to provide food and shelter for people living in Europe.

From the point of view of households, European economies changed by increased demand for consumer goods, on the one hand, and longer working hours, on the other. The theorem of the 'industrious revolution' has been developed by Jan de Vries (2008), borrowing the term but not the interpretation from Akira Hayami, who had used it for the economic history of Tokugawa Japan. The main idea is that an economic transformation emerged that was broadly rooted within European societies and demand driven, in contrast to the 'Industrial Revolution' that was started by capital owners and was supply driven (on which more in chapter 4). The increased availability both of consumer items, due to long-distance trade, and of stimulants, such as sugar, coffee and tobacco, which enabled longer working hours, may have played a significant role.

All these four aspects remain debated in global history, in particular in global economic history, some more than others. The significance that all individual aspects had in reshaping global and European history remains in dispute. Once taken together, though, it seems obvious that these changes brought about a major transformation of the 'terms of trade', as one should later say, on the one hand, as well as, on the other, a resource transfer between Western Europe and other world regions. Refraining from stronger assertions about their role in 'the rise of Europe' or the Great Divergence, we need to explore how far they signalled the emergence of a new economic-ecological regime. With reference to established debate, this can be done by asking how far these changes marked the beginning of modern capitalism, of the resource-intensive trajectory of modern societies, and/or of modern consumer society.

Inaugurating the capital logic?

As mentioned before, Immanuel Wallerstein dates the emergence of the capitalist world economy to the period around 1500. In the light of our explorations, he is right to speak of a new form of global social constellation, whose rise was not predetermined by the earlier constellation of world empires. Others speak for this period of trade capitalism or merchant capitalism, distinguishing this social configuration from later industrial or production capitalism. As said before, and as Wallerstein was aware, the long-distance trade regime went along with changes in production. Drawing on Wallerstein, Jason Moore (2003) extended the argument by emphasizing resource extraction and transfer, that is, going beyond trade and speaking about a capitalist 'world ecology'.

So far, so good, one might say. But there is a problem with using the term 'capitalism'. The term was coined in the late nineteenth century to make sense of the socio-economic transformations that European societies were going through at the time. Initially, moreover, the term 'capital' and the adjective 'capitalist' were more widely used, by Karl Marx for instance, than the notion 'capitalism' that claimed to describe an entire social formation or epoch. These conceptual origins, of course, do not rule out that the term can be applied to situations for which it was not coined. As Jürgen Kocka (2013: 20–1) recently argued, a 'working definition' of capitalism can start with determining which phenomena need to be present for us to reasonably speak of capitalism; for him, these are: individual property rights and decentralized decision making; coordination of economic actors through markets and prices; and 'capital' as a resource to be invested in the present to reap benefits in the future. (Interestingly, he explicitly does not include 'enterprises' as the space in which capital and labour interact, autonomous with regard to the state, in the definition.) This definition certainly permits the inclusion of many practices and institutions of the period between 1500 and 1800. Indeed, Kocka sees the inclusion of 'minority phenomena in non-capitalist environments' (2013: 21) in the analysis of capitalism as an advantage of this historically open approach.

Then, however, he immediately adds an important qualification: one should speak of a 'capitalist economy' or a 'capitalist system' only when capitalist principles dominate. By dominance, he is referring both to the mechanisms that govern the economy and the 'systemic-expanding' tendency of capitalism into other societal realms and into non-capitalist societies (Kocka 2013: 22). The imposition of capitalism as a 'dominant logic of steering' (2013: 70) starts to be reached, in Kocka's view, in the Netherlands and Great Britain only from the late seventeenth society onwards, underpinned by a new vision of society (on which more on pp. 72–80), elsewhere considerably later. At this point, Kocka introduces the term 'logic' and, indeed, logic of expansion, with which we have characterized theories of capitalism earlier in search of the reasons for the increasing the use of biophysical resources (chapter 1).

At the intersection of economic and environmental history, many scholars who analyse the exploitation of resources in long-term perspective indeed use the term 'capitalism' for the economic-ecological regime that emerged in the wake of long-distance maritime trade (for a very broad approach to 'profit' and capitalism, see Stoll 2023). Research on 'commodity frontiers' has turned into a specific approach, which combines the analysis of the transgression of resource frontiers with the conceptual focus on commodification as key characteristics of capitalism. In his comprehensive history of cotton as a commodity, thus, Sven Beckert (2014: XV–XVI) analyses the expansion of cotton production on plantations in America and largely for further processing in Europe as a form of capitalism that he calls 'war capitalism', emphasizing the alliance of political and economic actors reaching out beyond their own territory: 'Europeans united the power of capital and the power of the state,' and they did so 'in a global frame'. In parallel, he underlines the differences with later industrial capitalism: this early capitalism 'flourished not in the factory but in the field; it was not mechanized but land- and labor-intensive'; and it was 'based not on free labor but on slavery'. For our purposes, we conclude that the seventeenth and, more so, the eighteenth century witnessed the rise of phenomena that entailed an increased intensity of resource extraction and that can in some way be called capitalist.

At the same time, we also note that the politico-economic constellation of that period was clearly distinct from the one that arose during the nineteenth century, for which the concept of capitalism was originally developed.

Arguably, this distinction is related to the emergence of a 'logic' of capital (despite the fact that Kocka dates this to an earlier moment). Both the key critical scholars of nineteenth-century capitalism, Karl Marx and Max Weber, detected such a logic, even though in somewhat different terms. Karl Marx focused on commodification of social relations, whereas Weber emphasized rationalization and its impact on life conduct. These conceptualizations have in common that they claim to detect the emergence of a social phenomenon that, while having been created in long-term processes of human interaction, undermines the capacity for human agency and creativity. Weber is characteristically ambivalent, as he recognizes the increase of the reach of organized human power through rationalization but deplores the constraints that come with it. Marx is more decidedly critical of commodification but needs to define a new form of collective action, namely revolutionary action, to overcome the constraints that commodification imposed. In contrast, a later scholar, Karl Polanyi (1985 [1944]), gave a, so to say, Weberian twist to the concept of commodification. Defining commodities as goods that are produced to be sold, he identified three main 'fictitious commodities', namely land, labour and money, which are not produced to be sold and, thus the conclusion, should not be treated as commodities on markets. Given that the land constraint became a key topic in economies with an organic resource base, as we shall see in detail in what follows, this is a crucial observation.

A new resource regime?

The research on commodity frontiers aligns well with the notion of an emerging new resource regime with both wider spatial extension and greater extractive capacity, thus possibly paving the way for the global trajectory towards high-resource intensity that has generated climate change. Two major changes are rather incontrovertible. First, the emergence of transatlantic trade led to an exchange in the kind of resources that were known and used on each side of the Atlantic. This 'Columbian exchange' (Crosby 2003 [1972]) altered consumption and production patterns in an unprecedented and unpredicted way, making, for example, new foods available in Europe, such as the tomato and the potato, and new production and transport methods in America, such as the use of horses. Given the asymmetry of power, the outcome of this exchange favoured the Europeans; 'the winners were mainly located in Western Europe' (de Zwart and van Zanden 2018: 278). Second, given the way European settlers treated American soil as a frontier and African labour as a resource, the intensification of exploitation led to an overall increase of available resources, for example, sugar, coffee and cotton, again mostly for the use of Europeans. Even scholars who are extremely sceptical of any evolutionist reasoning, such as Graeber and Wengrow (2021: 256–7), see the Columbian exchange as marking the 'success' of the Neolithic revolution, whereas in their view there was no linear line of evolution in earlier human history.

Disentangling the components of this rupture in resource regime, we recognize three main elements. First, there is an increase in resource extraction; second, there is a substantive shift towards certain commodities; and third, there is a shift in the regional distribution and consumption of resources, in particular those for which also a quantitative increase can be detected. If kept separate, these components lend themselves to highly different interpretations: the increase in resource extraction can be seen as an evolutionary advance of humankind, allowing better satisfaction of material needs through a more systematic exploitation of non-human nature. A closer look at the substantive shift suggests that it may have supported the 'industrious revolution' in Europe by providing physical energy and stimulants for work through sugar and coffee and by increasing the supply of marketable commodities through cotton. Finally, the resource transfer towards Europe through 'ghost acres' (Kenneth Pomeranz) and similarly phantom labour enriched Europe.

Putting the components together again, two very different pictures can be assembled. On the one hand, one can argue that the share of American production and transatlantic trade in overall production and trade was too small to create a significant world-regional divergence between America (and Africa) and Europe (e.g., Emmer 1988), whereas in turn the innovations in production and trade were the seed of a new (modern and capitalist) economy that would fully blossom some time later, and the specific commodities provided steps for the emerging consumer society (on which more below) as part of that new economy. On the other hand, one can argue that the resource transfer to Europe, as proportionally small as it may have been, together with the additional physical energy input created a divide that, once existing, would tend to enlarge over time because of the initial advantage it created. One may add a variation to this second image by emphasizing that, rather than the increasing asymmetry of resource availability and, as a consequence, of resource surplus in Europe itself, it was the freeing of capacity for other activities that generated a new economic-ecological trajectory – other activities as different as knowledge production or industrial labour, both of which were hardly possibly in a situation of limited land and labour for food production, that is, in a context rigidly exposed to Malthusian constraints.

On the basis of the available evidence, I tend to see the latter interpretation as more plausible. Scholars who see limited significance generally base their conclusions on quantitative analyses of individual aspects. This is problematic for two reasons. As just hinted at, first, the resource changes were of such a kind that their combined effect on a socio-economic constellation is likely to be much greater than the sum of calculable individual effects. Second, a different picture emerges when one looks at the perceptions, assessments and interpretations by contemporaries, an approach which Maxine Berg has pioneered for 'luxury' (Berg 2007, on which more in a moment) and more recently for slavery (Berg and Hudson 2023). While contemporary misperceptions cannot be ruled out, contemporary observers and participants have a basis in experience that gets lost in the analysis of quantitative data and indicators (for a comparison of such approaches for the study of climate and society, see Degroot et al. 2022).

Speaking about contemporary assessments, another element needs to be added: by the end of the eighteenth century, the transatlantic constellation of production and trade remained almost exclusively based on organic resources. In this respect, it had changed very little in comparison to the earlier period of agriculture-based empires. While the per capita use of biophysical resources did increase, this rise was relatively small; in particular, while increasing, the share of paleo-organic resources, in relation to the subsequent nineteenth century, remained small. Only in a few regions, most importantly England, can one notice a significant augmentation in the consumption of coal during the seventeenth and eighteenth centuries. There was no element in the 'early modern' economic-ecological regime that so clearly pointed to a future step towards exploration of vertical frontiers and, in particular, fossil fuels that this step would have been envisioned by contemporaries (to be discussed in chapter 4).

The beginnings of consumer society?

There is a third aspect of the new economic-ecological regime that I have barely touched upon until now. Following the course of scholarly debate, I have first focused on trade – the 'trilateral Atlantic trade' regime (Barbier) – and then on production – the 'plantation economy'. More recently, though, changes in consumption have become the centre of attention, first through just observing a major transformation in Europe and then through considering this transformation as a driver of larger socio-economic change.

The core observation concerns a much wider diffusion of consumer goods in European societies than had been assumed earlier. In the sixteenth century, luxury items such as 'chinaware' predominantly came from China to Britain, and they were bought and used by the aristocracy. By the eighteenth century, though, there were many more items of such a kind, they were often produced in Britain itself and they were also bought and used by the non-aristocratic middle and upper classes. Significantly, these items came to be referred to and talked about as 'luxuries', thus indicating an affluence of material goods beyond those required for the satisfaction of material needs (Berg 2007). In more extended European analysis, it was even shown that some such items, such as pocket watches, were owned by a significant proportion of workers as early as the eighteenth century (de Vries 2008).

Jan de Vries (2008) indeed links changes in consumption to those in production and, to a minor extent, in trade. The 'industrious revolution', discussed on p. 64, brought increased household production of goods for sale, of 'commodities'. The monetary revenue, in turn, that came with the sale permitted the purchase of hitherto unaffordable goods. Through his examples, de Vries links these changes to the global maritime trade, underlining the new practice of adding sugar to tea or coffee or pointing out that, characteristically, a pocket watch might be purchased by a sailor of the

East India Company with his remuneration upon return to the Netherlands.

The theorem of early modern consumer society, if we can call it that, is potentially relevant for our analysis in two different ways. First, these analyses support my reflections on the economic-ecological transformations made above. Adding consumption, they close the circle of exchange and, one might say, complete the picture of the new economic-ecological regime. As a part of the reasoning about the 'industrious revolution', the theorem can be seen as underlining the conditions for the subsequent Industrial Revolution in terms of both the intensification of work efforts and the preparation of demand for emerging industrial products. While this claim has some plausibility, it does not fundamentally alter the analysis of the rise of industrialism and production capitalism in the nineteenth century. Second, though, the observations of an emerging consumer society can also be interpreted as introducing a new dynamic into social change. Rather than by the profit motive of early capitalist entrepreneurs, which led to exploring the maritime frontier and inventing the slave-based plantation economy, social change may also be brought about by the demand for non-necessary consumer items.

The cultural and economic historians who have focused on early modern consumption tend not to make the move to this more far-reaching claim. De Vries (2008), for instance, explicitly discusses the wide range of historical moments that have been referred to as marking the emergence of the consumer society from the seventeenth to, more typically, the late twentieth century, and he avoids emphasizing early origins and a subsequent unstoppable dynamic. Nevertheless, such findings can be connected to the theorem that demand for luxury is the main driver for humankind's embarking on the resource-intensive trajectory, a recent version of which has been provided by Ulrich Brand and Markus Wissen (2017) under the heading of 'the imperial mode of living'. From early modernity onwards, so the argument goes, the 'possibility of a more comfortable life in material terms' (Brand and Wissen 2017: 108–9) was extended to larger groups in European societies through the availability of new consumer items. This process of both extension and greater visibility led the 'wish for a fundamentally improved life' (Brand and Wissen 2017: 94) to become more widespread and turn into a demand for social change. As a consequence, a comfortable mode of living diffused across western societies, gradually and sometimes based on social struggles, and was emulated by the elites in non-western societies, both by settler elites and by 'traditional' elites. Given the material base of this mode of living, it is highly resource intensive and thus a major cause of resource extraction in general and, over the long run, of climate change in particular.

Summarized in this way, the reasoning has considerable affinity with the argument that modernity has been built on an ever-expanding foundation of fossil fuels, as promoted by Dipesh Chakrabarty and referred to at the outset. With its emphasis on emulation and diffusion, furthermore, it also resonates with modernization theory, except that it adds the twist that this process is no longer sustainable, thus providing a vision of negative modernization. The authors, furthermore, link this, as one might say, sociocultural approach with the politico-economic analysis of capitalism and imperialism, broadly suggesting that the provision of comfort to key social groups generates necessary support for the reproduction and imperialist extension of capitalism. In the terminology introduced earlier, they tie the two logics of expansion of modernity and capitalism together, assuming that the account thus gains in persuasiveness. At this point of our analysis, though, the approach rather multiplies the problems of explanation. We have not identified any linear logic of expansion to be at work in the history of human resource use before 1800, and much less the harmonious connection of two such logics. Nevertheless, the theorem of the imperial mode of living provides us with the task of systematically testing whether the profit motive of capital accumulation aligns with the social demand for more comfortable lives across socio-ecological transformations.

A new foundation for organized social life

In apparent support of some such connection of theorizing modernity and capitalism in trying to understand how humankind embarked on the resource-intensive historical trajectory, Pierre Charbonnier (2020) has recently emphasized the link between 'abundance and freedom' in the environmental history of political ideas from the seventeenth century onwards. Thus he goes back to what is seen as the origins of modern political theory or even, *tout court*, as the onset of political modernity. In the terminology adopted here, he looks at the societal self-understanding that was created in Europe during 'early modernity', and he does so in search of the new relation of human beings to non-human nature that is at the roots of the resource-intensive trajectory.

The conventional European reading of the history of political ideas underlined the invention of, or return to, the basic principles of freedom, democracy and popular sovereignty as the only legitimation of political power. This reading paid little attention to the problems to which the new principles were meant to be an answer, nor to the context which enabled those answers to be found. Therefore, the conditions under which the principles could be realized, or in other words the presuppositions on which they were built, fell into oblivion. Charbonnier's main thesis holds that the promise of freedom became sufficiently persuasive to usher in a major social transformation – the revolutions of the late eighteenth century – only when it was connected to the promise of affluence, to the possibility of enhanced material well-being (Charbonnier 2020: 49). We will return to his thesis in more detail on pp. 81–2, after having reconstructed the transformation in western societal self-understanding in a slightly different way than he does.

The discovery of freedom and America

As mentioned earlier, much of Europe was in crisis at the end of the Middle Ages and the beginning of 'early modernity'. The Great Plague led to a decimation of the population and was followed by the Little Ice Age, which is likely to have brought bad harvests and famines and rebellions in their wake. It is plausible to see the strengthening of state institutions and enhanced efforts at knowledge production as strategies for overcoming the multiple crises. This observation applies beyond Europe to other parts of Eurasia and North Africa as well (see chapter 2 above). But Europe is of key interest for our reasoning at this point because of two significant events that were located there: the seafaring missions across the Atlantic that led to the so-called 'discovery of America' with its encounter with unknown people, and the scission within western Christianity, with long-lasting religious wars in its wake. Separately, and even more so when taken together, these two events provoked radical new proposals for European societal self-understanding.

In contrast to members of other 'Old World' civilizations, who were perceived to be different in many respects but to some extent knowable and known, the Native Americans were the radical other. In a first discussion, at the core of which was the Las Casas–Sepúlveda controversy in 1550–1, their common humanity needed to be determined, and Christian thought helped towards that end, even though it could also be used for denying equal status (Pagden 2000). Subsequently, the otherness of contemporaneous Native Americans served to construct a dichotomous perception of world history, distinguishing a state of nature, in which the Native Americans lived, from civil society, which Europeans had reached. In parallel, the schism within western Christianity shattered all trust in fundamental harmony and shared cosmological bases. With the encounter of human beings in America whom they did not expect, whom they had not been aware of, and with the emergence of a divide in basic belief among people who used to live together, European thought entered into unknown territory with regard to what we may call the epistemic and political *problématique*: the question of reliable knowledge and the question of the rules for living together.

The outcome of the religious wars was the principle that the ruler of a territory should determine the faith of their subjects. Thus the principle of sovereignty over a territory was inaugurated at the same time as the spatial limits of the earth were recognized, together marking an intensified concern, as illusionary as it was, for complete territorial mastery. The Treaty of Tordesillas, dividing the – still largely unknown – territory of (South) America between Spain and Portugal in 1494, was mirrored by the Peace of Augsburg, introducing the – later so-named – principle *cuius regio, eius religio* in 1555. Inadvertently, thus, together with a notion of monarchical sovereignty, a notion of religious autonomy had been introduced, which later was extended to all individual human beings and other spheres of life. The lack of reasoned agreement on common higher principles, therefore, opened the path for turning the question around and starting philosophical reasoning with individual human beings, their capacities and their rights. This step was taken in radical ways by René Descartes for epistemic matters and by Thomas Hobbes for political matters (Shapin and Schaffer 1993; Toulmin 1990). To move beyond the state of nature required the elaboration of a social contract between the members of a collectivity. In the absence of other resources, the fundamental epistemic and political *problématiques* were now addressed in explicit and radical ways on the basis of an individualistic ontology. These authors, and some of those who followed them, such as John Locke, Nicolas de Condorcet and Immanuel Kant, came to be seen as those who created the philosophy of political modernity.

There is no reason to doubt the radical innovativeness of this thinking, nor the fact that it happened in Europe. But two insights need to be retained from our brief reconstruction. First, this innovation was generated in the face of severe problems and challenges to the prevailing self-understanding of just and effective authority. It emerged from the diagnosis of a crisis before it became constructive. At most, one may say that these thinkers made a virtue out of necessity. Second, this thinking wove two components tightly together that do not easily and self-evidently go together, namely the individual and the territory. Those mostly concerned with the need to sustain authority emphasized the clear delimitation of the territory over which, and over whose population, the state should exercise full and undivided control. Those mostly concerned with the justification of authority, in turn, concluded that this could only emanate, in some way or other, from the individual members of the political collectivity. Both of these aspects have problems of their own, which have been widely discussed in political theory ever since: how a state effectively controls a population and the boundaries of a territory, and how a common will emerges from a multitude of human beings (for a recent summary, see Wagner 2023). That the politico-philosophical link between a territory and a multitude of individuals generates specific additional problems, we may call them problems of political economy and ecology, has been less widely observed but is central for current purposes.

The conditional coherence of political modernity

The conceptual link between a territory and the individuals that reside in it was an implicit condition for the coherence of further reasoning in the philosophy of political modernity. It is widely accepted that the belief in, and commitment to, autonomy is the core component of modernity, often understood as referring to individual autonomy, to personal freedom. As a political concept, furthermore, some notion of collective autonomy is required, such as in terms of collective self-determination or democracy. The articulation of individual with collective autonomy is open to a variety of interpretations and historical transformations, but there is always some kind of articulation, at times more explicit than at others. Thus the early political philosophy of modernity presupposed a collectivity composed of individuals and was even hypothesized to be constituted by those individual members through the social contract. In historical perspective, though, the European states pre-existed any contract (read: constitution), and for a long time the inhabitants of the territory remained subjects without a say in the contract, rather than becoming citizens. Therefore, the territory and the population were de facto a given, and the relation between individual and collective autonomy was both theorized and practically determined within this framework.

Radical as the hypothesis of founding a polity through a social contract between its individual members was, it was not widely found very persuasive. The assumption that reason-endowed individual human beings would be willing to enter with others into such a contract for the sake of peace and survival was too abstract, failing to convincingly indicate why reason would prevail over human passions. To be sustainable, such a contract required additional conditions to be fulfilled, namely substantive bonds that tie the individuals to each other and create a common concern. The answer to this requirement was found in the extension of commercial relations and, thus, the creation of a division of social labour that would make people dependent on each other, or if one prefers, interdependent with each other. Specifically, the increasing role of trade in the relations between human beings was seen as giving more importance to – predictable – interests and reducing the role of – uncontrollable – passions. Fostering such interdependence through commercial ties would secure peace, as in the 'gentle commerce' (*doux commerce*) argument associated with Montesquieu. In a second step, it was furthermore argued that the ensuing specialization would increase productivity. A market society, therefore, would also enhance the wealth of nations in the reasoning developed by Adam Smith. Albert Hirschman (1977) famously saw this intellectual debate about passions and interests as providing 'arguments for capitalism before its triumph', but if we stay with our reflections on the concept of capitalism above, these were arguments for commercial society rather than capitalism as it would emerge later.

Specifically, wealth creation was linked to specialization, intensification of work and the division of labour rather than to increasing exploitation of biophysical resources. Relating intellectual history to economic history, one can see these arguments as provoked by the observation of the 'industrious revolution', which considerably extended trade relations between households, in particular in the Netherlands and Great Britain. It was not at all implausible to consider that the increase of wealth in parts of Western Europe and, more arguably, domestic pacification were due to this rise of commercial society.

As Charbonnier (2020: chs 2 and 3) compellingly shows, politico-economic thinking up to 1800 remained firmly aware of the limitations posed by available biophysical resources, in particular land. The connection between liberty and property has sometimes been seen as an ideological tool paving the way for the rise of the bourgeoisie and of capitalism. But rather than an expression of 'possessive individualism' (C. B. MacPherson), it linked the political commitment to personal autonomy with the economic concern for dealing with material necessity. Property referred foremost to property of land, and it was assumed that safe possession of land would entice landowners to make improvements on the natural endowment and, thus, enhance material well-being, as argued by Hugo Grotius and John Locke, for example. In addition, political economists were aware of the social consequences of their approach to resource limits. As Malthus (1798: 63) stated, 'When these two fundamental laws of society, the security of property and the institution of marriage, were once established, inequality of conditions must necessarily follow. Those who were born after the division of property would come into a world already possessed.' Writing *Wealth of Nations* more than two decades before Malthus's *Essay on Population* was published, Adam Smith was similarly concerned about finding ways to increase wealth against the background of a given resource endowment.

Therefore, one may well argue that the 'commercial republicanism' of the seventeenth and eighteenth centuries was a quite coherent political philosophy based on individual autonomy, on the one hand, and on sustaining the polity socially through commercial bonds and ecologically relying on renewable organic resources, on the other. True, the theory tended to justify an oligarchic regime based on unequal access to the ownership of land and, concomitantly, exclusion from political participation of the propertyless who supposedly could not be expected to act responsibly. But it did not necessarily work with a conceptual barrier to greater equality. Rather, the actual reality of the emerging commercial societies of the eighteenth century – only a few of which, such as the Netherlands and later the United States, were indeed republics – could be interpreted as an incomplete realization of the commercial–republican philosophy, to be completed in struggles for equality and recognition of those who were not yet fully included. Inspired by his reading of Hegel, Axel Honneth elaborated a proposal for interpreting world history after 1800 as an open-ended sequence of struggles for recognition, and we will come back to both the usefulness and the inconsistencies of this proposal in the next chapter.

At this point, that which was indeed a barrier to coherently realizing commercial republicanism and was recognized as such at the time is to be explored further, namely, the availability of land, which in the thinking of the time stands for biophysical resources in general. Combining the self-founding of a polity through the social contract with making this polity viable through commerce, commercial republicanism had created a tension between the stable territorial limits of the polity and the dynamic of commercial exchange, which after all was the engine of improvement, of wealth creation. One might say that this is a conceptual tension that does not need to become actual under all circumstances. But it was identified and critically discussed at the turn of the eighteenth century, and this in two strikingly opposed ways.

While clearly building his thinking on social contract theory and political economy, in *The Closed Commercial State*, published in 1800, Johann Gottlieb Fichte came to the conclusion that this tension could only be resolved by closing the borders of a state for individual commerce. A state should see that its natural borders are set in such a way that the material needs of its population can be met with available resource endowments, and subsequently the commerce with other states was to be limited and controlled. Thus the state would be enabled to take care of domestic justice, and it would not enter into conflict with other states, given that it could guarantee the basic material needs of its own population. While phrased as a politico-philosophical treatise, the proposal was motivated by the observation that contemporary reality was far from ideal. For this reason, Fichte was also well aware that it would not be received favourably by the Prussian government to which it was addressed. In a prefatory note, he wrote:

> Europe has, in the field of commerce, great advantages over the rest of the world; that it takes the resources and products of the rest of the world for itself, to an extent far greater than what its own resources and products could provide; that each European state, no matter how unfavorable may be its balance of trade with the other European states, nevertheless derives some advantage from this common exploitation of the rest of the world, and never gives up the hope that it can swing the balance of trade in its favor and thus derive a still greater advantage from the present arrangement. All these advantages it would surely have to forsake if it were to step out of the great European community of commerce. (Fichte 1800)

In other words, Fichte recognized the availability of biophysical resources as a constraint for the coherence of commercial republicanism, and he also saw that European commercial societies had overcome this constraint by drawing on resources of other societies, thus infringing the principles of the theory.

At the same time, on the other side of the North Atlantic, Thomas Jefferson also recognized the issue. He envisaged the recently founded United States of America as an 'empire of liberty' and connected his version of commercial republicanism explicitly with the 'agrarian question'. In his view, in line with neo-republicanism in general, freedom required independence of means and, thus, every citizen needed to have sufficient land for satisfying their material needs. In contrast to Europeans, who tended to see the earth as 'already possessed', though, he saw the United States as in a condition to meet this requirement, namely, through 'western expansion', a policy he actively and successfully promoted during his time as president of the United States at the expense of Native Americans. In other words, commercial republicanism provided a rather coherent political philosophy for the domestic concerns of a polity built on personal freedom, but republicans of the turn of the eighteenth century were aware that the existing polities tended towards relying on natural resources outside their own territory, the 'ghost acres' (Pomeranz). Fichte and Jefferson provided the most explicit recognition of the insight, with the former trying to put a statist check on this tendency and the latter finding a resolution in the special circumstances of his own polity.

The frontier thesis revisited

Resource availability and social change

At the end of the nineteenth century, Frederic Jackson Turner (2014 [1893]) proposed to read the history of the United States in the light of the exploration of the western frontier, placing the emphasis on the closure of the frontier at his time of writing and thus envisaging an upcoming social transformation (which we will address in chapter 5 below). In its detail, Turner's original frontier thesis is of remaining – and maybe increasing – interest because of the connection he makes between changes in resource availability and social change, including personality change. He suggested that the frontier experience created a new kind of human being. Even though he does not mention Jefferson, he can easily be understood as reading the nineteenth-century 'western expansion' as realizing the 'empire of liberty' in the United States. After the Second World War, Hannah Arendt (1970) – German-Jewish exile, naturalized US citizen and neo-Roman republican *avant la lettre* – saw the prosperity in the Thirteen Colonies as a condition of success for the 'American Revolution', whereas the unanswered social question doomed the French Revolution to failure, in her view. She did not reflect on the sources of US prosperity, though.

Walter Prescott Webb (1952) turned the frontier thesis into a key component of global history, beyond the specific experience of the United States, and Immanuel Wallerstein in turn elaborated his world-systems approach against this background. More recently, Jürgen Osterhammel (2009: ch. 7) tried to use the notion of frontier, again beyond the US experience, for a global history of the nineteenth-century 'transformation of the world'. This indicates that the dynamic of spatial expansion is increasingly considered a key to world history, and with it the increasing intensity of resource extraction, although the latter sometimes only implicitly. What gets lost in the generalization and – if I may say so – globalization of the frontier thesis is, first, the specificity of the US context and, subsequently, the possible link between changes in resource use and social change. In our attempt at providing a context-sensitive global history, in contrast, the way in which frontier exploration was seen as an answer to an open question of societal self-understanding in the United States needs to be taken in its specificity. In this light, we will have to return to the US case repeatedly in what follows. While running in parallel with European transformations, the articulation between (what should later be called) the social and the ecological question differed systematically between the two settings, and even more so from other world regions.

Charbonnier's thesis: the relation between freedom and affluence

In Pierre Charbonnier's approach, the relation between changes in resource use and social and political change is central, and he is without doubt right in emphasizing that the aspirations and struggles for freedom have been framed by a material history (Charbonnier 2020: 11). But in pursuing this hypothesis, as mentioned above, he claims that '[P]olitical autonomy initially relied on the prospect of material prosperity to make itself desirable. [. . .] There are reasons to believe that freedom without affluence would have been less attractive' (Charbonnier 2020: 49). However, the evidence for this connection is not at all as compelling as he claims.

For good reason, Charbonnier assigns a central place to Adam Smith as the scholar who explicitly connected freedom with wealth, thus inaugurating the 'liberal pact' (Charbonnier 2020: 103). In the Enlightenment intellectual constellation, in which republicanism is linked to political economy, there is little mention of wealth or affluence. Before Smith, the main argument for extending the realm of commerce was enhancing peace both within and between states; Smith's reasoning on the wealth of nations was a rather late addition to this debate (Hirschman 1977). The nexus of property and improvement does not as such entail a promise of affluence. While it linked liberty to efficiency, and thus potentially to greater material well-being, it did so by accepting the time-honoured natural resource constraint, and thus was far from any notion of abundance. Tying intellectual history again to economic history, the actual increase in wealth in Western Europe between 1650 and 1800 may well be related to liberty, but tenuously so, and in as far as it is, it is open as to what degree this is due to the freedom of domestic commerce and the industrious revolution and to what degree to external commerce that was more an exercise of domination over others than of freedom. It is telling that Charbonnier discusses at length Fichte's 'closed commercial state', which constrains the increase of material well-being in the name of justice, whereas he mentions Jefferson only in passing in a section of his analysis that refers to the mid-nineteenth century and without emphasizing the dependence of the 'empire of liberty' on 'western expansion'. Indeed, the promise of wealth is more closely related to what Charbonnier (2020: 130 and 150) calls the 'second birth of modernity' or the 'enigma of modern politics', located in the first half of the nineteenth century and linked to the systematic exploitation of the vertical frontier of deep coal mining. More than Charbonnier seems willing to grant, however, these second origins break the 'liberal pact', or at least transform it beyond recognition, as shall be shown in the following chapter.

4

Vertical Frontiers and the Great Divergence

The problem that the 'original' rise in CO_2 emissions meant to solve

The official objective of global climate policy, as expressed by the IPCC, is to limit the warming of the atmosphere of the earth to 1.5°C, or at least to 2°C, compared with the temperature before industrialization, the latter being specified as 'the reference period 1850–1900 [which] approximates pre-industrial global surface temperature' (IPCC 2022: SPM-7 and elsewhere). This definition places our search for the social causes of climate change squarely in the nineteenth century, even in the second half of that century, and it already identifies the causes, even though very summarily, in industrialization. This reasoning implicitly recurs each time when global climate change is evoked and climate policy defined on the basis of IPCC reports, as is mostly indeed the case. The objective of limiting global warming to a rise of 1.5°C is said to be future oriented, considering planetary boundaries, but as a measurement tool it is rooted in the past, pointing to the supposed moment when human action effectively started to change the climate. Even though the IPCC reports are not explicit on this issue, furthermore, one may even recognize there the underlying assumption that humankind embarked during that period on a basically linear trajectory on which it is still situated but which it needs to leave as a matter of urgency.

Data about CO_2 emissions appear to confirm this reasoning. From extremely low levels, emissions due to burning fossil fuels rise from the early nineteenth century onwards, accelerating from mid-century (see Figure 1.1 in chapter 1), and they rise in Great Britain, the original site of the Industrial Revolution, with other European countries and the United States significantly contributing only from the late nineteenth century (Figure 1.2). But rather than taking these data for an answer, we need to consider them as opening up questions. What were the problems that were meant to be solved by emitting carbon dioxide in Great Britain and later in other countries in the nineteenth century?

As we saw in the preceding chapter, West European societies had transformed considerably, albeit slowly, in the wake of the maritime expansion, drawing on additional resources and developing a new self-understanding. Great Britain and the Netherlands, in particular, had become commercial societies generating 'wealth' and even 'luxury'. By the end of the eighteenth century, nevertheless, critical concern was increasingly voiced. In current terminology, this concern is best understood as addressing the consequences of economic growth, even as pointing out unavoidable 'limits to growth' under the prevailing assumptions (Wrigley 2010: 191).

One major expression of this concern was about a supposed scarcity of wood. With growing populations, forests had been cleared both to provide for firewood and timber and to convert land for use as pasture, for agriculture and for dwelling purposes (e.g., Richards 2003: 221–7). There was hardly any absolute scarcity: the supposed scarcity was one of effective demand, of success, rather than of supply. The debate about wood shortage reflected rising prices due to increasing demand, as well as changing conventions of wood usage, including increased commercialization and explicit moves towards forest management. Incidentally, the term 'sustainability' (*Nachhaltigkeit*) was coined in the German scholarship of forest management in the eighteenth century, although it found wider usage only in the late twentieth century (Radkau 2012 [2007]).

In broader terms, the debate about the supposed wood shortage signalled scarcity of land. Wood prices rose because of increasing demand for wood itself, as well as because of the pressure to convert forests for other uses. Thus we return to Malthus and his theorem that land availability necessarily limits population growth. Why, one may want to ask, was this notion developed at the end of the eighteenth century? What was the precise concern Malthus wanted to express? The finiteness of the globe had already been known, in principle, for three centuries. In practice, though, planetary bound-

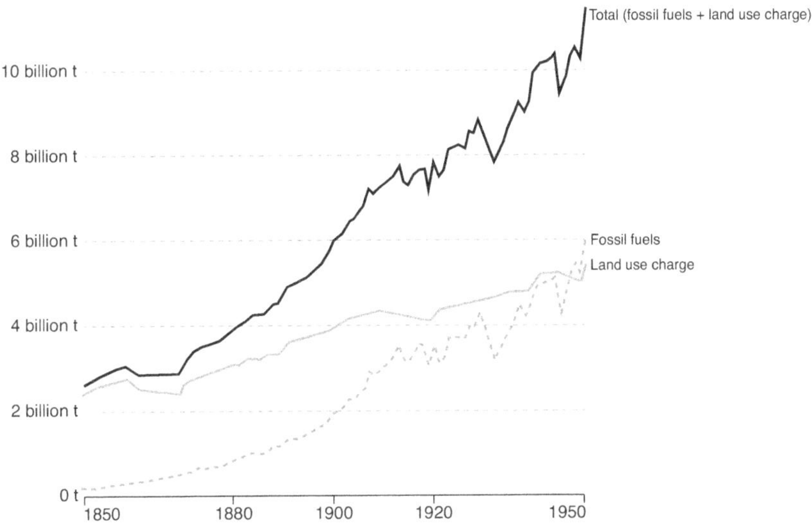

Figure 4.1 Global CO_2 emissions due to fossil fuels and land-use change, 1850–1950

Source: Hannah Ritchie, Max Roser and Pablo Rosado, 2020, *CO_2 and Greenhouse Gas Emissions*. Published online at OurWorldInData.org. at https://ourworldindata.org/co2-and-greenhouse-gas-emissions

aries, as one says today, were not yet in sight by 1800. In global perspective, indeed, land-use change, which in most cases involved deforestation, even remained the main source of CO_2 emissions into the atmosphere until far into the twentieth century (see Figure 4.1 above), due to both the destruction of carbon sinks and the burning of wood. From the eighteenth century onwards, however, land-use change takes place mostly outside Western Europe, very significantly in America, both North and South. In Western Europe, deforestation had occurred earlier, and further land-use change was limited precisely because of the insight into the need for forest management and the comparatively high population density (e.g., Marks 2020: 117–18).

While Malthus addressed the scarcity of land in a particularly pointed way, other political economists, including Adam Smith and David Ricardo, were similarly aware of the issue (Wrigley 2010: ch. 1; 2016: ch. 2). They were reasoning against the background of a society reliant on organic resources because this is what they observed, and they did not imagine an alternative resource base. Thus we have broadly identified the problem but not yet the way towards a solution because none was known at the time. 'Energy became a problem in the early modern period. [. . .] Ultimately, coal burning proved to be the way out of the energy cul-de-sac' (Richards 2003: 621–2). Today, we seem to know that the solution was 'industrialization', which occurred through the 'Industrial Revolution', but the meaning of these terms remains contested. 'Coal burning' on its own did not amount to a revolution.

The use of coal in England increased from the sixteenth century in response to a combination of the rising price of wood and coal's easy accessibility for surface extraction. Coal production increased more than tenfold between the middle of the sixteenth and the beginning of the eighteenth century. By 1700, coal accounted for almost half of the total energy consumption, a share that rose to almost 80 per cent by 1800 and more than 90 per cent by 1850, with production increasing fivefold between 1700 and 1800. This rise was not only due to population increase, as per capita energy consumption almost doubled between 1700 and 1800 (Wrigley 2010: 37). Coal was used for heating, both for residential use, significantly in the rapidly growing city of London, and in commodity production. As such, it was replacing wood and charcoal without any major change in the form of use. Thus we observe a gradual transformation of the resource base in a commercial society, moving beyond organic resources. 'The coal transformation of the sixteenth and seventeenth centuries opened up a new, strategic resource to add to the influx of wealth gained by mercantile and colonial expansion' (Richards 2003: 240). It added a 'subterranean forest' (Sieferle 2010 [1982]: part III) to the range of available energy sources.

This transformation, though, precedes the Industrial Revolution, if by the latter we refer to the use of inorganic (better: paleo-organic) resources for the generation of mechanical energy, rather than only thermal energy, the key example being the coal-fired steam engine. 'Coal became the fuel of choice [. . .] well before the steam engine created a new, ravenous demand for coal' (Richards 2003: 194). The move to paleo-organically generated mechanical energy was practically significant in two main steps, succeeding each other. First, the steam engine was used to drain mines and, thus, permit deep shaft mining, making vastly more coal deposits accessible. While the early steam engine was very inefficient, this mattered little for this purpose because it was running on the coal that its employment itself helped to extract. In other areas, such as cotton weaving, the steam engine was adopted very slowly and hesitantly because producers had to pay for the coal, whereas hydro energy was freely available, albeit site dependent (Malm 2016). The gradually increasing use of the steam engine went along with improvements in its energy efficiency and in its mobile use, and it is these steps for which James Watt is known, rather than for inventing the steam engine as such. These improvements, second, extended the range of its use, most importantly for transportation, namely by railroad and steamship. In turn, the new means of transportation enhanced possibilities for (long-distance) commerce, while at the same time further increasing the demand for coal, namely for the production of iron and steel. This rapid development set in by the 1830s, not earlier, and within decades spread from England to other European countries and the United States. Furthermore, it was not predicted, either by the classical political economists, as we have seen, or by other knowledgeable observers in the early nineteenth century.

While, as mentioned earlier, this is not the place to intervene in detail in the debate about the timing of the Great Divergence and the causes of 'the rise of Europe', the preceding description both draws on and leads to conclusions about this debate. It suggests that the Great Divergence did not happen during a short identifiable period but was a long-term process, with a marked point of acceleration at its end, though (for a recent comprehensive discussion, see O'Brien 2022). Given the long duration, it is also evident that many factors played a role in this process. While these insights are overall congruent with the state of debate, one additional observation needs to be made, given that we here are searching for the driving forces in the increasing use of fossil fuels. Some current scholars emphasize the role of political and legal institutions, not least property rights, and the role of scientific and technical innovation, of human ingenuity, but they show little awareness of the fact that institutions and ingenuity rarely generate material 'wealth' *cum nihilo*. Mostly, they enable a different way of exploiting biophysical resources, which is scarcely, if at all, addressed in institutional and techno-epistemic approaches.

The discussion of one example helps clarify the issue. In a recent overview, Mark Koyama and Jared Rubin (2022) aim to explain 'the historical origins of economic growth'. While painting a broad picture, they quickly sidestep the arguments by E. A. Wrigley (2010, 2016, and earlier) and Kenneth Pomeranz (2000) about the crucial significance of coal (both) and the 'ghost acres' made exploitable for Europe in the transatlantic trilateral trade (Pomeranz), but they do so in an ad hoc and unsystematic way. Exploring the question of why the Industrial Revolution took place first in Britain and not elsewhere, they point out that Germany and China also had coal deposits, but they overlook the fact that Germany's deposits required deep mining from the beginning, unlike England's, and that China developed other means to successfully deal with the emerging limits of the advanced organic economy until the middle of the nineteenth century (Marks 2020: 110–17). Furthermore, they do recognize that the society that was most similar to England in the eighteenth century was the Netherlands, but they fail to develop a comparison of these two societies' relevant features, which would quickly have revealed that the Netherlands did not have coal but used peat instead to satisfy rising energy demand and came up against resource limits in the eighteenth century, while coal-using England became the richest society on the globe.

No reasonable scholar will claim now that a single factor explains 'the rise of Europe'. But Koyama and Rubin fail to understand the particularity of Wrigley's and, in my reading, also Pomeranz's claim, even though the former at least is quite explicit. Saying that it is hard to identify a 'sufficient cause or combination of causes', Wrigley argues that it 'may be possible to make a claim of a different type – that *without* the presence of a given factor that change in question would have been impossible' (Wrigley 2010: 21; emphasis in original). And in conclusion, '[*W*]*ithout* coal no industrial revolution was possible in the circumstances of an organic economy' (Wrigley 2010: 193, emphasis in original; see also Wrigley 2016: 202–3; despite his critique of Pomeranz, Vries 2001: 224–5, appears to accept the argument). One might say that the claim is tautological, namely, if the Industrial Revolution is defined as a historical economic transformation based on the diffusion of coal-fired machines and production processes. But it is not if it is read as pointing to the way in which the problems of advanced organic economies – in Europe, India, China and Japan – were defined and overcome or not. Counterfactually, we may just ask, without being able to give an answer, what course world history would have taken if the perceived problems of the advanced organic economy had been addressed by further improving the use of organic resources, as was done in China and Japan, rather than switching to paleo-organic ones.

Discarding the focus on energy for understanding the Industrial Revolution, Koyama and Rubin's reasoning denies the relevance of biophysical resources in a way that became dominant in economics by the middle of the twentieth century, even though at the time of the Industrial Revolution it was not. Let us briefly look at how the history of economic developments feeds into – or feeds from? – this mainstream economic thinking. All scholars agree that the resource constraint that had informed the Smithian view of growth through specialization and division of labour had been overcome during the Industrial Revolution. Institutionalists argue that the stable institutional framework of western societies, in particular property rights and markets, had enabled this growth (e.g., Acemoglu and Robinson 2012: ch. 7). Techno-epistemic approaches point to the technical innovations, prompted by a 'culture of growth' (Mokyr 2016), that increased productivity and continued to do so, driven by market competition that stimulated processes of 'creative destruction' (Joseph Schumpeter). Thus what came to be called Schumpeterian growth, based on a new relation of human beings to nature, tended to replace Smithian growth, which relied on relations between human beings. Mokyr (2016: 16) speaks briefly about a 'game against nature' but does not specify the rules or the adversary and never comes back to the issue after this opening salvo. In both views, there is some notion that an arrangement for 'sustained growth' had been reached for the first time in human history. Institutional arrangements and innovation were seen as mutually supportive. Future growth only required the stability of the existing institutions and further inventions. The term 'sustained' (still used by Wrigley 2016; Koyama and Rubin 2022: 6) is meant to refer to the introduction of a mechanism that overcomes fluctuations in economic activity due to dependence on population developments and climate and weather variations, which existed in the prior organic economy. Clearly, though, as Wrigley was aware, it is exactly the economy of 'sustained growth' that is unsustainable in the long run. The two main scholarly approaches for understanding the 'rise of the West' have little conceptual place for this feature, a question to which I return when discussing the hegemony of a concept of economic growth in the middle of the twentieth century (chapter 6).

The market-industrial and the liberal-democratic revolutions

Once more coal deposits had thus been made accessible and the range of coal uses enlarged, the trajectory of increasing fossil fuel use seems to have unavoidably been embarked on, or this is as it might look from a current perspective. And, indeed, the basic argument stands: the transgressing of the 'first vertical frontier' (Edward Barbier) is at the origins of fossil fuel-induced climate change. There is good reason to see the 1830s as a social tipping point, after which changes take place which are difficult to reverse, but we still need to understand exactly how and why. The analysis of the both long-winding and initially place-bound path towards fossil fuels complicates the standard picture by inviting further questions about both the social causes and the social consequences of the intensification of fossil fuel use. The remainder of this chapter will raise these questions for the nineteenth century and coal, whereas the subsequent one will do so for the first half of the twentieth century and oil. The analysis here will start by disentangling the components of the reinterpretation of the social world after 1800 and thus allow for a non-linear view of social change in the interconnection of these components. This view will be spelled out in the following steps through explorations of: how industrialization and resource use were perceived in the nineteenth century; how the social (or labour) question arose in the industrializing societies while the colonial question was neglected; and how the question of democracy was returned to political debate after having initially been sidelined after 1800. The whole set of questions was without convincing answers at the end of the nineteenth century. And this was the context in which the 'second vertical frontier', the one of crude oil and natural gas, was transgressed.

The decades around 1800 are often seen as the moment of world-historical rupture that brings modern society and/or modern capitalism about in a supposedly conjoined political and economic transformation, epitomized by the Industrial Revolution and the French Revolution. The Industrial Revolution indeed became part of a dominant narrative during the later nineteenth century, and this narrative stayed central in societal self-understanding at least until the 1960s (see Landes 1969), if not today (see chapter 9 below). The narrative connected scientific-technical progress with economic growth and enhanced material well-being. While immediately seen as an event of world-historical significance, in contrast, the French Revolution came to stand as a symbol for a new era, but it was less clear what this symbol stood for, the meaning of the three principles of the revolution – freedom, equality, fraternity – remaining contested. There was not even a consensus over whether the revolution was successful or defeated, again in contrast to the Industrial Revolution.

On a closer look, the interpretations of the social transformation around 1800 emphasized, though unevenly, four components of change – markets, industry, liberty, democracy – whose relations to the two events – the Industrial and French Revolutions – were complex and not free of ambiguities (see also Stråth and Wagner 2017: chs 4 and 5). As we have seen in the preceding chapter, the political theory that most coherently captured the West European transformations of the seventeenth and eighteenth centuries, commercial republicanism, placed the emphasis on markets and liberties through its articulation of social contract theory with political economy. As such, it was without doubt a highly innovative way of thinking about political orders and, as said before, it may even have had a certain coherence. However, it was at odds with the societal self-understanding that evolved during the nineteenth century, and it was ever more so as the nineteenth century went on. In basic conceptual terms, we may phrase this as the question of what happens once industry and democracy become key characteristics of societies that saw themselves as committed to (unequal) liberties and markets. Saying this, I need to underline that this did not happen any time soon after 1800. Rather, the term 'industry' was proposed to capture a transformation that emerged slowly, and the term 'democracy' came to be used as a claim to deal with the consequences of industry, both from mid-century onwards.

Before 1800, the word 'industry' referred to diligence and activity, as in 'industrious'. The adjective 'industrial' was used to refer to the making of commodities through the use of inanimate energy sources only from the 1830s, and the term 'Industrial Revolution', the first documented use of which dates to 1799, came into wider use only around 1840 and was made a key reference by Arnold Toynbee's lectures under this title published in 1884 (Osterhammel 2009: 909; Wrigley 2010: 48). Its coinage reflects the economic transformation brought about by transgressing the first vertical frontier. Expressing the change in Polanyian terms, the markets of the organic economy started to treat land as a commodity despite its fictitious character; the industrial economy included subterranean resources in commodification, even though they clearly were not produced to be sold either.

In turn, the aspect of democracy can be said to be at least implicitly present before 1800, as the notion of social contract hypothesized the citizen's consent to the agreement. In substance, though, neo-Roman republican thought was oligarchic, given the elaborate reasons why certain categories of persons could not be included in political participation. Equal universal suffrage came briefly onto the agenda during the French Revolution, but this is the dimension on which the revolution can be deemed to have failed. Suffrage remained restricted during the constitutional monarchies and the short-lived Second Republic, whereas even the Third Republic kept excluding women from the vote.

Thus, while we may say that the components of industry and democracy were added to the political philosophy of markets and liberty during the transformations around 1800, this occurred in a rather uneven and incoherent way. The second birth of modernity during the early nineteenth century, as Charbonnier calls it, remains enigmatic if the elements of continuity and rupture are not well defined. Charbonnier tends to see the new conceptual constellation as merely spelling out the liberal pact of abundance and liberty, which had been elaborated during the seventeenth and eighteenth centuries, under new circumstances owing to the introduction of 'industry', making abundance resource-dependent in a new way. He jumps from the connection of liberty with markets to one of industry with democracy (Charbonnier 2020: ch. 5) and pays little attention to the sequence of changes in the politico-conceptual arrangement, for which 'pact' is hardly an appropriate term in the nineteenth century. In my reading, this sequence should roughly be reconstructed like this. First, the promise of abundance was added to the societal self-understanding only tentatively and late, the land constraint making such a promise unfeasible except for Jefferson's spatially expanding 'empire of liberty' or through the colonial exploitation that Fichte tried to fend off. Second, it emerged only fully when the vertical-frontier resource addition made it feasible without adding land, which is what Charbonnier would characterize as the second birth. But even then, third, the promise of abundance only reached out to the propertied classes. And this limitation, fourth, was socially sustainable because democracy kept being rejected. A true connection between industry and democracy was only made at the end of the nineteenth century, and it was pushed onto the agenda by the workers' movement. We have discussed the first element in the preceding chapter. In what follows, the link between abundance and vertical-frontier resources will be shown in a brief discussion of contemporary interpretations of industrialization. Subsequently, the explicit social limitations of abundance and their consequences will be analysed. Thirdly, the return of democratic claims will be seen as a political project for overcoming those limitations. The guiding question, here as throughout, is which issue and what purpose is it that drives increasing resource use and, in this period in particular, the transition to fossil fuels.

The industrial 'transformation of the world' and its interpretations

By 1900, it was evident that the nineteenth century had witnessed a major 'transformation of the world', as well as a Great Divergence between Western Europe and North America on the one side, and most other world regions on the other, in terms of economic growth and material affluence. There was widespread agreement that industrial production methods made possible by fossil fuels were the core ingredient of this transformation, even though not necessarily the causes, which could be found in as different phenomena as religious ethics, institutional arrangements or alleged 'race'-related capacities.

Inaugurated in 1851 by the 'Great Exhibition of the Works of Industry of All Nations' in the purpose-built Crystal Palace in London's Hyde Park, regular world fairs became the international showroom for the advance of commodity manufacture (on the presentation of coal in the exhibition, see Jonsson 2020). The London exhibition responded to the 1844 *Exposition des produits de l'industrie française* in Paris and set the stage for the recurrence of the events in cities of different industrial nations. The 1893 fair in Chicago was meant to commemorate the 400th anniversary of Columbus's voyage. Frederick Jackson Turner gave his lecture on the American frontier on this occasion. The 1904 exhibition in St Louis commemorated the US purchase of Louisiana from France a century earlier, as instigated by Thomas Jefferson as key to the 'western expansion'. It was attended by Max Weber, who broadened his view on 'Occidental rationalism' and the relation between religion and society on a three-month journey through the United States and gave a lecture in St Louis. The world fairs illustrate the self-understanding of western elites through their celebratory self-presentations at the peak of western power. Their main themes wove a narrative of the rise of western civilization; many of them included the 'display' of colonized people. For our purposes, they provide evidence of how far western societies saw themselves as based on steadily advancing industrial production by means of energy gained from fossil fuels.

The world fairs certainly also meant to demonstrate increasing human mastery over nature. Current ecological debate often emphasizes the separation of nature and society in western thought that makes an instrumental attitude of human beings to nature possible (Latour 1991 is a key text). By implication, so the argument goes, the dependence of human life on non-human nature tends to fall into oblivion. Without denying that a transformation in the understanding of human–non-human relations took place in the course of the rise of fossil fuel-based industry, however, a closer look at European social self-observation during the nineteenth century shows that, in some way, the awareness of human dependence on non-human nature even increased because of the reliance of the new affluence and grandeur on fossil fuels. By the middle of the nineteenth century, coal was being used on a larger scale, and the spread of railways and steamships began to perceptibly change the mode of production and ways of working and living in European societies. Concern about the consequences had started to be raised even earlier (Jonsson 2020). Significantly, this concern came to address both core ecological themes, the emergence of which we tend to trace to the late twentieth rather than the late nineteenth century: the limited availability of natural resources and the planetary impact of resource use, specifically climate change as a consequence of burning fossil fuels.

The nineteenth-century version of the limits-to-growth argument was provided by William Stanley Jevons in *The Coal Question* of 1865, which was widely read and discussed after its initial publication and has been referred to again recently. (In between, its author was mostly known as one of the founders of the marginal utility school in economics.) Jevons's analysis contained every element of the reasoning on scarcity and frontiers set out here: he characterized coal as 'the material energy of our country' with 'miraculous powers'; he acknowledged that the Malthusian land constraint had been overcome thanks to this fossil resource; but he argued that Malthusian reasoning had not therefore been vanquished. While increasing use of coal had permitted rapid population increase, coal itself was a limited resource, and its exhaustion, the date of which he tried to calculate, would create a crisis of larger dimensions than those that Malthus had envisaged. At about the same time, the visibility of smoke from burning coal entering the atmosphere had also raised environmental concerns. Air pollution became a recognized issue for cities, in particular London. But even the hypothesis of a relation between the level of CO_2 in the atmosphere and global temperature was formulated, first as a general hypothesis by US scientist and women's rights campaigner Eunice Newton Foote in 1856, long fallen into oblivion, then by the British scientist John Tyndall in 1859, and in a first attempt at calculation by the Swedish climatologist Svante Arrhenius in 1896 (see, e.g., Weart 2008: 3–8).

The second half of the nineteenth century was a period of 'Great Acceleration' (see Figure 1.1), minor in terms of resource use and transformation of the earth compared to the post-Second World War Great Acceleration (Steffen et al. 2015), but perceivable in a similar way, maybe even in a more pronounced way because of the almost complete absence of fossil fuels from economy and society before.

It is quite widely known that Max Weber considered the possibility of sociocultural challenges to modern capitalism, namely the return of old ideals or the rise of new prophets. He did not believe that modern capitalism was immune to all contestation, even though according to him it did not rely on motivational support any longer once the 'steel casing' had been firmly established. It is less widely perceived that he also envisaged the end of capitalism due to exhaustion of its material support, namely when 'the last ton of fossil fuel will have been burnt'. Weber polemicized against the proposal of an energy-based social theory, made by Wilhelm Ostwald in a debate at the newly founded German Society for Sociology (Osterhammel 2009: 928). But he acknowledged that material resources mattered for social change and should be considered in any analysis of social life.

Thus far, I consider we have established two insights about resource use across the nineteenth century: first, the transgressing of the first vertical frontier unleashed major economic growth while making western economies and societies reliant on fossil fuel, a fact of which the elites in those societies were well aware. Second, there was also awareness of the unsustainability of this new economic-ecological regime because of both inherent limitations and ecological damage, but the risks were seen as lying rather far in the future, even mostly not yet amenable to a sufficiently precise assessment. If we left the analysis at this point, it would be possible to understand the rather triumphant self-understanding of western elites, including their attitude of postponing action on the consequences of fossil fuel reliance into the future. One might conclude that, for the time being, the liberal pact of joining liberty with affluence had worked and had, as Charbonnier tends to think, become a driving force of history. If so, we would have fulfilled our objective of identifying a logic of expansion that led to the resource-intensive trajectory and ultimately to climate change. Today, we would just live at a more advanced moment on this trajectory and face urgent action without possibility of further postponement. However, the account is too selective and linear, and the jump towards identifying a logic is premature.

The social question, domestic and global

Again, taking the world fairs as an illustrative indicator, we can note that the glorious self-presentation of industrial civilization really takes off (if one may use this phrase) only by the middle of the nineteenth century, sparked by competition for attention and recognition between Great Britain and France, rather than earlier. This provides one more element for holding that the link between the improved steam engine and the storming of the Bastille in the 1780s, on the one side, and major social transformations, on the other, is more tenuous than often assumed – which is not to say that it is entirely absent. It is far-fetched to suggest that the gradual realization of the promise of affluence marked social change throughout the nineteenth century.

But before elaborating on this observation further, we need to introduce a distinction as to the social location of the promise. One can either assume that it applied only to European commercial societies, given that it was being voiced in European thought and made conditional on a particular organization of social relations. Or one can assume that it was a universal promise that, sooner or later, would be fulfilled across the globe, as in later modernization theory. During much of the nineteenth century, though, it was for most people fulfilled neither in Europe nor in other world regions (with the partial exception of North America, to which we will come back). But the promise was broken in rather different ways in different locations, due to the way Europe had been connected with other world regions. In Europe, the deviation from the expectations that had been raised came to be called 'the social question', which moved to the centre of public debate in the closing decades of the century. It referred to the discrepancy between the increasing wealth in a small section of society and the misery of large parts of the population in European metropolitan states. This question could also have been posed for the populations of colonized territories or for the indigenous or slave populations in 'settler' societies, but it was not, or at least not generally, in the same way as for the 'domestic' social situation.

The sites of early industrialization in Europe were marked by impoverishment and worsening living and working conditions, despite increasing use of fossil fuels. People were working longer hours compared to pre-industrial times, and health had declined, not least due to living in worse hygienic conditions, in particular in the cities. Life expectancy did not increase during much of the nineteenth century in Europe and North America (e.g., Osterhammel 2009: 259). This situation was a major topic of public debate and of numerous investigations, such as those by Friedrich Engels on the working classes in England, by Charles Booth on the London poor, or by Frédéric LePlay on France, and of fictional accounts in literary realism, especially in England, such as in Benjamin Disraeli's novel *Sybil* with its notion of 'two nations' in 1845 or Charles Dickens's 1854 invention of 'Coketown' in *Hard Times*. More recent historico-sociological accounts have confirmed a picture in which the elites meant to 'govern misery' (Procacci 1993) rather than spreading abundance and let much time pass before they acknowledged the existence of a 'social question' (Castel 1995) or 'labour question', as it was called with a different emphasis in the United States and Great Britain, as a consequence of industrialization.

Rather than considering these developments as an aberration from an otherwise promising course towards general wealth and material well-being, they should be seen as an expected outcome of the recourse to fossil fuels in the very hierarchical societies of nineteenth-century Europe. Early industrialists knew about the promise of 'affluence', but they had no immediate intention of spreading it societywide. In his *Treatise on the Steam-Engine* of 1827, John Farey, whom one would today call a business consultant, underlined that the working class, aided by machines, would produce more 'surplus wealth' for the 'educated class in society', which might gradually also include a new 'middle class', whose members applied their minds rather than their hands to work (Farey 1827: v; cited in Malm 2016: 122).

By the mid-nineteenth century, one response in Europe to the deterioration of working and living conditions was the mobilization of the workers' movement to whom Marx and Engels aimed to give guidance, then rather unsuccessfully, in their *Communist Manifesto* of 1848. In turn, governments reacted to protests and strikes, often with oppression and censorship. In the absence of improvements, millions of Europeans emigrated to America, both South and North, as well as Southern Africa and Australia, in the hope of better conditions (e.g., Bayly 2004: 411; Hatton and Williamson 2005; McKeown 2004). In some cases, governments organized and stimulated emigration with the explicit purpose of reducing the likelihood of revolt at home. Often, those who became settlers had been rather poor and even faced famine in Europe. They were told about resource abundance and hoped to significantly improve their living conditions as well as social status in their destination societies. Their arrival changed the social structure in those societies, creating or reinforcing a hierarchy in which natives and (descendants of) slaves occupied the lower ranks, which entailed having less access to the resources that were used.

These movements of people were so sizeable that they marked a significant change in socio-ecological constellations, both in Europe and in the destination regions, but in highly different ways. In terms of resource use, emigration further eased the constraints in Europe as millions of European emigrants came to use resources elsewhere directly, rather than as 'ghost acres' made available through trade.

Outside Europe, settlers partly contributed to horizontal frontier transgression, be it in the United States, where this term came to be used, or in Australia, southern Africa and some Latin American countries such as Argentina. Land was not 'scarce' there, and the settlers' view was that it was not 'possessed' either. Towards the end of the nineteenth century, partly due to the closure of the horizontal frontier, they also moved into industry and mining. Native inhabitants of these regions were further displaced, as in the United States or Australia, or mobilized for low-paid work under high surveillance, such as in gold and diamond mines in South Africa. The latter also held true for slaves, in particular in the United States and Brazil, in continuation from earlier periods working in plantations.

The democratic political imaginary

Before moving from resources to self-understandings, we should again briefly recapitulate. The idea that freedom and wealth creation go hand in hand was developed in late-eighteenth-century political economy, arguably reflecting the experience with the industrious revolution in Western Europe. This thinking acknowledged the land constraint, though, which arguably posed a limit to further wealth creation along the lines of this model. Subsequently, the land constraint was overcome by transgressing the vertical frontier of deep coal mining, opening up a new avenue of wealth creation. However, living and working conditions worsened in the industrial areas of Europe, and wealth increased only for small groups in society. As a consequence, Europeans emigrated to other world regions, where they occupied land or extracted resources and/or dominated the native population. The supposed link between freedom and wealth within one space turned out to be illusionary. Charbonnier suggested that freedom only became attractive because it was connected with the expectation of increased wealth. In the light of the above, one may be inclined to think, vice versa, that wealth creation was highly unequal because freedom was denied to the majority of the population. This hypothesis will now be explored in two steps: first, we will briefly see how the economy was transformed in such a way that Smith's expectations were undermined. Second, we shall show how particular claims to freedom arose because of the denial of participation in wealth creation. This particular freedom was collective freedom, or democracy.

By the middle of the nineteenth century, two aspects of the ongoing economic transformation in Western Europe were clearly discernible: the organization of production in ever-larger factories, and the rising number of people working in those factories. The former change tended to replace market coordination with a hierarchy of command chains, the latter questioned the vision of a society of independent property owners. Karl Marx was to describe these changes as a trend towards the 'concentration and centralization' of capital, on the one hand, and, on the other, as the class division of society into the owners of the means of production and those who had only labour power to sell. Calling his analysis a 'critique of political economy', he was quite explicit about his conclusion that these changes undermined the commercial republicanism of which 'political economy' was a key component. Doing so, he broke with critics of society whom he himself called 'utopian socialists' (later to be referred to as 'early socialists') and who had stayed connected with the political philosophy of republicanism (Honneth 2015). Even though he focused on socio-economic changes, which he came to see as inevitable, the underlying cause lay in the change in 'productive forces', not least new kinds of machinery powered by fossil fuel.

In Marx's view, the socio-economic changes would equally inevitably bring political changes about, namely the rise of the factory workers to become the dominant political force. To develop the argument, he drew on the intellectual heritage of the French Revolution, which had brought equal universal suffrage briefly onto the political agenda, and linked it with his observation of an emerging majority of the population that shared an oppressed condition, the industrial proletariat.

In the course of – or, at the very least, in the aftermath of – the Philadelphia Declaration of Independence, the French Revolution and the Haitian Revolution, the preferred term for the emerging political order became 'republic' rather than 'democracy'. This can well be seen as appropriately due to the way in which the political actors of the time drew on the Greco-Roman politico-conceptual heritage. The term 'republic' was used as a translation of Aristotle's *politeia*, which referred to the political order, whereas Aristotle had mostly used the term 'democracy' for a particular extent of participation in a political order, namely the government of the many. Significantly, the emerging preference for the term 'republic' left the extent of participation open. Looking at the outcome of the struggle, it is clear that most European societies strongly restricted participation, be it in the emerging republics or in the majority of constitutionally bound monarchies. To offset tyrannical tendencies of one-person rule, well known from ancient debates, the monarchs were increasingly flanked by parliaments elected by small – though growing over time – numbers of property-owning male citizens and limited in their actions by the idea of rights of the individual. But nothing that would have been recognizable as 'democracy' was stably created in Europe until at least the 1860s. Even the historian who made the expression 'democratic revolution' popular for the political transformation of the period, R. R. Palmer, stated categorically: 'No "democrats" fought in the American Revolution' (Palmer 1953: 205; see also Palmer 1959). Without forcing a shortcut from intended meaning to outcomes, political developments after the revolution tended to confirm that eighteenth-century republicanism was an oligarchic political philosophy, which could avoid addressing explicitly the question of political participation until institutional change required an answer to it. Without exception, the answer lay then in providing justifications for exclusion. In the eighteenth and nineteenth centuries, '[t]he advocates of representative government had seen it not as a first step towards democracy but as an oligarchic alternative to it' (Mitchell 2011: 17). Rather than seeing the nineteenth century in Europe as the period of the rise of a bourgeoisie to power which combined market-industrial enrichment with a liberal-democratic political self-understanding, the historian Arno Mayer (1981) provocatively, but with good reason, identified this period as 'the persistence of the Old Regime'.

Nevertheless democracy, understood as equal universal suffrage as the norm of political participation, remained on the horizon and came to be demanded more strongly from mid-century onwards. Marx's correspondent Arnold Ruge called for the 'overcoming of liberalism by democratism' (cited in Conze et al. 1972: 884). As Reinhart Koselleck (Conze et al. 1972: 850), more than anyone else, has pointed out, 'democracy' became a 'universal expectational concept', a term that went far beyond the political experiences of the time but expressed the expectation of future political development. Observing US politics during the 1830s, Alexis de Tocqueville concluded that a process had been set in motion that would not be stopped until universal suffrage was reached. We can speak of a democratic political imaginary that was available in the aftermath of the French Revolution and that could be activated according to the circumstances. This was true not only for Europe, but the conditions for forceful activation of the imaginary varied widely, as I shall argue in the next chapter (e.g., for a historical political sociology of Chile, see Silva Pinochet 2017).

To speak about a democratic political imaginary is different from speaking about 'democratization' as one component of 'modernization'. The latter terms suggest a linear process driven by an incontrovertible logic, which may temporarily be halted and even reversed but can always be measured according to a concise scale. The term 'imaginary', in contrast, refers to a difference between the present and the future that is in need of interpretation and contestation, which is highly context dependent.

In the context of the mid-1800s, the call for democracy (re-) emerged when the discrepancy between wealth creation in the emerging industrial economy, on the one hand, and worsening living and working conditions, on the other, widened due to the denial and oppression of material claims by the workers' movement. Even a revolutionary-minded thinker like Marx agreed that 'political emancipation' due to suffrage rights would be an important step ahead, given the expected future electoral majority of the working class, even though it fell short of full 'human emancipation'. Importantly, the material claims and their plausible urgency were articulated in a different register than the connection between independence and responsibility in – tendentially oligarchic – republican thought. Instead of such a market society of independent producers, a conceptual possibility of which Marx was still aware, a capitalist society had emerged in the course of the nineteenth century in which most members remained dependent on others because of the need to sell their labour power in the absence of other property. For this reason, rather than being found convincing in its own right, full inclusion was gradually forced upon the elites of the persisting Old Regime by social movements in the course of the nineteenth and early twentieth centuries. As a consequence, critics of inclusive, equal-suffrage democracy had an easy target because the tension between the idea of independence as a condition for citizenship and the fact that the majority of voters depended on others for their livelihood was not resolved during the nineteenth century (see, e.g., Hirschman 1991, about electoral reform debates in Britain).

However, there is a line of reasoning in the history of socio-economic thought that suggests that it has been resolved since. 'Modern' societies are both commercial and democratic societies. A division of social labour exists in them that enhances productivity and wealth, yet makes all members of these societies interdependent with all others, thus creating strong social bonds between them – 'organic solidarity', as Emile Durkheim (2007 [1893]) called this link. This interdependence, no longer the individual property earned through the right to the product of one's own labour, is the new basis for responsible political behaviour. It is common to all members of a nation, not limited to a class of property owners; and the nation became the new agent of collective responsibility (Evers and Nowotny 1987; Wagner and Zimmermann 2004). There was broad awareness, but little detailed reflection, that this responsibility could be shouldered by the nation-state only because of the gains in resources due to the transgression of the vertical resource frontier.

The sociopolitical constellation in Europe towards the end of the nineteenth century contained a double tension: first, between the enhanced possibilities of material well-being, on the one hand, and its denial to the majority population, on the other; and second, between the imaginary of inclusive democracy, on the one hand, and its denial through suffrage restrictions, on the other. Historico-sociological and socio-philosophical accounts of this constellation recognize this double tension but tend to see it as being resolved, after considerable class conflict and wars, in a progressive, emancipatory way. Thus political rights were added to civic rights in the nineteenth century, and social rights in the twentieth, according to T. H. Marshall (1950). Or, in a more recent perspective, struggles for recognition fostered individualization and led to greater inclusion (Honneth 2011). But the emphasis on such accomplishment merely creates what we may call a doubly limited philosophy of history, which is exclusively 'domestic', focusing on the institutional containers of existing nation-states, and exclusively 'social', ignoring the material preconditions of the diagnosed progress. Such philosophy of history has marked the political imaginary of modernity, but it has largely ignored the reliance of 'modern' sociopolitical configurations on external resources, both land, horizontally and vertically exploited, and people elsewhere. Or rather: it denies these resources the conceptual place that they should have because such recognition would undermine the foundations of the theory.

At around 1900, the awareness of this denial was very limited, even though not entirely absent, as shown above. In theoretical terms, it was only the internationalism of the workers' movement that envisaged full global inclusion of people. But the practice of unions and workers' parties was very different. Later, from the middle of the twentieth century onwards, the implicit assumption was that processes of recognition could and would be extended globally, as they were extended within western societies to gradually include workers and women. This was the core of the post-Second World War sociology of 'modernization and development'. But, again, the practice in international politics was very different. In turn, availability and use of natural resources, including fossil fuels, was largely considered unproblematic, at least in the medium term, by 1900. By the end of the twentieth century, this was no longer the case. However, this insight stands in direct contradiction with the assumption that 'development' means following the West on its resource-intensive trajectory. I shall subsequently address this contradiction as it unfolded across the twentieth century.

The special case of the United States

The period around 1900 was the high point of European world domination, in the double sense of European states and European settlers dominating large areas of the globe and of European world interpretation imposing itself on other world regions, not least because of its apparent success. The debate about imperialism at the time and the ones about colonialism and decolonization from the middle of the twentieth century to the present are testimony to the asymmetric power relations between Europe and other world regions. As a consequence, the specific constellation of fossil fuel extraction, the arising social question and the democratic political imaginary that characterized Europe did not exist in other world regions. As briefly mentioned above, a 'global social question' in an equivalent way to the European 'domestic social question' did not emerge, partly because of the great variety of colonial or quasi-colonial situations, partly because of the dominance of the European world interpretation, which left other world-regional interpretations, which well existed in China, Russia and elsewhere, in the shadow of the European one.

The one major exception is the United States. In the preceding sections of this chapter, I have been speaking somewhat alternatingly about 'Europe' or 'western societies' The main difference in the spatial reference is the inclusion of the United States, and the answer to the questions if and at what point in time one includes the United States depends on the account one wants to provide. By the middle of the eighteenth century, the region of North America that was to become the United States was a set of settler colonies like others. By the end of the century, it had become one of the origins of the political revolution towards 'modernity'. Thus, if we focus on societal self-understandings, the United States should seemingly be part of the narrative from the late eighteenth century onwards on equal terms with Europe (and arguably Latin America, even though this is often overlooked). If we focus on resources and the transgression of the first vertical frontier, the picture looks different. This transgression is adequately located in Britain (and small areas of Western Europe) in the early nineteenth century, and it occurs in the United States much later in the nineteenth century, with a considerable acceleration at century's end. By century's end, though, the situation had thoroughly changed. In resource terms, the United States (as well as Germany) overtook Britain in coal mining and industrial output and was among the first countries (together with Russia) to explore the second vertical frontier of crude oil and natural gas. The Chicago World's Fair of 1893 was a demonstration of this new status. From this time on, it is rather appropriate, as a shorthand, to speak of the industrializing societies as 'the West'. In parallel, the United States also acquired – some may want to say strengthened – their particular societal self-understanding, of which the frontier thesis was one expression. Another indicator is that European travellers increasingly recognized the United States as a highly modern society, but as a modernity that was different from their own.

The United States is the only European settler colony that, as we may want to say, left the colonial condition of being subordinate to Europe and dependent on Europe for its own development during the nineteenth century. Numerous explanations have been offered for this particularity, including early institutional arrangements, Protestant religion and the Lockean worldview that the early settlers brought along with them. Without entirely discarding any of these explanations, one obtains a more comprehensive picture when one focuses on the constellation of resources, social structure and self-understanding, as we do here. Even by the early nineteenth century, the United States of the western expansion had abundant resources that were relatively easily accessible, both in terms of territory and climate, as well as exploitable for existing demand, such as cattle and cotton. It soon had a strong majority of its European settlers and their descendants, who lived mostly in segregation from the native and slave population but dominated them or pushed them off the usable territory. As a result of both features, the settlers became relatively wealthy and developed self-government of male property owners, as sketched in the republican tradition. Other settler societies had some of these features but not all of them. They had less, or less accessible, natural resources, again considering both territory and climate, and often a minority of settlers dominating a native and/or slave majority. As a consequence, these societies became very hierarchical, based on exclusion of a majority from both wealth and political participation.

In comparison with the social and the democratic questions that arose forcefully on the European public agenda during the second half of the nineteenth century, racialized minorities, poverty and political exclusion of Native Americans and African Americans were less recognized as public issues in need of resolution in post-Civil War United States. Thus the United States could appear as combining material abundance with democratic freedom, an early testimony of which is Tocqueville's account of 1835–40, even before fully exploring vertical resource frontiers. This view, clearly, can only be upheld if both the oppression and exploitation of the non-settler population and the rapid over-exploitation of the resources from the transgression of the horizontal frontier are ignored. Nevertheless, one can argue that this combination of resource endowment and relative economic and political equality among the white majority population created a virtuous circle that led to the United States becoming a world power by 1900. This is a widespread view among institutional economists (such as Acemoglu and Robinson) and economic historians (such as Barbier). The virtue appears in a different guise, though, when seen as an emergent attitude towards biophysical resources and people, shaped by the experience of abundance. More than at any earlier point in human history, one could detect here an emerging logic of expansion based on the apparently unending availability of resources and of the people who would (be made to) exploit them. The former impression was due to the horizontal westward expansion, and the emerging attitude was transmitted when moving towards vertical expansion, whereas the latter was due to the steadily increasing population both through immigration from Europe and Asia and, until it was halted, through the slave trade. Let it just be noted that there is, to the best of my knowledge, no diagnosis of constraint equivalent to Jevons's *Coal Question* in the United States during the nineteenth century, or at least not until 1893 and Turner's *Significance of the Frontier*.

To avoid misreading, this is here not an observation of an emerging US national character, as it was in Turner's frontier thesis. Rather, it is an observation of a world-historical juncture at the end of the nineteenth century. Economic development after the first vertical frontier had created class-divided societies in Europe in which questions were raised that could not be answered. European colonization, in turn, had created domination and resource extraction in the colonized and most of the settler societies, which generated racialized hierarchies without clear prospect of development. Only in the United States was a similar deadlock absent, and the rise of the United States in world politics and in the global economy gave the US experience a world-historical significance that would fully emerge during the twentieth century.

One could object to this interpretation by pointing out that within the United States itself a barrier to further development was identified, namely the frontier thesis itself. Turner had analysed the nineteenth century in the light of steady frontier exploration, but the point of his analysis was that the frontier had closed at his time of writing, that is, with the full extension of the United States to the Pacific Coast. In this sense, *The Significance of the American Frontier* was a crisis report, even though a veiled one. The diagnosis had some prima facie plausibility, but its author was not aware that the means for overcoming the crisis had already been found. From the middle of the nineteenth century onwards, crude oil started to be extracted in the United States, creating a new kind of boom town. In parallel, oil started to be extracted near the Black

Sea coast in Imperial Russia, (e.g., Barbier 2011: 481–4; see also the comprehensive overview in Smil 2021: 121). For the time being, let it just be noted that the United States benefited from the conjunction of new energy resources with the existing industrial fabric in a similar way, *mutatis mutandis*, as Britain did a century earlier with coal. The argument about the closing of the frontier should not be exaggerated, but the United States had started to face a resource constraint, a situation to which the society had not been used. As a socio-ecological constellation, this moment had similarities with the one of the late eighteenth century in Europe, when Smithian growth had appeared to reach its limits and Malthus had diagnosed constraints that, in his analysis, could not be overcome. The transgression of the first vertical frontier was the answer in Britain, the one of the second vertical frontier in the United States.

5

Fordism and the Path Towards the Great Acceleration

The second vertical frontier and the socio-ecological transformation of modernity

The decades around 1900 are often referred to as the period of the Second Industrial Revolution, driven by new technical innovations leading to the emergence of the electrical and chemical industry. Both types of innovation were powered, in the literal sense, by fossil fuels – electricity was produced in coal-fired power stations (as well as by hydropower – see chapter 7 for further discussion), and chemical production required derivates of oil as did the combustion engine, which found increasing diffusion for transport purposes. If one asserts, quite rightly, that the innovations led to the emergence of new industries, then one should not overlook that the diffusion of the innovations depended on further advances on the first vertical frontier of coal mining and the transgression of the 'second vertical frontier' of crude oil and natural gas extraction. The use of coal kept expanding beyond the middle of the twentieth century; the use of oil and gas initially expanded only slowly but accelerated during the interwar period and much more rapidly after the Second World War.

This change in resource regime is visible in the late-nineteenth century hike in CO_2 emissions. Since the late nineteenth century, furthermore, a world-regional shift can be observed. The United States became a globally significant user of fossil fuels, overtaking the sum of European countries in carbon dioxide emissions for the first time in 1917 (Figure 5.1).

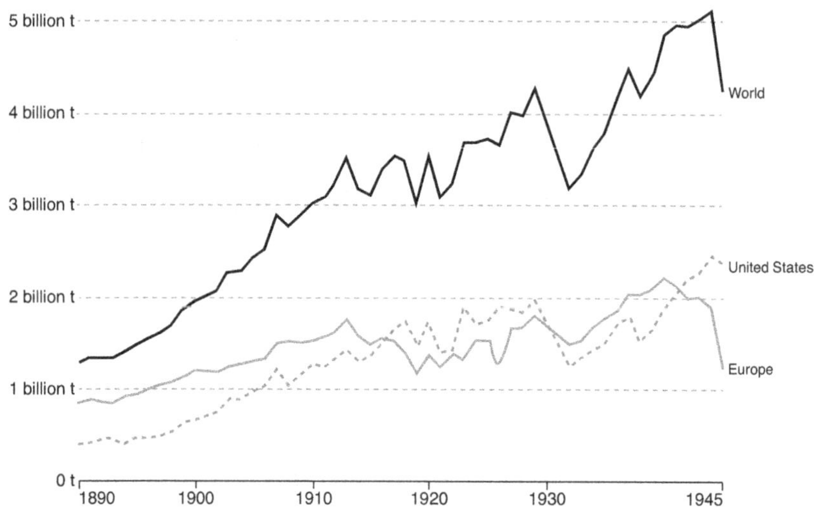

Figure 5.1 CO_2 emissions, world, United States and Europe, 1890–1945

Source: Hannah Ritchie, Max Roser and Pablo Rosado, 2020, *CO_2 and Greenhouse Gas Emissions*. Published online at OurWorldInData.org. at https://ourworldindata.org/co2-and-greenhouse-gas-emissions

The upward move of the emission curve between 1890 and the beginning of the First World War is pronounced. In a way, it mirrors the experience of many contemporaries in Europe and North America of living through a period of rapid social change. With a view to further developments during the twentieth century, however, one should be cautious in identifying here the embarking on a path which determines further social change and from which it is difficult, if not impossible, to deviate in the future. Rather, one needs to take a careful look to precisely discern the sites and kinds of social change that were enabled by the use of fossil fuels.

During this period, the term 'infrastructure' was coined, first in French to refer to railway tracks and later, after the Second World War, widened to mean 'the basic equipment and structures (such as roads and bridges) that are needed for a country, region, or organization to function properly' (*Britannica Dictionary*). The late nineteenth century was the high moment of expansion of the railway network in European societies, as well as of the building of the transcontinental railway lines across North America. In turn, the post-Second World War decades witnessed the accelerated building of double-lane motorway networks. Émile Durkheim, even though always suspected of separating the social from the material, noted at the end of the nineteenth century that '[T]he social fact sometimes materialises itself to the degree that it becomes an element of the exterior world. [. . .] This is so for the tracks of communication and transport [. . .].' The material infrastructural developments created new foundations for social life and gave it 'a determined direction' (Durkheim 1897: 354, cited in Charbonnier 2020: 186; my translation). They marked the societal transformation towards 'organized modernity', as I have proposed calling the emerging social configuration (Wagner 1994), one in which full coverage of space went along with a higher degree of collectivization, both aiming at greater control and stabilization of society. The matter with which this was achieved was steel and concrete, in turn based on coal and oil, for creating these materials and making vehicles to run on them. The world fairs, as discussed above, were events of self-presentation of this new kind of society. In parallel, the permeation of society with products and services dependent on fossil fuels also changed the perception of social life and the social world, particularly in urban settings. The emergence of nature conservation movements is an indicator of the experienced transformation of landscapes.

Thus, following up on the contrast between the period around 1800 and the one around 1900 in the preceding chapter, it is appropriate to recognize in the latter period the rise of industrial society, now extended to much of Western Europe and North America. Later debates, in particular after the Second World War, have also seen a line of continuity from 1900 to the 1960s. The social policy innovations from the 1890s onwards were then considered to have formed the early welfare state, and the introduction of universal (male) suffrage to have been a major step in democratization, to be consolidated after 1950. This claim of continuity, though, is much more doubtful. While the rise of industrialism truly meant a break with earlier socio-ecological configurations, there was no clear way forward from there in the prevailing perspective of the time. The availability of resources from the first and second vertical frontiers had sustained a sense of possible progress, but it alone did not generate common expectations for the future.

In this light, the task of this chapter is to reconstruct the path from the transgression of the second vertical frontier to the post-Second World War Great Acceleration. The argument will be developed in four steps. First, it will be shown that Europe's domestic social divide and its hierarchical relation to other world regions led to divided expectations about future social development. Second, an alternative emerged gradually in the United States, which was based on a wider diffusion of the supposed benefits of frontier resources across society. Third, this US alternative imposed itself across western societies after the Second World War, partly due to the outcome of the two wars, and led to the Great Acceleration, or as we will later more precisely say, to the Western Great Acceleration. Fourth and finally, namely, the 'energy divide', created by the cumulative effect of the transgression of two vertical frontiers, led to a global social divide and the distinction between developed and developing countries.

The 'stagnation' of European societies

During the decades before the First World War, the social and the democratic question had begun to be addressed, with considerable variation, in European countries. However, with hindsight, the answers to these questions were not as straightforward as T. H. Marshall (1950) presented them, namely as the gradual granting of political and social rights. Equal universal suffrage, at least for men, was on the horizon, but it was seen as desirable and necessary by some and as a merely unavoidable evil by others. The answers to the social question diverged more widely, from a socialist overcoming of capitalism to minimal care for situations of poverty. Tensions arose, in particular, because the gradually emerging answer to the political question, namely widening of political participation, heightened the electoral pressure for providing stronger answers to the social question, answers that kept being resisted by the elites. The British television series *Downton Abbey* (2010–2015) shows in vivid scenes the long-lasting persistence of an old regime with its class, gender and political divides, taking its symbolic starting point from the sinking of the *Titanic* in 1912 and leading the plot until the middle of the 1920s.

For our purposes, I may bluntly state that the increased recourse to fossil resources was not used to enhance the material well-being of the whole society but only of a minority in the very hierarchical settings of Europe. In the preceding paragraph, I described the issue in sociopolitical terms, but it has also been described in economic terms. Theories of imperialism, mostly but not exclusively in Marxist terms, diagnosed a situation of either overproduction or underconsumption, equally leading to a crisis of capitalist accumulation. This crisis was expected to either spell the end of capitalism, in Vladimir Ilyich Lenin's view, or be temporarily resolved by imperial expansion, in Rosa Luxemburg's view. After the outbreak of the First World War, Luxemburg saw the tension heightened, leading to a moment of world-historical decision and bifurcation, 'socialism or barbarism'. Relating the sociopolitical to the economic elements, one recognizes that European industry produced consumer goods for a small, even though growing, minority in their own societies while relying on the low wages of their workers and the low cost of their raw materials, increasingly in imperial competition with enterprises in other industrial countries.

As mentioned in the previous chapter, European societies started to turn the social question into a domestic issue and declared the nation-state as the site of collective responsibility for the well-being of the entire population. However, this commitment remained largely incomplete, not least because of the persistent divide between elites and the majority population, with the former refusing resource diffusion to the latter. Under the pressure of domestic social claims, as well as due to inter-imperial competition, furthermore, resource extraction outside of the metropoles was increased.

The First World War, one of the causes of which arguably resided in this tension, altered the constellation but exacerbated, rather than alleviated, the unanswered questions in European societies. The end of the war was marked, on the one hand, by geopolitical changes together with the wider acceptance of the notion of collective self-determination, which left the elites in the states that lost the war weakened and further debilitated by a peace agreement without much concern for future coexistence in Europe. On the other hand, the end of the war witnessed the Russian Revolution and the increased strength of the socialist movement in general, not least by the elites' dependence on workers and soldiers during the war effort, including women who took the places of male soldiers at worksites. In other words, some societies had emerged in the West in which the claim to political equality went along with the considerable social power of the dominated groups. The suffrage was widened in western societies, not least under pressure of the workers' and the women's movement, leading to the granting of universal male – and in some cases also female – suffrage. In those formal-institutional terms, the end of the First World War marks a watershed, some would say a breakthrough, in the history of democracy.

While this is true, what is often overlooked is that politico-theoretical debate remained dominated by critics of democracy, rather than supporters of it. Few were those who, like maybe most significantly Karl Mannheim in 1935, both recognized the major challenge of (what he called) 'fundamental democratization' and remained committed to democracy. Much more forceful was the voice of those, on both the political right and left, who considered universal suffrage and competitive-party democracy unstable, undesirable or both (see Bolsinger 2001 for a comparative study of Vladimir Ilyich Lenin and Carl Schmitt; also Strong 2012). While the elites resisted ceding power and resources, they could no longer control the composition of governments that emerged from the popular vote. These societies were politically volatile, and the apparently successful communist revolution in Russia encouraged a variety of transformative projects. In some countries, such as Germany and Italy, these elites allied with other groups in society – sometimes the 'mob', to use Hannah Arendt's (1951: 106) expression – to put an end to the short-lived democratic commitments through fascism and Nazism. In Spain and Portugal, alliances between the hierarchies of the Catholic Church and the military led to the creation of clerical-authoritarian regimes that would last until the 1970s. In the Soviet Union, Bolshevism turned into Stalinist totalitarianism. In Sweden, in contrast, it was an alliance between workers and peasants, together forming a popular majority and both represented by democratic political parties, which tried to overcome the blockade of liberal-imperial Europe.

As it contains a notion of a logic of expansion, Rosa Luxemburg's concept of 'land seizure' as a persistent need for capitalist reproduction is currently widely cited in analyses that join a critique of capitalism with analyses of environmental degradation and climate change. We do not know whether her vision of socialism would have avoided the resource-intensive trajectory since barbarism dominated the scene in much of Europe for decades to come, including her own murder in 1919. But one can get glimpses of alternatives, or at least variations, by looking beyond Europe at the articulation of political, social and ecological issues in other world regions during the first half of the twentieth century, starting with the society whose transformative project of liberal capitalism would become the dominant one in due course, the United States. (Alternatives will be more systematically discussed, with a focus on the period after the middle of the twentieth century, in chapter 7.)

The combustion engine and mass consumption: the US answer

I borrowed the expression 'stagnation' for the sociopolitical and economic development of European societies during the first half of the twentieth century from Burkart Lutz's (1989 [1984]: 64, 87) historico-sociological analysis of 'constellations of prosperity' in Europe, in which he emphasized the discontinuity between the imperial-industrial prosperity before the First World War and the democratic-industrial prosperity after the Second World War (see also Stråth and Wagner 2017: ch. 8). To explain the stagnation during the interwar period, he mobilized the comparison with the 'counter-example' (Lutz 1989 [1984]: 79) of the United States. We have already noted (in chapter 4) that the United States had overtaken the United Kingdom in terms of industrial production and fossil fuel use by 1900 and had also taken a lead in transgressing the second vertical frontier of crude oil and natural gas. Abundant natural resources and capacity for expanding resource exploitation further could be considered sufficient explanation for advancing on the track of economic growth, modernization and development. By 1900, though, no such track had yet been designed, and our preceding discussion of European developments showed that there could be considerable dispute about which path to take.

Taking a very broad view, the United States and some European societies faced similar issues, a process of rapid fossil fuel-based industrialization combined with open issues about political participation and social inclusion. But this would be too broad a view, neglecting differences that became crucial for future developments. Voting rights of African Americans were a specific contested issue regarding political participation, and the 'labour question' hardly raised exactly the same issues as the 'social question' in Western Europe. Furthermore, the United States had an experience of growing wealth that supposedly was available to everyone, in principle, and indeed attracted migrants from Europe. Nevertheless, the imbalance between sectors of production existed in the United States, too. At around 1900, literal 'land seizure' in the West had slowed down, if not stopped, and, as a former colonial society, the United States had few colonies of its own that could serve, in Luxemburg's terms, for solving the underconsumption problem for capital accumulation. In contrast, rationalization of production through Frederick Winslow Taylor's 'scientific management' and the assembly line tended to further increase production capacities. Henry Ford's motor company was a leading enterprise in this rationalization process, but Ford also recognized wider social consequences. When he greatly raised the workers' wages in one of his plants in 1914, he intended to address problems of turnover and motivation, that is, of production efficiency, but he was also aware of the consumption side (Boyer and Orléan 1991). As he said in his autobiography, 'No question is more important than that of wages – most of the people of the country live on wages. The scale of their living – the rate of their wages – determines the prosperity of the country' (Ford and Crowther 1922: ch. 8). If we read this more instrumentally, Ford saw the long-term prospect for car production conditioned by gradually enabling workers to buy the products of their own work. Having advanced techniques of mass production, Henry Ford's diagnosis paved the way for a mass-consumption economy. Given that his particular product, the motor car, needed fossil fuels for its operation and that it would become the most emblematic household item in the United States, a significant step on the trajectory of fossil fuel intensity was thus taken. (Thomas Alva Edison had asked Henry Ford to oversee the production of electric cars, but Ford turned that offer down, a potential critical juncture to be discussed below, p. 166; Smil 2021: 21).

The twentieth-century variety of capitalism that emerged in the United States was called 'Fordism' by the Italian communist and intellectual Antonio Gramsci (1971), identifying a transformation of capitalism with political consequences that the European workers' movement should take note of. Half a century later, 'Fordism' has been analysed as a response to an accumulation crisis in US capitalism, focusing on its connection of mass-production technology with significant wage increases for industrial workers (Aglietta

1976). While the regulation school goes beyond a standard analysis in terms of capital logic, this transformation needs to be seen in yet broader sociopolitical terms. Like Gramsci, his conservative contemporary Friedrich von Gottl-Ottlilienfeld (1924: 37) recognized this and referred to Fordism as 'white socialism', suggesting that the claims of the socialist movement could be fulfilled by transforming instead of overcoming capitalism. More than just raising wages, Fordism satisfied democratic demands for equality by raising the material standards of living throughout society, with the corollary however of increasing the use of biophysical resources (see also Maier 1970).

Over the medium term, this energy-intensive social transformation proved to be the most long-lasting political project of the twentieth century, even though it initially failed to consolidate and remained crisis driven. More than Ford's initial steps, it was the reaction to the Great Depression of 1929 through the New Deal that consolidated the mass-production, mass-consumption economy and spread a way of life at the centre of which stood the consumption of commodities.

After the Second World War, social thought tended to see this social transformation in the United States as irresistible, but for divergent reasons. It could be seen as a superior form of social organization combining freedom, democracy, equality and material well-being in an unprecedented way, or it could be seen as a way of preserving capitalist domination under conditions of accumulation problems, worker shortage and political participation. (It was not widely seen as leading to environmental or ecological problems until the 1970s.) Thus either a logic of modernity or one of capital was supposed to impose itself. Jumping to one or the other conclusion, however, means neglecting or at least underestimating the fact that this transformation occurred in one world region – and in this region only, as Max Weber might have said, could he have observed the phenomenon – with very special circumstances, unique at least in their concatenation, such as: abundance of land and availability of coal and oil; the lack of an established hierarchy among the majority population; domination of this majority over a minority brought to the country for enforced labour; and scarcity of free labour under conditions of political equality. These conditions did not exist and could not easily be created elsewhere. Therefore, those who claim that the irresistible logic of modernity and/or capitalism merely asserted itself first in the United States to then diffuse across a 'West' that hardly existed by 1900, and later across the globe, would need to either discard the view that the above concatenation of conditions was necessary for the observed social change in the United States or provide additional evidence about the ways such logics spread across space.

A world regionally comparative note

Here, I do not assume that any of those logics are irresistible but want to investigate whether they exist and in which way they operate. To better understand the specificity of the United States in this light, we will take a brief look, as an intermediate step, at the conditions for a transformation to a resource-intensive mode of working and living in other world regions.

In interwar Europe, the closest parallel could be found in the social-democratic version of emerging industrial and consumer society in Scandinavia. We will briefly discuss below the specific relation between resource endowment and social transformation in Sweden (chapter 7). And as it was already suggested above that other European societies were blocked in a way that the United States was not, we will look at the ways in which this 'stagnation' was overcome subsequently (in chapter 6). But we should consider briefly the conditions of and experiences in other world regions, starting with the Soviet Union.

The Soviet Union

Leaving the town of Khorogh, capital of the Autonomous Region of Gorno Badakhshan in Tajikistan, in an easterly direction, one encounters an unusual monument at the roadside, namely a black historic car, dating from the 1930s, placed on a concrete pedestal. The monument recalls and celebrates the completion of the Pamir Highway, the second-highest road on the globe, leading first east-wards and then northwards to Osh, Kyrgyzstan, along the border of the Union of Soviet Socialist Republics, of which Tajikistan was a member, with Afghanistan and with China, then not yet a People's Republic. The car is supposedly the first car that travelled the newly constructed road. The completion of the road through high mountains was a major accomplishment, possibly serving more military than economic purposes, and an object of pride for the Soviet Union, a sign of its modernity. The notion of organizing society by creating a physical infrastructure across the territory, mentioned above, is easily applicable to the endeavour: a firm foundation is built that – literally – underlies all future traffic and makes it possible at higher speed and with greater reliability. (It is worth pointing out that the road was not entirely new as it leads along the historic Silk Roads, which were largely unsuitable for cars and hardly usable for long periods of the year.) The building of the Pamir Highway was a large-scale public investment in a collective good. Given both the time and the place of its construction, it stands at a transition between railroad building, as a collective means of transport, and motorway building, with its penchant for individual use, bearing in mind that there was hardly any private car use in the region at the time. After the end of the Soviet Union, the road started to decay due to lack of public investment in independent but rather poor Tajikistan, while in parallel it regained importance due to increasing long-distance trade with China.

This extreme case of physical investment – far from the decision-making centre, high in the mountains – is exemplary for the Soviet Union's commitment to frontier exploration and consolidation. Imperial Russia had before expanded on its eastern frontier and was in imperial competition over Central Asia, including what came to be Tajikistan. After difficult consolidation during the first years after the revolution, the Soviet Union's leadership saw itself in competition with western capitalism, which it identified as both industrial and imperial, exploiting both vertical and horizontal frontiers. In 1920, Lenin had defined communism as 'Soviet power plus the electrification of the whole country', thus indicating energy-intensive development similar to the West but under new political guidance. From the late 1920s onwards, the five-year plans foresaw a rapid process of heavy industrialization, in a way repeating the western capitalist emphasis on production of investment goods rather than consumer goods, but now with the intention of catching up with a West that had entered into an accumulation crisis. Even though falling short of the very ambitious envisaged growth rates, the heavy industrialization is mirrored in the increasing use of vertical-frontier resources, both coal and oil, and rising carbon dioxide emissions.

With the motive of private profit absent, explanations of climate change that draw on classical theories of capitalism do not apply to the early Soviet Union. But neither do theories of capitalist regulation that, as we have seen, identify the intensification of the fossil fuel regime in the United States with the shift to higher wages and consumer goods, in particular cars with combustion engines and electrical household appliances. Given that the Soviet Union was created under war conditions and in an unlikely context according to historical materialism, and given the absence of a bourgeois class, a perceived need to be capable of defending socialism both militarily and economically certainly played a role. Furthermore, though, early Soviet socialism was also characterized by what we may call a high-modernist self-understanding focused on technical progress and mastery (Khomyakov 2016), mirroring but also going beyond western imaginaries in the early twentieth century. Planned industrial cities like Magnitogorsk in the Ural Mountains are outcomes of such an orientation. In any case, the Soviet Union was the only world region outside the capitalist West in which fossil fuel use rapidly increased during the first half of the twentieth century. Having presented itself as a kind of alternative modernity to the western one (and having been interpreted as such, e.g., Arnason 1993; Maslovskiy 2018), the Soviet Union could possibly also be discussed as a non-western perspective on development (see below, chapter 7), but in terms of its historical location, its ideational inspiration and not least its use of biophysical resources, it is more appropriate to mention it here as a transformative political project that emerged in the context of the socio-ecological transformation marked by the transgression of the second vertical frontier.

'Settler societies' beyond the United States

Those societies that emerged from the migration of significant numbers of Europeans to America, Africa and Australia are often referred to as 'settler societies', though quite misleadingly so since the (descendants of) the settlers cohabited with the native, and in some cases also the slave, populations, forming more precisely 'new societies' (Hartz 1964). These societies were dominated by the settler elites, sometimes formally limiting the rights of the native and (former) slave population, in other cases dominating by other means. Given the high standard of living of these elites, many

Latin American countries, Australia and South Africa continued to attract immigration during the first half of the twentieth century, including the early years after the Second World War. Brazil became known as a model country for diversity, not least against the background of obsession with homogeneity in European nationalism.

While resource endowment and resource use varied considerably, most of these countries relied on their abundance of land, the products of which were largely exported to Europe, such as beef from Argentina or coffee from Brazil. Some societies also extracted and exported mineral resources, such as copper in Chile or gold and iron in Brazil. The Union of South Africa, a member of the British Commonwealth until 1961, had a marked vertical-frontier economy, mining gold and diamonds, again mostly for exportation. However, fossil fuels were not a significant part of the mining economy in these societies, with the exception of some Latin American countries, reflected in the rather small share of these societies in global carbon dioxide emissions until far into the twentieth century. Some Latin American societies, notably Argentina, Brazil, Chile and Mexico, had embarked with some success on industrialization strategies through import substitution policies since the 1930s. Overall, however, the 'new societies' remained dependent on the importation of industrial commodities. For that reason, fossil fuels were also less needed. Coal deposits were explored rather slowly, given that coal was not a very suitable export commodity due to the cost of long-distance transport; and major oil deposits were not discovered during the first half of the twentieth century.

Persistence of low-resource economies

With the exception of Japan, other world regions did not witness major transformations of their economies and resource bases. The colonized regions of Africa, South and South East Asia suffered from domination often going along with resource extraction, but to highly varying degrees. A particular position was taken by the Middle Eastern region, politically composed of protectorates and new states, where oil was extracted by western companies for exportation to fuel the western 'carbon democracy', as the arrangement was called by Timothy Mitchell (2011). Self-governed societies, most importantly China, traded with European societies but aimed to limit western impact overall, be it economically, politically or culturally. Only Japan embarked on an industrialization strategy, which proved to be fully successful after the Second World War (on the conflict between Japan and China over Manchuria and its coal mines, see Seow 2021). Otherwise, the contributions of all these world regions to climate change remained minimal until long after the Second World War.

The social divide and the energy divide

This brief comparative sketch of economic development and resource use across world regions provides a background to what became known during the twentieth century as uneven development and led during the 1960s to the formal distinction between developed and developing countries. While the Great Divergence between western societies and all other world regions had opened up by 1800 at the latest and was at least partly due to the transgression of the first vertical frontier of coal mining, the crossing of the second vertical frontier created a deeper 'energy divide' (Osterhammel 2009: 936), as western companies tended to exploit fossil fuel resource sites even in other regions, in particular the Middle East. To reiterate, coal needed to be used near to the mining sites in the early nineteenth century. This was one of the reasons for rapid industrial development in Britain and sections of Western Europe, and later in the eastern United States. Resource transfer from other world regions to Europe between 1500 and 1900 remained largely limited to agricultural commodities (including 'waste' such as guano) and mining resources of smaller weight and volume (such as initially gold and silver, later copper). Crude oil, in contrast, could not only be extracted and refined with less human labour than coal, it could also be transported across long distances more easily, such as through pipelines and in tankers of ever-increasing size.

Mitchell's (2011) analysis of 'carbon democracy' aims to grasp the connection between domestic and global politics in the transgression of the second vertical frontier (see also Black 2012). Starting out from the beginnings of oil extraction in the United States and in Imperial Russia, his reasoning soon moves to the discovery of oilfields in the Middle East and highlights the interest of the imperial powers of Great Britain and France, as well as the US-based oil companies, in a context in which the Wilsonian call for self-determination was interpreted through the creation of protectorates and new states. The interest in the resource was very pronounced, as otherwise states and businesses were more likely to have abstained, given the complex regional situation. Mitchell explains this interest with the increased capacity, the 'power' and 'agency' (his terms), of the working class for successful struggle in the metropoles, with coal miners in a central position. Miners were providing the 'miraculous' (Jevons) resource on whose steady supply societies had become dependent. They were working under rather similar working conditions, including significant autonomy at work underground, and with a high concentration of numbers at worksites. Thus they had great power of mobilization and disruption in a context of high workers' mobilization in general. Oil, in contrast, could be extracted and transported with much smaller numbers of workers who, furthermore, would be located outside of industrial society, if operating in the Middle East. One may have doubts about the direct connection between carbon and democracy as seen by Mitchell, but the argument about an elite interest in a dislocation between resource supply and democratic pressure is significant (we come back to this issue from the angle of functionality of energy sources in chapter 7, and in terms of problem displacement in chapter 9).

The cumulation of the effects of the first and second vertical-frontier transgressions in the late nineteenth century turned the energy divide into a global social divide as the European, then western, societies underwent a major socio-ecological transformation, as described above. As a consequence, the structure of global social inequality changed drastically between the mid-nineteenth century and the late twentieth century. At mid-nineteenth century, the material situation of the lower social classes, that is, the majority of the population, in much of Europe had not been very dissimilar to the one in other world regions, whereas a strong divide had existed in Europe between the rich and the poor, today technically called 'within-country inequality'. Up to that moment, the politico-economic transformation often seen as the onset of both modernity and capitalism had not at all provided the wealth and liberty in Europe that had been evoked in writings of the late eighteenth century. The further one moves into the twentieth century, in contrast, the greater the divide becomes between rich and poor societies, or 'between-country inequality' (for two different approaches with similar findings, see Korzeniewicz 2018; Korzeniewicz and Moran 2009; Milanović 2012, 2015, 2016). For several decades, for the reasons given above, the United States was the only country that was both wealthy and appeared to offer upward social mobility, therefore attracting immigration from Europe as well as from Asia. After the Second World War, exploiting fossil fuels in the US way, West European societies became both richer and more equal. Thus the divide gained sharper contours and let a new terminology for world regions emerge, now distinguishing a 'First World' or later 'Global North', on the one side, from a 'Third World' or 'Global South', on the other. This transformation is related to a major reinterpretation of social organization, which became effective in the North but not in the South.

Elevated to high symbolic level in and around the French Revolution, the question of equality became central for the dynamics of change during the nineteenth century. From the late eighteenth century onwards, the notion that political orders should and could be built on a principle of equal rights became widely diffused across the globe. It did not spread everywhere and not with the same intensity and degree of acceptance, but it became a focal point of the political imaginary, orienting much political action (see, e.g., Rosanvallon 2011). However, the conditions for success in implementing this principle varied widely across world regions. In Western Europe, emigration limited the population (growth), and industrialization concentrated workers in factories and facilitated their organization. In regions of European settlement, again with the partial exception of the United States, in contrast, the divide between the (descendants of) settlers and the indigenous and (in some countries) slave populations was reinforced, and hierarchical command at workplaces was imposed against a background of abundant 'labour supply' (Mota and Wagner 2019 on Brazil and South Africa). Claims for equality were in both settings combined with calls for democracy as a means to enforce the will of the majority. Under those different conditions, however, only in the West did the elites become dependent on the majority, due to the threat of strikes at the workplace and to the commitment to the war effort during the First World War, both in the military and on the 'home front'.

In this global constellation, thus, a specific social configuration emerged in one world region, which availed itself of biophysical resources to an unprecedented degree and, partly for this reason, was in a dominant position relative to other world regions, on the one hand, while on the other hand the majority of its population was in a position to exert considerable, even if unfocused, power on the dominant elite. This historically new social configuration, while materially rich in global comparison, encountered problems that were found difficult to interpret and to handle.

The Western Great Acceleration and its interpretations

The post-Second World War view that European societies had finally re-embarked on a trajectory that they had initiated in the nineteenth century but abandoned during the interwar period overlooks, first, that there were alternatives early on, and second, that the supposed 're-embarking' was not sustainable.

Thanks to the International Biosphere-Geosphere Programme (IBGP), we now have a greater consciousness of the radical change in resource use and its effects that was brought about after the middle of the twentieth century (McNeill and Engelke 2014; Steffen et al. 2015). The introduction of the term 'Great Acceleration' has the welcome effect of focusing attention on relatively recent change, with something like a 'take-off' that really happens only after the Second World War. As the IBGP diagrams include the accumulation of CO_2 in the atmosphere, this emphasis challenges all claims that climate change is the outcome of capitalism or modernity, as the origins of these forms of human social configurations date back much further. At the very least, an argument would need to be made as to why capitalism or modernity generated this unprecedented acceleration only so recently.

However, the diagrams and their popularity also have an unwelcome effect. They show global aggregates and, thus, tend to suggest – without saying so or even meaning to – that we are looking at a phenomenon that is global not only in its effects but also in its causes. But while the accumulation of carbon dioxide in the atmosphere is a global phenomenon, the emission of carbon dioxide is not. A look at CO_2 emissions, as we have seen throughout this volume, shows that this aspect of the Great Acceleration is generated by the

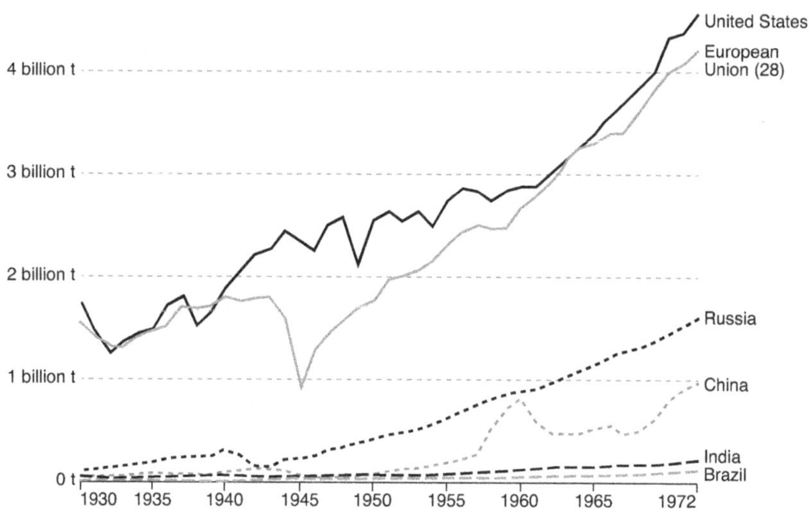

Figure 5.2 CO_2 emissions, selected countries, 1930–1972 ('European Union (28)' refers to the current EU plus the United Kindgom)

Source: Hannah Ritchie, Max Roser and Pablo Rosado, 2020, *CO_2 and Greenhouse Gas Emissions*. Published online at OurWorldInData.org. at https://ourworldindata.org/co2-and-greenhouse-gas-emissions

western societies, and to some extent by the Soviet socialist societies, in particular the Soviet Union. The contribution of other world regions is comparatively small, or almost negligible, and hardly accelerating, even though rising emissions from China can already be observed (Figure 5.2). As we know, this was to change later in the twentieth century, in particular for China and India (more on this below in chapters 7 and 9), but if we look at the first three post-war decades, we should speak of a Western Great Acceleration rather than a global phenomenon, at least with regard to fossil fuel use and responsibility for climate change.

Repeating Jevons's term about the societal impact of coal, a social transformation once again was described as 'miraculous' as it was going on. In West Germany, Italy and some other western countries, the economic growth in the post-war decades was described as an 'economic miracle'. Of course, the term only meant to indicate that the growth was spectacular, not that it was not explainable. Among the explanatory factors that were referred to in public debate, the exponential growth in the use of oil was not given particular significance. Natural resources figured in assessments of the place of states in international competition, for instance, with coal and iron entering into the 'formulas for power' in a 1966 study widely read in West Germany (Fucks 1966). But otherwise, fossil fuel was mentioned but taken for granted, and mostly it was only implicitly seen as crucial for economic growth and social change before the 1970s. With hindsight, that is, from the late 1970s onwards, namely when the growth rates had diminished and there was no realistic expectation that they might return to earlier heights, the first three post-war decades kept being characterized as 'glorious' (Fourastié 1979) but also as a 'short dream' (Lutz 1989 [1984]). By that time, resource constraints had moved (back) to the centre of attention, but even then the centrality of fossil fuels was rarely at the core of analysis.

Even though no longer miraculous, the Western Great Acceleration remains enigmatic – both its causes and its persistence. We now know that this socio-ecological transformation set the planet on course for barely reversible global warming, and we also know that this was the result of a deliberate exponential increase in the burning of fossil fuels. As countercultural author Kurt Vonnegut said with hindsight about the 1960s, 'Dear future generations: Please accept our apologies. We were roaring drunk on petroleum' (from the movie *Kurt Vonnegut: Unstuck in Time*, 2021). It clearly would have been preferable if this could have been avoided, but it was not. There are two common arguments for dissolving the enigma, or indeed to deny that an enigma exists, which should be mentioned before elaborating my own answer. One may think that the question of the *causes* of the rise of the fossil fuel society has not yet been asked simply because the answer to it is rather obvious, for two main reasons. First, arguably, western societies intensified fossil fuel use because of the immediate benefits in better satisfying material needs. And second, there was no reason for not doing so because knowledge of the enormous adverse consequences only became available much later. While not entirely without validity, these responses beg further questions. Considering increasing fossil fuel use being equal to enhancing material well-being was unprecedented and not at all self-evident before it happened. Thus it remains a relevant question to understand the context in which this happened, and what more specific problems were meant to be solved by burning fossil fuels (see chapter 6 below). Furthermore, some critical knowledge had been available early on, and it needs to be understood why it was sidelined or discarded in this socio-ecological transformation (see chapter 8 below).

A second, separate set of questions concerns the *persistence* of the fossil fuel regime. By the early 1970s at the latest, the link between fossil fuel use and material well-being had started to be strongly questioned in public debate. And knowledge had accumulated showing: the limited availability of biophysical resources, including fossil fuels; the severe environmental damage and degradation due to industrialization in general, and fossil fuel use in particular; and, somewhat later, the trend towards global warming due to carbon dioxide accumulation in the atmosphere. Thus a whole range of evidence provided reasons for phasing out fossil fuels. Nevertheless, emissions have continued to rise up to the present day. Here, the denial of any enigma works by rejecting the way the question is posed. Based on data for carbon dioxide emissions, it is argued that western societies indeed started to change course after knowledge of climate change became more fully available and incontrovertible, and that any slowness was due to dependency on the path that had been embarked on and would soon be overcome. Therefore, so such an argument goes, the main problem today is the intensity of fossil fuel use in so-called 'emerging' societies, in particular in Asia, and hence the difficulty of reaching a working international agreement. This reasoning, however, underestimates the – historical and present – global connectedness in terms of the cumulation of CO_2 emissions and the entrenchment of global social inequality. In turn, it overestimates the degree to which a change of trajectory has already been undertaken in the West and underestimates the resistance to any such change, which remains strong.

These all-too-common explanations for the rise and the persistence of the fossil fuel-intensive society stand in the way of adequately understanding the phenomenon and, by implication, changing the resource trajectory of our societies. Up to this point of our analysis, we have seen how concerns for biological reproduction, freedom, comfort and profit under conditions of power differentials have worked together, in various combinations and degrees of emphasis at different times and varying across world regions, to generate over the long run the global socio-ecological constellation of the middle of the twentieth century, which is the point in time at which anthropogenic climate change truly 'takes off'. In the remainder of this volume, I will provide a more fine-grained analysis of this global socio-ecological constellation. The further pursuit of the resource-intensive trajectory of social development since the end of the Second World War will be traced in more detail, switching from a mainly chronological presentation to a focus on the key mechanisms at work that, despite alternative options at certain moments, kept western societies on this trajectory and made many, though not all, societies in other world regions embark on it.

Part III

The Social Logic of Fossil Fuels: Climate Change and the Politics of the Great Acceleration

The preceding part II has provided a long historical perspective on a sequence of transformations in resource regimes in world history. While fossil fuels started to be more systematically used from the early nineteenth century onwards, and played a key role in the industrialization of West European societies, the move towards high fossil-fuel intensity occurred in western societies in the middle of the twentieth century. Part III analyses in detail the reasons for this latter shift, which is at the origins of the current climate crisis. Chapter 6 shows how fossil fuels were deliberately used to solve sociopolitical problems in western societies that had remained unsolvable since the late nineteenth century, that is, as an answer to the 'social question' and the stabilization of democracy without challenging the power of the elites. Having thus created what is here called the Western Great Acceleration, this approach enters into a profound crisis by the 1970s when two of its basic assumptions prove untenable, namely that one can burn fossil fuels over extended periods without causing major ecological problems, and that one can separate one world region from all others and maintain privileges without provoking destabilizing reactions in those other world regions. Against this background, chapter 7 considers in more detail the material features of fossil fuels that made them lend themselves to providing this solution and also explores alternatives to fossil fuels that existed during the post-Second World War years. Chapter 8 questions the widespread view that environmental consciousness only arose forcefully from the 1970s onwards and, in turn, explores how knowledge attitudes alternate between emphases on limits that cannot be overcome, on the one side, and frontiers that can and need to be transgressed, on the other. Both these chapters lead again to recognizing the 1970s as a critical juncture in the global socio-ecological constellation. Chapter 9 synthesizes the findings up to this point and identifies problem displacement, instead of problem solving, as the key political mechanism that led to the climate crisis. Against this insight, it moves to analysing post-1970 developments as a 'problem squeeze' in western societies, the reaction to which generates two further, uncontrollable displacements: the warming of the atmosphere; and the move of Asian societies to high fossil-fuel intensity, creating the Asian Great Acceleration.

6

Capitalism, Socialism and Democracy: The Politics of Material Well-Being

Reinterpreting the world at mid-century

The Great Acceleration data show that western societies fully embarked on the fossil fuel-intensive trajectory after the Second World War. This trajectory was designed in a socio-ecological transformation in the United States during the interwar period, but there was nothing inevitable about its adoption in other countries and world regions. In contrast, one could argue that other world regions either did not have the resource endowments to embark on this trajectory – this would hold for Western Europe with its limited known oil and gas reserves (this situation only changed with the discovery of large amounts of oil and gas in the North Sea from the 1970s). Or they did not have the technical and industrial capacity to exploit or even explore existing reserves – this would hold for all other world regions in the middle of the twentieth century, except the Soviet Union. Thus the situation of the United States was rather exceptional. If European societies nevertheless emulated the path that had emerged and that became consolidated in the United States, as a consequence of which 'the West' was formed, one needs to ask what the diagnosis of their own situation was that drove them in this direction and what enabled them to do so despite the lack of resources. Therefore, the task now is to show what the problems were that European and then 'western' societies were facing at the end of the Second World War or, more precisely, what their elites perceived as the key problems that needed to be dealt with in this global moment of reconstruction and transformation.

At the end of the Second World War, the United States had risen as a global power, now in a comprehensive sense in economic, political, ideological and military terms. Totalitarian regimes in Europe had been defeated in the war, but a new geopolitical situation of opposition between liberal capitalism and Soviet socialism had emerged, with much sharper contours compared to the first three decades after the Bolshevik Revolution, that became known as the Cold War. Across the future 'Global South', furthermore, there was widespread mobilization for decolonization after the adoption of the principle of collective self-determination by the United Nations, with the partition and independence of India and Pakistan being an early and major example. Against this background, one can state, in very general terms, that among western elites a common self-understanding of their societies as liberal-capitalist emerged, an arrangement that was seen as a fragile achievement to be safeguarded from demands for socialist transformation, on the one hand, and the consequences of the end of colonial rule, on the other. The arrangement was considered as fragile because both the socialist and the decolonial challenge arose from earlier sociopolitical tensions that had not been resolved by mid-century, only temporarily pushed into the background by the necessities of the war. Several aspects of these tensions can be distinguished, but they were sequentially related to each other.

Within this new geopolitical context, first, the experience of the totalitarian breakdown of democracy in Europe overshadowed political thinking in the emerging West. Since this breakdown was associated with the mobilization of supposedly politically immature masses, one could have expected a revival of the critique of democracy. However, one consequence of the oppression and mass murder under totalitarian regimes was the renewal of the commitment to universal human rights and popular sovereignty, first voiced during the late eighteenth-century period of the 'democratic revolution' and now reiterated in the United Nations Universal Declaration of Human Rights of 1948, which maintains (article 21, pt 3): 'The will of the people shall be the basis of the authority of government; this will shall be expressed in periodic and genuine elections which shall be by universal and equal suffrage and shall be held by secret vote or by equivalent free voting procedures.' Even though elites were hesitant and far from being convinced of the merits of inclusive-egalitarian democracy, no justification for exclusion from formal political participation could any longer be provided. Given the experiences of breakdown and the risks of its recurrence, though, political thought concentrated on developing a new model of democratic politics, often now referred to as the Schumpeterian model, in which democracy means the selection of political decision makers by an inclusively defined citizenry that remains apathetic outside of the brief moments of election campaigns and elections (see Almond and Verba 1963; Schumpeter 1976 [1942]; for later discussions, e.g., Wagner 1994: ch. 6). The combination of, on the one hand, a division between a political class and the wider citizenry, in contact only at the moments of election, and on the other, the apathy of the latter otherwise was meant to provide democratic legitimacy and stability of government at the same time.

While arguably rather successful in the West for several decades, this model was empty of substance, focusing only on procedural requirements. Second, in parallel, therefore, the substantive reasons for the earlier collapse of democracy were explored. A broad consensus emerged that identified the main reason in the failure to give an adequate response to the 'social question' that had arisen with the class division of industrial capitalism during the later nineteenth century (as discussed above, chapter 4). Again, the UN Declaration on Human Rights of 1948 can serve as an indicator, as it included a section on 'economic and social rights', of which only the framing of this social commitment as a right was controversial, not the commitment itself (Moyn 2018: ch. 2).

With the consolidation of the Soviet Union and of communist parties in some western countries, third, answering the social question was no longer a purely domestic but an international geopolitical issue, given that communism had a declared commitment to equality and social justice. Thus it became of paramount importance to delimit any attraction that Soviet socialism might have as a political project that might provide a better answer to the social question. Finally, fourth, the potential attractiveness of socialism was also a concern with regard to those world regions that came to be called the 'developing countries' or the 'Third World'. Unlike that with Soviet socialism, the relationship with the Third World had a particular component for the western elites. There was no concern that answers to social questions there might arise that would be attractive to North American or West European citizens.

However, the West had become dependent on the availability of biophysical resources at convenient economic terms from the Third World, and any political realignment might endanger the supply of those resources.

The main task of this chapter is not to show that these were indeed the key concerns and perceived problems of western elites – there is already ample evidence that this was the case, some of which I will refer to in what follows. Rather, the aim is to demonstrate that these elites were searching for a specific kind of solution to these problems, one which they had not been able to find before, and that the post-Second World War period witnessed the emergence of indeed an entirely novel answer. The quest was for a solution that entailed neither the relinquishing of their position of power and privilege nor the resort to overt oppression and violence against the citizenry of their own societies. The novel answer was the massive recourse to fossil fuels.

A few more explanatory remarks are in order before proceeding, be it only to avoid misunderstandings. First, some readers may say that we know all this already. Western liberal-democratic, capitalist welfare societies are the main site of fossil fuel use between the middle and the late twentieth century. The point here, however, is not to restate this well-known fact. Rather, the aim is to show how the intensification of fossil fuel use was the deliberate answer to a certain interpretation of the key problems of the post-Second World War era from the angle of the dominant groups in western societies. Thus these highly consequential actions and decisions of western elites are understood against the background of their problem identification and interpretation. Second, some readers may object to the focus on western elites as an apparent continuation of some kind of Euro- or western centrism. This choice, though, is imposed by the fact that, as indeed we already know, it is the actions and decisions of western elites that brought about the Western Great Acceleration. As the analysis proceeds, though, it will become clearer that these actions were conditioned by the power and actions of actors in other world regions as well as within western societies. The constellations of power have been undergoing changes, and both the western and the subsequent Asian Great Acceleration are the outcome of struggles over problem interpretation and problem-solving actions under asymmetric conditions but without the chance for any actor to impose their view and will.

Third, in terms of method of presentation, this chapter will proceed by analysing exemplary texts that interpret contemporary problems and propose solutions. These texts were widely read in their time and have lastingly influenced further debates. Nevertheless, no claim can be made for them to be representative; the selection is small, and it is here proposed to stimulate further research and debate. The focus on problem interpretation, though, suggested such exemplary text analysis over other approaches, such as the analysis of indicators or institutions.

The social requisites of democracy

Capitalism, Socialism and Democracy, first published in 1942, is the book in which Joseph A. Schumpeter (1976 [1942]: 269; the following quotations are all from this volume) set out 'another theory of democracy', which should become the new model as sketched above. This theory, though, was not the main theme of the book, rather a part of the conclusion of his reflections about the possibilities for capitalism to survive, given the challenge by socialist critique and claims. A sibling to Karl Polanyi's *The Great Transformation* (1985 [1944]), published two years later, Schumpeter's book assessed the historical dynamics and future perspectives of western societies at the moment of polarization between freedom and socialism, in Polanyi's terms, or capitalism and socialism, in Schumpeter's. Its last chapter, in the revised version of 1946, addresses the consequences of the Second World War and starts out by stating, 'England and the United States are struggling to maintain some influence in Central and Western Europe. The fortunes of socialist and communist parties reflect these conditions' (376), and it then relates these struggles and fortunes to industrial success in the United States and possible political success of Russia. Having grown up in the Austro-Hungarian Empire and emigrated to the United States in 1932, he had witnessed the rise of socialism in Europe after the end of the First World War as well as the one of the Fordist mass-production and mass-consumption economy in the United States.

Against this double background, he recognized, on the one side, the deteriorating living and working conditions of the majority of the population due to the spread of industrial capitalism in the late nineteenth and early twentieth centuries, which gave rise to the socialist demands for radical social transformation. Mixing a functionalist and a power-theoretical argument, he diagnosed 'the capitalist order [as] not only unwilling but also quite incapable of guaranteeing' a decent standard of life of the masses, using the plight of the unemployed as his key illustration (68–70). At least until the end of the nineteenth century, there prevailed 'the impossibility of providing adequately for the unemployed *without impairing the conditions of further economic development*' (70; emphasis in original), thus leading to the claim of the need for overcoming capitalism. On the other hand, his US experience told him that capitalism had radically transformed there, to the degree of letting the 'great possibility' (380) emerge that its 'colossal industrial success [. . .] may annihilate the whole case for socialism' (382).

Based on a plausible, though somewhat off-the-cuff, estimate of production growth in the United States between 1928 and 1978 and observing the existing trend towards 'production for the purposes of domestic consumption', further enhanced by the conversion of the war economy, by 1950 'the huge mass of available commodities and services [. . .] promises a level of satisfaction of economic needs even of the poorest members of society' (384). The upcoming 'avalanche of consumer goods' will entail 'that all the desiderata that have so far been espoused by any social reformers [. . .] could be fulfilled *without significant interference with the capitalist process*' (68–9; emphasis in original), the latter being so important to the author that he repeats the assertion later: 'all this can be accomplished without violating the organic conditions of a capitalist economy' (384).

Schumpeter's 'great possibility', the realization of which he himself barely dared to hope for, sketches a path on which capitalism, democracy and material well-being across the whole society can be combined. In a moment, we will discuss in detail the conditions for such a path to be embarked on. But it should be mentioned now that Schumpeter, given that his analysis is based on the United States, explores the possibility that 'new land' may have been a precondition for the colossal success, thus pointing to a possible exceptionality. He also mentions the 'presence of coal and iron ore in England or of petroleum in this and other countries' as 'an opportunity that is no less unique' (109). Therefore, the question arises whether the 'achievements of capitalism [. . .] may conceivably be achievements that cannot be repeated', and

Schumpeter indicates 'another forty years' as the horizon of time for his reflections (110). Even though this thought arises in the context of land, coal and petroleum, however, he does not see limited availability of biophysical resources or negative consequences of their use as a problem for economic development. We will see in a moment why.

One and a half decades later, the path that Schumpeter had laid out had indeed been embarked on in the West, against his odds. Growth of production had reached unprecedented levels, and much of it was production for consumption. Democracy appeared to have consolidated, as political scientists should say, as social-policy measures financed by taxing business profits secured citizen apathy. This was the moment at which one could start to systematically analyse the 'social requisites of democracy', as Seymour Martin Lipset set out to do in the late 1950s (1959; the following page numbers refer to this article).

Drawing on Schumpeter's understanding of democracy, and developing a systematic comparative perspective, Lipset configured indicators of 'economic development' and 'legitimacy' as the two complex characteristics of social systems that correlate with stable democracy. Economic development was seen as 'comprising industrialization, wealth, urbanization, and education' (71). Operationalizing these features, Lipset measured wealth through 'per capita income, number of persons per motor vehicle and per physician, and the number of radios, telephones, and newspapers per thousand persons' (75), thus including prominently the durable consumer goods that Schumpeter had also focused on. In turn, one of the indicators of industrialization was 'the per capita commercially produced "energy", being used in the country, measured in terms of tons of coal per person per year' (78), thus going straight to what still was the key fossil fuel used at that time. Lipset finds that English-speaking and European democracies on average burn two and a half times more coal per person than European dictatorships and even six times more than Latin American democracies, which he at that time considered unstable (76). As a result, his analysis confirms the 'most widespread generalization' about democracy, namely 'that the more well-to-do a nation, the greater the chances that it will sustain democracy' (75).

With hindsight, we may say that Lipset validated a politico-economic strategy that western societies, led by the United States, had embarked on since the end of the Second World War. At the same time, he contributed to making this strategy more explicit and more generalized. His article was highly influential, giving rise to a whole research area, (macro-quantitative) comparative political research (e.g., Przeworski, Alvarez, Cheibub and Limongi 2000), including an offspring focusing in particular on the relation between democracy and capitalism (e.g., Rueschemeyer, Stephens and Stephens 1992; Streeck 2013). Critical scholars created a version of Lipset's thesis that held that welfare policies, financed by the surplus made available through economic growth, were designed to generate mass loyalty and stabilize late capitalism, rather than democracy (Narr and Offe 1975 for an anthology). Jumping slightly ahead in time, it is also worth noting that Lipset employs a notion of 'crisis of legitimacy', which came to be used by critical scholars during the early 1970s when energy prices rose and economic growth rates declined (Habermas 1973; Offe 1972).

In addition to these widely received scholarly diagnoses, some examples of public-political discourse of the early post-war period will be referred to. Rather than being analytical, the selected texts are part of a 'powerful discourse that, while not true, is able to make itself come true', a 'prophecy which contributes to its own realization because those who produce it are interested in it being true and have the means to make it come true' (Bourdieu and Boltanski 1976; see also Jens Beckert 2016). The examples come from the Federal Republic of Germany (West Germany) and France, two of the 'unstable democracies' in Europe in Lipset's (1959: 74) view of the time. The West German minister of economic affairs, Ludwig Erhard, if not the inventor at least the popularizer of the concept 'social market economy', published a kind of extended manifesto in 1957 under the title *Wealth for All* (*Wohlstand für alle*). In France in 1962, the planning agency Commissariat Général au Plan, at the request of the prime minister, created a study group called Groupe 1985 whose task it was to envision the state of French society in 1985 and which published its findings in 1964 under the title *Reflections about 1985* (*Réflexions sur 1985*).

Neither of the two publications placed much explicit emphasis on democracy. After totalitarian dictatorship and military occupation *cum* authoritarianism respectively, it may have felt safer not to explore in too much explicit detail the requisites for democracy. Rather, the assumption was that these societies had consensually embarked on a new path of development based on higher insights and overcoming cleavages of the past.

Erhard (1957: 7) starts out from stating his conviction as early as 1948 that an economic constitution was to be aimed at that 'could lead ever wider and broader strata of our people towards wealth' (translating *Wohlstand* as Adam Smith might have done; a more current expression would be 'material well-being'), thus overcoming the old hierarchical structure with a divide between a thin and rich upper class and a large lower class with 'insufficient purchasing power'. In turn, Groupe 1985 (1964) evokes that 'tensions within solidarity' will be mitigated in 'a climate of greater well-being' and by 'a sufficiently diffused progress [that] will overcome the society of needs by going beyond the coverage of elementary needs' (1964: 11). In both cases, old divides are overcome, and Groupe 1985 indeed calls for a 'solidarity of individuals and a solidarity towards the next generation', rather than connecting the term with social groups or classes (1964: 37). The basis for this new social order is in both texts the growth of production, and in particular the growth of production of consumer goods. The German minister looks back to the achievements of the first post-war decade, whereas the French group has the task of looking two decades ahead. Erhard sounds like Schumpeter when he claims that 'the most revolutionary transformation of our social order would never have been able to raise the private consumption of this or that group by even a fraction of the actually achieved increase' (1957: 11); and one influential member of Groupe 1985, Jean Fourastié (1979), would later speak of an 'invisible revolution' that had been accomplished.

The key expression that recurs in both texts is 'increase in productivity'. Increase in productivity is seen as the condition for the greater satisfaction of material needs, in particular for those groups in society that had been disadvantaged before. And it provides the magic formula that makes enhanced material well-being of all compatible with a capitalist or market economy, namely increasing wages in parallel with the increase in productivity, as explicitly mentioned by Erhard (1957: 8). It is this formula that allows the demarcation of the new order from the divided societies of the preceding epoch. Following a wider shift in public discourse in the light of social contestations (Fuhrmann 2017), Erhard distinguishes the concept of 'social market economy' from both the 'liberalistic' market economy, in which monopolistic companies can block innovation, and from the attempts of the social-democratic opposition, as he claims, to appropriate more than the gains achieved through productivity increase for raising wages.

For further reference below, it shall be noted that neither of the texts devotes much attention to biophysical resources. Erhard is concerned about the supply of coal in the early post-war years, a problem since solved, and does not mention oil at all. Groupe 1985 discusses the upcoming major transformation of agriculture in terms of productivity increase. It does point out that the available fossil fuel resources on French territory will be insufficient for the expected economic growth but looks at supply through importation, and substitution through nuclear energy, to resolve the issue. Future concerns for resources hitherto perceived as unlimited, such as air and water, are pointed to but are seen as a management problem only.

These two texts have been selected because they formulate a view on the ongoing social transformation that shaped the societal self-understanding of the period in Europe. In (West) Germany, Erhard is credited with creating the 'economic miracle' of the 1950s and 1960s, even though, his own claims notwithstanding, the West German record did not deviate that much from those of other West European countries such as Italy or France. The members of Groupe 1985 were a key component of the producers of the newly 'dominant ideology' (Bourdieu and Boltanski 1976) in France arguing for an expertise-based politics of balanced increase of well-being in an era after the end of ideologies (see Bell 1960 for the 'exhaustion of political ideas').

The requisites of 'economic development'

It is now well known that 'economic growth' became the guiding orientation in post-Second World War politics, fully formulated around 1960 (Lane 2014; Schmelzer 2016; see Angeletti 2023 for the French debates and a longer historical perspective). While increase in production of investment as well as consumer goods had already been a key theme in economic and political debate, the term 'economic growth' emerged as an aggregate concept synthesizing and, at the same time, measuring changes in production. The creation of this term was dependent on two steps: first, the separation of economic activities from all other social life, which Karl Polanyi (1985 [1944]) characterized as the 'disembedding' of the economy from society; and second, on a tool for the measurement of the course of this 'economy', which was accomplished with debates during the 1940s about 'national income accounting', leading to the creation of the indicator Gross National (or Domestic) Product (GNP or GDP). Despite the fact that its creators had underlined its limits and shortcomings from the very beginning (Schmelzer 2016: 97), the indicator became widely accepted as a key measure of economic policy success, in an almost religious way, by the late 1950s. For current purposes, it is important to see how the sources of economic growth were understood at the moment when such growth became the overarching component of government policy and, indeed, the guarantor of a stable social and political order.

From the times of classical political economy onwards, the economic sciences had aimed at identifying the ingredients that constituted the production of goods. The most common view distinguished land, labour and capital as 'factors of production'. The emphasis given to these factors varied over time (as well as between scholars and approaches). Land was the crucial factor for the physiocrats in eighteenth-century France, whereas labour gained dominance in the late eighteenth century in political economy and in the nineteenth century most pronouncedly in the work of Marx. As the question of economic growth moved to the centre of debate in the twentieth century, not least because of the experience of the Great Depression, economists aimed to empirically attribute growth to the individual factors, by this time mostly considering labour and capital only. The search for a general theory of economic growth gained significance because growth became the key economic policy objective, and the main academic contributors such as Nicholas Kaldor (Káldor Miklós), Roy Harrod and Robert Solow also acted as government advisors. Nevertheless, no consensus about the explanation of economic growth could be reached, in contrast to growth as a policy objective, even though this, too, was contested until the late 1950s – and again from the early 1970s.

For current purposes, rather than reconstructing the barren academic debate about the sources of economic growth, it is more fruitful to go back to the reconstruction of historical transformations of economic regimes (in the preceding chapters). Thus three sources of wealth – as the earlier terminology had it – can be distinguished, one of which was rather new and significantly altered the relation between the other two.

As we have seen, first, classical political economy based the increase in wealth on a deepening of the division of labour. Arguably, this was the first significant deviation from seeing land as the key, or even the only, source of wealth, which was something like a common wisdom before physiocrats formalized the issue. Clearly, this implicit 'theory' had been underpinning core policies over centuries, those of territorial expansion. The focus shifted to the division of labour with the rise of 'commercial society', with hindsight including the 'industrious revolution', and it had also early on been applied to international commerce, based on the theorem of 'comparative advantage'. To some extent, factory organization, including the plantation economy, and the 'scientific management' known as Taylorism at the beginning of the twentieth century can be seen as applying the maxim of deepening the division of labour through evermore specialized and fragmented work tasks (i.e., that which Marx had called the 'real subsumption' of labour under capital). After the Second World War, this maxim was meant to be applied throughout the economy as 'modernization', clearly seen in the report of Groupe 1985. Furthermore, economic growth was to be enhanced by internationalization of trade, in response to protectionism and even moves towards autarchy before the Second World War, which were seen as partly responsible for the Great Depression from 1929. The creation of the International Monetary Fund (IMF) and the World Bank in 1944 and the General Agreement on Tariffs and Trade (GATT) of 1947 were meant to consolidate and further international trade.

Second, as shown earlier (chapter 4), economic growth had also been seen as dependent on an increasing input of resources. Malthus had seen here limits that could not be overcome. But even before him, West European societies had appropriated resources from other world regions, with the 'ghost acres' being the means for overcoming the Malthusian land constraint in one world region by drawing on land resources in others. The move towards systematically transgressing vertical frontiers, first coal around 1800, then oil and gas around 1900, opened completely new horizons. Contemporary scholars and observers were well aware of the novelty as well as of its possible limits, Jevons being a key example. But entering into the twentieth century, this awareness gradually diminished, even though it never entirely disappeared. The examples of Ludwig Erhard and Groupe 1985 show only a general awareness of the issue which was given rather little significance.

The reason for this declining significance of biophysical resources for economic growth resides in the detection of a third source for such growth, namely the increase in productivity, central in post-war thinking as just shown exemplarily. However, this explanation only begs further questions. Generally, the term 'productivity' refers to the rate of input for a unit of output. In the period under consideration, rise in productivity was mostly measured by a decreasing amount of labour time required for the same product. It was exactly this relation that permitted the link between wages and productivity in the magic formula. Such rise in productivity could be achieved by specialization of tasks, as in Taylorism, in which case we are back to the first source of growth, namely division of labour, without requiring additional resources. And this is indeed a partial explanation. Later explorations of productivity and economic growth added other sources – or rather, concepts to stand in for sources – such as human capital, education and scientific knowledge (Schmelzer 2016: ch. 5), all of which do not centrally depend on biophysical resources for their mobilization either.

However, the core explanation for productivity increase that was offered during the post-war decades was another one, namely 'technical progress'. In an attempt to attribute economic growth to factors of production, Robert Solow had found that a considerable 'residual factor' was left after accounting for the contributions of capital and labour. Not knowing what this residue consisted of, it came to be referred to as technical progress, initially left as a black box and later investigated in studies of innovation and technical change (such as those by Giovanni Dosi and Thomas P. Hughes, and generally in the rising studies of science and technology). At first sight, such 'explanation' does not appear surprising, rather it is patently obvious considering the visible transformation of western societies during the early post-war decades through the erection of large-size factories and extended infrastructure, as well as consumer technologies such as motor cars and a range of household appliances. On second thoughts, though, two major problems arise when referring to the source of this transformation as 'technical progress'. First, most of the technologies evoked in the preceding sentence were invented in the late nineteenth or early twentieth century in the course of the so-called Second Industrial Revolution, the main exceptions being the jet plane, television and nuclear energy. Thus, the post-war decades are rather a period of diffusion of technology than of major technical progress. This being so, second, the question arises as to how the diffusion of such technologies contributed to the economic growth of the period. A comparison of the US economy with West European ones during the 1950s is revealing. There was an enormous 'productivity gap' between the two, which led to the debates mentioned above in Europe. This gap, though, can be explained by quite straightforward means without evoking the enigmatic concept of technical progress: 'US industry used between two and three times as much electrical power per worker' than the West European industry, drawing on its abundant supplies of coal and oil (Schmelzer 2016: 131; see also Mitchell 2011: 29; and for a general reasoning along these lines now Pineault 2021). European production and consumption became much more energy intensive, too, during the 1960s and 1970s, following the US path without ever coming close to the level of per capita resource use, though. At least during this period, therefore, the first hypothesis should have been to see use of biophysical resources, in particular fossil fuels, as the main source of the high rates of economic growth, as growth rates of GNP and of energy use aligned neatly (which would later become a topic of debate; see below, chapter 8). While the use of biophysical resources experienced exponential increase and reached unprecedented levels, though, the economic sciences, supposedly dealing with allocation of resources and questions of scarcity, basically ignored the issue and reasoned in terms of 'factors of production' to which they tried to attribute their respective contributions to overall growth. (The more policy-minded OECD set up an Energy Committee, which studied oil and gas supply as 'fuel for growth'; see Schmelzer 2016: 201).

With his more comprehensive perspective, Joseph A. Schumpeter (1976 [1942]; the following page numbers refer to this volume) had considered the question whether 'new land' (109), as mentioned above, and also 'technological progress' (110) are basic requisites for economic growth. He did not deny the importance of these factors, but he subordinated their significance to his broader view of the 'capitalist process'. From this perspective, the availability of land, such as the western frontier of the United States in the nineteenth century, should be seen as 'objective opportunities' – that is to say, 'opportunities that exist independently of any social arrangement'; and such opportunities 'are always prerequisites of progress, and each of them is historically unique' (109). Such uniqueness, though, does not entail that the destruction of this opportunity by making use of it creates a limit or a constraint for future 'progress'. On the contrary, the disappearance of one opportunity will lead to the search for a new one: 'The whole capitalist process, like any other economic process that is evolutionary, consists in nothing else but exploiting such opportunities as they enter the businessman's horizon and there is no point in trying to single out the one under discussion in order to construe it as an external factor' (110). Even though that expression was not available to him, Schumpeter reasons in terms of planetary boundaries – or rather, frontiers.

> It is gratuitous to assume not only that the 'closing of the frontier' will cause a vacuum but also that whatever steps into the vacant place must necessarily be less important in any of the senses we may choose to give to that word. The conquest of the air may well be more important than the conquest of India was – we must not confuse geographical frontiers with economic ones. (Schumpeter 1976: 117)

Schumpeter was probably thinking of air traffic, maybe even of space traffic, and not of air pollution and even less of climate change. But for him, anyway, air was just an arbitrary example of an 'opportunity'. He may well be right that one must not confuse geographical frontiers with economic ones, but one may need to think more on what the difference between them is and what possibly the connection. Twenty years later, Groupe 1985 stated that it would have been sheer fantasy to consider air a primary resource a decade earlier. But by their time of writing 'the consumption of air, its destruction' had reached worrying levels (Groupe 1985 1964: 128–9). This was three decades before the creation of the UN Framework Convention on Climate Change (UNFCCC).

Democratic capitalism in one world region

Up to this point, my analysis has focused on the 'domestic' identification and interpretation of key problems within the emerging world region that was to be called 'the West'. In short summary, the key issue was that, by the early twentieth century, European and North American societies had found democratic political institutions unavoidable but had largely failed to consolidate them in the face of strong social cleavages and high political mobilization for greater equality. By mid-century, thus, there was a perceived need to enhance material well-being throughout society, expecting greater acceptance of the sociopolitical order and decline in critical political participation as an intended consequence. The means to achieve this outcome was called 'economic growth', and it was made possible by exponential increase in biophysical resources, even though the latter was rarely made central on the public agenda until the early 1970s. With hindsight, one can say that this strategy 'worked', at least temporarily. The liberal-democratic capitalist welfare state of the period was widely seen as a 'model' and has even remained a point of reference for many current scholars. Before we take a closer look at its mode of operation with a view to understanding its later challenges, transformation and partial demise, we need to situate it in a global perspective, to understand democratic capitalism as a world-regional phenomenon.

We have already pointed out that, next to the collapse of some European democracies, the rise and persistence of Soviet socialism with its flagged commitment to social equality was a main reason for focusing on the enhancement of material well-being. Even though this may be difficult to recall after the demise of the Soviet Union, western societies saw themselves in a competition with existing socialism that they feared losing on the 'social' more than on the military front, at least until the 1970s. The relationship between the West and Soviet socialism was considered to be 'system competition', with firm boundaries between them. In contrast, the relationship with what came to be called the 'underdeveloped', later 'developing', countries, some of which were still under European colonial domination at the end of the Second World War, was in need of being (newly) defined.

Towards that end, US scholarship in the social sciences soon created a tool in line with the emerging diagnoses of western societies as oriented towards economic growth and a functionally ordered set of institutions. Closely related to the theories of economic growth, as just discussed, the economic theory of modernization was based on a stage model of economic development, and 'developing' countries merely needed to be advised and supported so that they could reach their 'take-off', following the path of western societies (the classic statements are Rostow 1956, 1959; see now, e.g., Schmelzer 2016: ch. 6). Similarly, the sociological theory of modernization assumed that western democratic capitalism was a model for social and political development to be emulated across the globe (for a classic statement, see Parsons 1964).

Even if one accepted that 'modernization and development' was a desirable direction of history, it would be highly questionable to assume that states and societies were separate and could be considered as independent from each other so that they were, in principle, capable of pursuing development strategies in search of their own growth trajectories. While the developing countries were at a different stage from western societies to start with, they were just seen as somewhat behind on a general line of evolutionary development. Prima facie, though, it had always been more plausible to consider that the fact of being 'ahead' or 'behind' impacts on a society's possibility for action and change. Implausible as it was to assume that the exit from an era of imperial and colonial domination would entail equal capacity for 'development', the theory of modernization was widely accepted for some time and has never entirely disappeared (Knöbl 2003; Latham 2003).

Placing these conceptual considerations in a historical context, two observations stand out. First, by the end of the Second World War, large parts of the globe, in particular in Africa and Asia, were still under colonial domination; those societies could not therefore develop and embark on their own strategies for change. Indeed, even though posing as a general theory, the theory of modernization was developed for a decolonized context of a globe consisting of formally equal states. And second, while many world-regional settings were marked by scarcity, resource constraints were not in any way seen as globally significant. Theories of modernization and development did not consider the possibility that the resource intensity of this 'model' made it inapplicable on a wider scale. Despite the devastation they brought, the two world wars and totalitarianism appeared rather to testify to the enormous human capacity of mobilizing social and biophysical resources for specific purposes. As the report *Science: The Endless Frontier* (Bush 1945), presented to the US President in 1945, had it, the problem was only to redirect this capacity towards socially beneficial purposes.

On a closer look, this new purpose becomes recognizable as the broad commitment towards enhancing domestic social well-being, later to become known as the welfare state. In the immediate post-war context, the urgency to adequately address 'the social question' was acknowledged as a global issue. The fact that, as mentioned above, the UN Declaration of Human Rights included social rights shows a wide consensus on the matter. At the same time, the general expectation was that these rights would be realized and protected within national welfare states, the creation of which had already started in Europe. There were calls, though, maybe most explicitly by the Swedish scholar Gunnar Myrdal, to organize social solidarity globally, to create a world system of welfare states. Just as national states had started to recognize the social question and to build social policy institutions, so one would now need to recognize world poverty and build global redistributive institutions that spread material well-being more equally. 'The concept of the welfare state, to which we are now giving reality in all the advanced nations, would have to be widened and changed to the concept of a "welfare world"' (Getachew 2019: 160–2; Myrdal 1956, cited in Moyn 2018: 107).

However, '[a]t the end of the Second World War the economic and social recovery of vast portions of the globe was simply not on the agenda of the victorious nations' (Garavini 2012: 20). The key actors were mostly colonial powers who did not consider the colonized peoples on equal terms, and their key concern was to stabilize the metropolitan societies, not least in the face of totalitarian threats to liberal-capitalist settings, both in the form of prior fascisms and in the ongoing Cold War context (Moyn 2018: ch. 4). Rather than erecting global redistributive institutions, therefore, 'development aid' was introduced by national governments and included in national budgets. There it not only remained marginal in terms of size but was often subordinated to specific interests in bilateral relations between an 'advanced' and a 'developing' country. Thus the resource-intensive industrial welfare state was created with strong boundaries to sustain the difference in material well-being from its outside. These boundaries have not always been state boundaries. Apartheid South Africa created a welfare state for the white minority only; and the United States had colonial features through the way it segregated its Native American and African-American population from the WASP citizenry (see Korzeniewicz 2018: 21–2 for a reflection on the setting of boundaries to maintain welfare differentials, going back to Adam Smith). As Gunnar Myrdal had said at the end of the 1950s, we have to 'squarely face the fact that *the democratic Welfare State in the rich countries of the western world is protectionist and nationalistic*' and that if this situation persists '*there is no alternative to international disintegration*' (Myrdal 1956: 119 and 130; emphasis in original).

Beyond being thus scaled down, the theories also did not come to be fully tested in their heyday because neither leading political decision makers nor globally acting business people ever intended to put them into practice. This was left to some development 'experts' and a few decision makers, influential in small countries but marginal globally (Marklund 2020). Debates among western elites about the relation to the 'developing' countries were dominated by two other issues: how to avoid 'Third World' countries adopting a socialist political orientation and aligning with the Soviet Union; and how to maintain access to the biophysical resources that western 'economic growth' depended on, as was admitted in practice though denied in theory.

As decolonization proceeded further and post-colonial states were established, new actors made claims for global solidarity and political responsibility for colonialism. The Asian-African (Bandung) Conference of 1955 (e.g., Umar 2019), the United Nations Conference on Trade and Development (UNCTAD) created in 1964, and the New International Economic Order (NIEO), approved by the UN General Assembly in 1974 (e.g., Gilman 2015), were key foci for this attempted reinterpretation of global politics, which has recently been profoundly analysed as an attempt at deliberate 'world making after empire' (Getachew 2019). Reflecting the future articulation of nation-building and global order in the light of the right to post-colonial self-determination, the attempt left space for different visions of 'development' and their resource implications (see below, chapter 7) but was founded on the right to the biophysical resources on the territory of the newly independent states.

However, these attempts were largely rejected or only formally accepted by the western powers. Rather, one can observe a gradual process of abdication of political responsibility of the colonizing states for the former colonies, which are more and more charged with taking care of themselves (Karagiannis 2004). By the 1970s, therefore, the divide between the 'First' and the 'Third World' was well entrenched, with the former achieving social and political goals while exceeding planetary boundaries of resource use by far and the latter failing to reach social and political goals while living way below their 'share' of biophysical resources – to employ a language that came into use only recently (O'Neill et al. 2018). The 'First World' had apparently successfully solved its sociopolitical problems by spatially displacing them to the 'Third World'.

The Rawlsian moment: the self-understanding of post-colonial democratic capitalism

One may be inclined to say that the double process of democratic 'consolidation' in western societies and decolonization in Africa and South and South East Asia spelled the end of the liberal-imperial and oligarchic world order that had been created during the nineteenth century, materially based on coal as the main energy source. Certainly, this was an interpretation that was promoted as a new societal self-understanding from within western societies that presented themselves as the 'free world' in explicit contrast to Soviet socialism and in a more unclear relation to the 'developing' societies.

For our purposes, we can consider John Rawls's *Theory of Justice* of 1971, accompanied by 'the law of peoples' of 1993, as a snapshot of this new societal self-understanding. While his thought can obviously not be considered as representative of such a self-understanding, given its academic nature and the widespread criticism it also faced, I treat it here as exemplary. *A Theory of Justice* was hailed as a refoundation of political theory, and it has triggered reactions far beyond its original ambition, not least the academic and public debates about global justice that indeed made Rawls write 'The Law of Peoples' to address questions of justice beyond the domestic polity. I will ignore all questions about the status of the theory, such as the distinction between ideal and non-ideal theory, and discuss Rawls's work contextually as an expression of the spirit of the epoch within the West (for a detailed contextual reconstruction of Rawls's work, see Forrester 2019).

Let us first recall the architecture of Rawls's political thought. He imagines a political order based on equal freedom of its members and, on this basis, aims to develop criteria for justice within this polity. This polity is democratic, given that its members are thought to arrive at these criteria of justice themselves; they are not externally given. But on the assumption of freedom and equality, Rawls surmises, one can theoretically determine these criteria, with just the additional assumption of the 'veil of ignorance', that is, citizens are supposed to express their view in ignorance of their own social position within this polity. This construction impressed many readers since it aimed to provide a strong underpinning for liberal-democratic polities. Furthermore, Rawls arrived at an understanding of justice that involved some redistribution in favour of the poor. As one might say, he provided theoretical arguments for the welfare state, which increased the attractiveness of the proposal at the time. Beyond the widespread praise, the key perceived problem was the limitation of justice to the relation between members of a polity in the face of a global reality that, as it seemed to many, was evidently unjust. In response to calls for considering global criteria for justice, Rawls came up with a distinction of types of societies and argued that 'liberal' societies have some very limited 'duty of assistance' towards 'burdened' societies.

In this light, two historical-contextual observations can be made. First, Rawls theorized a globe composed of formally equal states, many of which have liberal-democratic constitutions, and he does so precisely at the historical moment of the end of colonial domination. As an indicator, one can just look at the number of member states of the United Nations, which has rapidly been increasing from the late 1950s onwards. Such a situation was entirely unprecedented. From the beginning of global consciousness at around 1500, the globe had always consisted of imperial formations, often with uncertain control of their outer reaches, combined with territories that had not been integrated at all into any world system. Rawls, thus, takes his own moment and turns it into a baseline for political theorizing, first by implicitly erecting a boundary between a 'well-ordered society' and the rest of the globe, and subsequently, in 'The Law of Peoples', by thinly defining the relations between societies. One would not be culpable of undue reductionism if one saw here just a mirror image of a globe composed of a number of liberal-democratic welfare states, which erect a boundary between themselves and poorer societies to whom they provide 'development aid'.

Second, for his reflection on just institutions, Rawls reasoned from the point of view of individuals entering into a social contract precisely at the moment when 'collective concepts' (Max Weber), including those of class and nation, were widely criticized, both in scholarly debate, including sociology, and in the public sphere. On the one hand, leading critical sociologists, such as Alain Touraine, Anthony Giddens and Michael Mann, insisted explicitly that there is no 'society' *sui generis* but only social relations of variable extension and different kinds. Subsequently, the rise of individualist-rationalist thinking in the social sciences seemed unstoppable, even though not endorsed by these scholars (see, e.g., Wagner 2010). On the other hand, the collective political projects of the twentieth century, socialism and post-colonial nationalism, became increasingly discredited due to malfunctioning and oppression in their 'actually existing' forms. This was the context in which the idea of individual human rights became the 'last utopia' (Moyn 2010) and turned hegemonic in the combination of 'human rights and democracy', leading to the 'fall of self-determination' as a world-making project (Getachew 2019).

In other words, Rawls elaborated a rather coherent self-understanding of liberal-democratic capitalism in one world region. Like the theorists of commercial republicanism two centuries earlier, though, he sidelined any consideration of those preconditions for coherence that in some way lay outside the polity in the way he defined it. Doing so, he ignored the material bases of the supposedly rather 'well-ordered' societies of his time.

Displacing the global urgency: from the social to the ecological question

The debate on criteria for justice beyond the boundaries of polities initially focused on social justice. Rawls's term 'duty of assistance' was seen as referring to social needs, and the resource claim in the New International Economic Order (NIEO) was also read as enabling 'developing' countries to achieve economic and social development. In parallel, one can observe that the status of such social claims was downgraded during the closing decades of the twentieth century. Domestically, western countries faced the 'crisis of the welfare state' (O'Connor 1973) and a change in economic policy orthodoxy, giving greater emphasis to balanced public budgets than to the reduction of unemployment. Internationally, the expectations of 'development' faded away, and aid to 'burdened' societies was refocused on basic needs and poverty reduction (Getachew 2019; Moyn 2018).

During the 1970s, global political debate witnessed a shift from social to ecological concerns, including a shift from social to environmental justice. The failure of the NIEO and the first UN conference on the environment in 1972 signalled respectively the downgrading of the former concern and the upgrading of the latter. The 1970s mark a moment of global transformations, both in terms of discourse and of material resources, that we will address from different angles through all of the following chapters. At this point, only a few features of this shift will be mentioned that form the background for the subsequent analyses.

First, we can here indeed speak of a rather short moment, marked by events, most importantly the close coincidence of the publication of the Club of Rome report *Limits to Growth* in 1972 with the so-called oil-price crisis in 1973. The well-publicized diagnosis of rapidly depleting resources came together with the apparent – not real – shortage of a key energy resource for western societies.

Second, the rapid shift in problem definition and interpretation raised suspicions of several kinds. On the one side, the western path of economic growth and well-being seemed to be questioned, and with it possibly the profit-based capitalist economy. On the other side, from the perspective of southern countries, the shift seemed to renege on the promise of modernization and development. If resources became scarce because they had been used up in western development, southern development was postponed from 'not yet' to 'never' (see, e.g., Agarwal and Narain 1991).

Both of these possibilities were highly critical. Thus, third, considerable effort was undertaken to hold the social and the ecological together in a global problem definition.

The work of the so-called Brandt Commission (Stråth 2023) aimed to halt the conceptual movement by diagnosing a huge resource divide between North and South (creating the 'Brandt Line', which separates the Global North from the Global South) and deriving responsibility for resource transfer from this diagnosis. With the so-called Brundtland Commission, some years later, a conceptual link between the social and the ecological was established through the term 'sustainable development', which has remained central, even though vague, up to the UN Sustainable Development Goals of 2015 (Borowy 2013).

The work of both these internationally sponsored commissions keeps being referred to in global debates, but its actual impact on global action is uncertain. One aspect, though, is noteworthy. With regard to social justice and material well-being, the attempt to establish an 'expansive account of political responsibility' (Getachew 2019: 35) at the global level has failed, whereas for environmental and resource matters, and more recently for climate change, we have witnessed the gradual emergence of a principle of global justice. Accelerating global environmental debates (e.g., Walker 2009) have often been led in terms of 'unequal ecological exchange' and 'global environmental justice'. Since the 1970s, and increasingly so, the notion of 'common but differentiated responsibilities' has been a guiding principle and has been integrated into international declarations from the Earth Summit in Rio de Janeiro in 1992 to the Paris Agreement in 2015 (Paris Agreement, Art. 2.2 and elsewhere; Josephson 2017; Stone 2004). Thus both the global reach of the problem and the different degrees to which (state) actors are responsible are widely accepted. There is even little general doubt about the spatio-temporal trajectory of problem causation, roughly as discussed in part II of this book. In other words, for environmental and climate matters, an interpretative tool is at hand, even though the step from principle to action has not been taken. The Paris Agreement provides only a few guidelines for interpreting the principle, and its application remains widely contested in detail (e.g., Ekardt, Wieding and Zorn 2018; Pauw, Mbeva and van Asselt 2019; Rajamani 2016).

7
Why Fossil Fuels? Alternatives to 'Development'

Growing up during the glorious years

The house in which I grew up in the north of West Germany did not have a bathroom when I was small, and the toilet was situated across a courtyard. A metal bathtub was moved into the kitchen when it was time for us children to have a bath, normally on Saturdays. The water was heated in large pots on a stove that was run on bottled gas located just outside the window. The living room was heated by a large tiled stove, fuelled by wood and coal, and so was my grandmother's room. The other rooms did not have heating. On winter mornings, the windowpane showed a frost pattern in the morning, called 'ice flowers' in German. Elements of the fossil fuel economy were present, but nevertheless I grew up as one of the 'sons' who would largely be separated from their 'mothers' by a change in era, namely during the tail end of the domestic 'energy transition' to fossil fuels in Western Europe (Smil 2021: 3–7). Before I was born, my parents were digging peat in a nearby moor and selling it for heating and cooking purposes. I may have been eight years old when warm-water central heating was installed in the house, but it was still fuelled by wood and coal. My father prepared the back boiler in the morning to light it in the evening. One day, I wanted to see how it worked and looked inside. Not seeing anything, I lit a match and threw it in. As the paper that my father had included for lighting the fire immediately started to burn, I panicked and poured water on it to put it out. My father never found out why the paper, wood and coal were wet in the evening, but I imagine he had a suspicion.

In two further stages, the central heating fuel was changed, first, to oil and, later, to gas. I was told that these were changes that one made at the time, but I recall little of the broader context. The local supplier of energy for heating remained the same in the small town where we lived. The business switched from supplying coal to oil to gas, and my parents probably followed their recommendations. Oil and later gas were then cheap and abundantly available, but I doubt whether any of these further steps made heating cheaper for my family. Rather, they increased the 'convenience'. After moving to oil, my father did not need to prepare a fire any longer in the morning – nor my mother, after my father died when I was ten. A 2,000-litre oil tank was installed in a shed that probably had housed wood and coal before, and something like twice a year my mother had to call the supplier to fill the tank. This was no longer necessary when the fuel moved to gas, which came in pipes. The tank was taken out, and the shed remained empty.

All this happened during the West German 'economic miracle', or the 'thirty glorious years'. We are now well able to criticize the commodification of everyday life. When I was a child, much of our food came from a small fruit and vegetable garden, potatoes and apples being stored in the basement for the winter and other produce being conserved under vacuum in glass jars by my grandmother. A local farmer brought a truck full of additional potatoes in October to feed the family through the winter. Second-rate apples were brought to a neighbour to be turned into juice. Later in my childhood, though, we went once a year by bus to a consumer goods fair in the regional capital, where we bought novel domestic appliances and ordered apple juice to be delivered by van. But in what sense exactly were we tricked into dependency on working for a wage and buying what we needed rather than producing it ourselves or exchanging with locals? Or vice versa, to what degree were our material living conditions actually improving and this improvement appreciated in everyday life?

Biophysical resources and material well-being

Having gone through the history of the human use of non-human resources, we can return to the question of whether increased resource use was a necessary condition for enhancing human material well-being. The close correlation between the two was the basis for the hegemonic answer to this question in the West during the first phase of the Great Acceleration and in other world regions since. We need to readdress this question because it often remains a baseline assumption in public debate, not least as a justification for why climate change policies cannot straightforwardly be based on reducing the use of biophysical resources. As the debate goes on – lingers on, we may say, because there is little evolution – critical observers start to agree with this presupposition, the most prominent example being Dipesh Chakrabarty (as stated at the outset).

Let us first recall that Malthus made a direct connection between human survival and biophysical resources, the latter for him expressed in usable land. Inadvertently, his thinking provided a new perspective on reading prior human history, namely as the repeated attempt to overcome this constraint by expansion in space – first mostly terrestrial, then also maritime. Through such expansion, control over more non-human resources and/or over more human beings on whom productive work could be imposed was aimed at and often achieved. For current purposes, we can consider extension of long-distance trade relations as a similar form of expansion, that is, when the terms of trade can be set rather one-sidedly, as was largely the case. Thus far, biophysical resources are closely tied to human material well-being but also to inequality and hierarchy.

From the sixteenth and seventeenth centuries onwards, as we have seen, two notions were developed that tended to make this link more tenuous. One of them is what we now call, after de Vries, industriousness. It includes longer working hours, specialization and an increasing domestic division of social labour. None of this necessarily requires more biophysical resources, even though we have seen before (chapter 3) that the 'industrious revolution' took place in parallel with the increased acquisition of biophysical resources on 'ghost acres' overseas. The other notion is 'technological progress', that is, an increase in knowledge that can be applied to support and enhance production processes (chapter 6). For our purposes, the term conceals more than it elucidates. We can imagine here the improvement of a tool, say a plough, that increases efficiency. However, the notion leaves open whether the new plough will keep being advanced by animal or human energy or by a combustion engine. In the former case, evidently, such progress is rather resource neutral; in the latter case, it is not. In historical context, again, the realization of technological progress as an outcome of what came to be called the scientific revolution became highly oriented towards machinery run by fossil fuels, initially mostly coal (chapter 4).

During 'early modernity', in sum, we find two notions that potentially decouple enhanced material well-being from increased use of biophysical resources. At the same time, the emergence of these possibilities was accompanying historical transformations towards greater use of biophysical resources, thus making it difficult, if not impossible, to disentangle the effects on material well-being that were due to resource use from those that were not. This problem became exacerbated by the increasing detachment of economic and managerial thought from the material aspects of production. Fossil fuels had remained central for Jevons and significant for Weber, but after the combined onslaught of the subjectivation of economic action in the marginal utility school, the focus on work organization for productivity increase in Taylorism, and the circularity of macro-economic thinking, the material base of production was lost from sight. It appeared, paraphrasing Cornelius Castoriadis (1975; see recently Mouzakitis 2014) for a different purpose, as if production innovation could occur not only *ex nihilo* but also *cum nihilo*.

While economic concepts performed their work of hiding biophysical resources, the statistical figures gave a different account that could be mobilized when this was found suitable. In the context of the rising ecological consciousness and the oil price increase of the early 1970s, it was argued that the high rates of economic growth during the preceding decade and a half were closely correlated with increasing consumption of energy. While this was statistically accurate for the past, the argument was that this was a necessary relation and that, thus, the energy supply needed to be secured for future economic growth and, by implication, material well-being. In response, ecologically minded economists developed counter-modelling showing that growth and well-being could be decoupled from resource use. Significantly, even then such critics tended to keep economic growth and well-being connected, for easier political acceptability, while insisting that resource use did not need to increase further.

Those debates reflected what we can now recognize as the emerging ecological crisis, and they were marked by their context. Ecologically minded critics had to combat the double absurdity of dominant thinking, namely the claim in economic theory that natural resources were not required for economic growth, on the one hand and, on the other, the claim in applied economics that growth of gross domestic product required proportional growth of energy input. We may recognize here Bruno Latour's (1991) distinction of 'purification', which means separating the social (here, the economy) from the natural (here, coal and oil), and subsequent 'hybridification', which creates new entities (here, refineries and thermal power stations), as the two core components of the 'modern constitution'. Given this attempted immunization of mainstream economic thinking from critique, it is understandable that ecological criticism at times tends to discard the question of the relation between biophysical resources and material well-being altogether. From the original 'affluent society' detected by Marshall Sahlins (1972) to the *buen vivir* in the Andean countries, there are supposedly plenty of alternatives, reachable once the growth dogma (and the interests behind it) has been effectively denounced and resolute 'de-growth' policies are being adopted (Muraca and Schmelzer 2017). The merit of these debates is the interpretative opening to a variety of possible resource bases for current societies. Their frequent deficiency, though, is to neglect the constraints, which are always twofold: on the one hand, the constraints residing in the characteristics of the various resources themselves, and, on the other hand, the constraints that emerge from the social forms of use of these resources. In line with the general approach taken here, we will keep our eye on the resources and the problems their use was meant to solve. We will start by looking at the characteristics of fossil fuels that may help an understanding of their adoption over other types of resources and will, in a second step, review the historically existing alternatives. These reflections will serve to better grasp the shift from the Western to the Asian Great Acceleration and, subsequently, the likelihood of the current, incessantly evoked but hardly practised, energy transition.

The multiple convenience of fossil fuels

The brief autobiographical introduction to this chapter was meant to signal arguments from everyday life for fossil fuels, and specifically also for oil and gas against coal and wood (and peat). The move from stoves, which needed to be prepared and kept going all day while only heating two rooms of the house, to a system that heated the whole house at the push of a button marked a considerable functional advantage. I cannot provide figures, but the superior system was probably not, or not much more, expensive than its predecessor, at least after the initial investment, because my far-from-affluent parents could not have afforded it otherwise. As much as we know about business strategies to lure potential customers towards their products, intensified in the West after the Second World War (Packard 1957 remains the classical reference), unless we believe that every supply creates its own demand there must be some benefits buyers receive from steady consumption, even if they are not fully 'rational'. Therefore, we need to look at the characteristics of fossil fuels that made them functionally advantageous.

The key functional features of fossil fuels are their high energy density, their transportability and their storability. First, stating that fossil fuels have a high energy density means that the energy that is released by burning them is high in relation to their volume. The energy density of coal is higher than that of wood, and in turn, that of oil and gas is higher than that of coal. The difference is so significant that even high losses of energy, such as in coal-powered steam engines or in the combustion engine, do not, or at least not always and not immediately, eliminate the advantage in relation to other energy sources. Second, in comparison with wind and water, fossil fuels are transportable energy sources. The user does not have to move towards the energy source, but the energy source can be delivered to the user. Transportability of fossil fuels varies. As we have seen earlier (chapter 4), one of the reasons for the early diffusion of coal use in England was the proximity of exploitable coal deposits to urban economic centres. With the then available technology, long-distance transport of large amounts of coal would have required significant effort and cost. From the late nineteenth century onwards, in turn, oil could be transported in (ever larger) tanker ships and through pipelines, which made bulk transportation across large distances feasible. Oil deposits in regions far away from established sites of industry or large consumer populations, such as the Middle East, started to be exploited, mostly under the direction, if not always ownership, of companies based in the United States, the United Kingdom, France and the Netherlands (chapter 5). Third, fossil fuels are natural stores of energy, which can be left in their sites for later exploitation or extracted and stored in the areas of their use. This was a historical advantage over wind and solar energy, increasing the reliability of supply when needed. As is well known, the further expansion of wind and solar energy in the current 'energy transition' remains dependent on the development of forms of storage.

We have started out looking at the characteristics of fossil fuels from the angle of their functionality for heating purposes for private consumers, and as such the advantages are fairly evident. However, such functional assessments vary highly with context and purpose. Even in the autobiographical example, it is clear that my parents could not have made the fuel transitions on their own but depended on businesses providing the fuel (and possibly governments encouraging the transitions). For business and government, though, the rationales can be quite different, as two key examples show.

Andreas Malm (2016) analysed the introduction of the coal-powered steam engine in the British weaving industry during the first half of the nineteenth century. The industry was located along rivers at sites of significant inclination because it was using water power for the processing of cotton, and it worked with home-based weavers to whom the cotton was delivered. Under these conditions, the coal-powered engine long remained unattractive because coal was costly whereas water came for free, and because coal had to be delivered whereas water was available at the already existing sites of industry. The dependence on the river with variable flow, though, required coordination between companies located at the same river further up- or downstream. When companies started to liberate themselves from this coordination requirement through coal-powered engines, they set a transition in motion that not only led to fossil fuel dominance but also involved new locations at urban sites and concentration of workers in factories, thus an entire new production system. Malm (2016: ch. 13: 71–3) tends to interpret his findings as evidence that a capital logic – in broad terms of class relations, not straightforward profit maximization – was driving the move towards fossil fuels. However, this is not as evident as he assumes since we observe a move from one to another production arrangement, both of which were reliant on wage labour and were profit driven and, in this sense, capitalist.

Instead, we may recognize that the characteristics of fossil fuels can work for or against their adoption, dependent on the context. For a more long-term analysis of a resource trajectory, the important question arising from this analysis is whether coordination requirements tend to be seen as a burden under modern or capitalist conditions and, if so, whether fossil fuels are adopted because they reduce such requirements.

In his analysis of the rise of oil as an energy source, Timothy Mitchell (2011: e.g., 7, 41) is clearly hesitant about assuming that a straightforward 'capital logic' is at work. Instead, he emphasizes domestic and international political factors, setting the increasing move towards oil in the context of the strengthening of the workers' movement in western societies, on the one side, and the late- and neo-imperial context around and after the First World War, on the other. Like Malm does with coal, Mitchell pays attention to the material characteristics of oil, in this case the less labour-intensive extraction compared to coal and the easier transportability, which allows the separation of the point of use from the point of extraction, with the important qualification that the latter increasingly lies outside the domestic territory of the extracting companies and of the consumers. Thus his main conclusion is that the shift from coal to oil permitted breaking the power of the coal miners' unions, seen as the core of the labour movement with the capacity of bringing society to a standstill. However, this reasoning lacks compelling evidence and plausibility while containing a conceptual bias.

Mitchell pays little attention to the long time span during which oil and coal were both key energy sources in western societies, but without fully being substitutable, as coal was mostly used for generating electricity and for thermic industrial processes (as well as for heating, though to a declining degree) whereas oil was predominantly used for motorization in combustion engines and for new industrial products. Without spelling this out, Mitchell's interpretation seems to be shaped by the breaking of the National Union of Miners in the United Kingdom by Prime Minister Margaret Thatcher at the moment when North Sea oil became an available energy resource for the United Kingdom. But this was an exceptionally reckless repression, conditioned by the circumstances, which had no equal in other western countries. The key interpretative problem is that Mitchell analyses the characteristics of oil only compared to coal and only in view of the conditions of production.

Thus he disregards other energy options (to which we come in a moment) and the functionality of energy sources at the point of consumption.

We can illustrate the latter point with a comparison. In line with her world view, Margaret Thatcher also favoured the use of private cars over public transport and invested in the motorway system while letting the railway services further deteriorate. Strikes of railway workers can bring a whole country even more quickly to a standstill than miners' strikes (and have done so). But to the best of my knowledge no one has argued that the quick and wide diffusion of private cars in the post-Second World War period in Europe, which reduced the social and economic significance of trains, was promoted by business in collusion with governments in capitalist societies to break the strength of the railway workers' unions and, thus, of the workers' movement in general (on the attraction of cars see, e.g., Urry 2011). In other words, while paying attention to the characteristics of fossil fuels, both Malm and Mitchell ultimately consider these features in their functional role within a preconceived theory of society, to which the empirical analysis is subordinated. Therefore, it becomes impossible to conceive of a biophysical resource as altering the very hierarchies and forms of domination within and – keeping Mitchell's international perspective in view – between societies.

Critical junctures

Economic and political forms of power are at the centre, in different ways, of Malm's and Mitchell's analyses, and there is no doubt that they are highly significant. From a resource perspective as taken here, however, these forms of power, including their crystallization in institutions, are framed by the resources' resistance to, or compliance with, the uses to which they are being put (see further the discussion on enabling and constraining knowledge in the following chapter), on the one side, and the driving forces on the part of the users of these resources, on the other side. The latter can be described with a wide range of terminologies, ranging from value, utility, profit and benefit to convenience and comfort, each with their own connotations more or less clearly embedded in social theories in the broad sense of the term. As stated earlier (chapter 1), my favourite term is societal self-understandings or, borrowing from Castoriadis, social imaginaries, emphasizing openness to interpretation. In other words, standard theories of economic and political power fail to capture two core aspects of the human condition, namely being embedded in, and dependent on, non-human nature, and having the power of imagination to shape this embeddedness and dependence. Critical junctures (e.g., Hogan 2019) in the history of energy use can be explored as examples of the significance of these aspects.

In Malm's account, as a first example, the choice between water and coal remained open for a long time in the British weaving industry. We can assume that developments outside Malm's view played a significant role in tipping the balance, such as the increasing use of coal in other industries, most importantly iron and steel, and the experience with factory work and discipline, starting in the colonial plantations. Nevertheless, his account leaves open the possibility that weaving would not have resorted to fossil energy were it not for the disembedding from space that coal enabled, and thus the avoidance of coordination with others.

We are used to thinking that motor cars were invented as operated by a combustion engine, and this is true for the first prototypes by Daimler and Benz in the late 1880s. But, in my second example, Thomas Alva Edison was convinced that electric cars were a better option and even tried to get Henry Ford on board of his project. Electric cars were indeed built in the United States and France from the late 1890s, and it was a French car that first reached a speed of 100 km/h in 1899. Charging stations were built between New York and Philadelphia, and Edison set to work on better batteries (Smil 2021: 21). At that time, Henry Ford worked for an electrical company while experimenting with combustion ('gas') engines, to the discontent of his boss who said to him (according to Ford's autobiography): 'Electricity, yes, that's the coming thing. But gas – no.' Ford continues:

> He had ample grounds for his skepticism – to use the mildest terms. Practically no one had the remotest notion of the future of the internal combustion engine, while we were just on the edge of the great electrical development. [. . . But] I did not see the use of experimenting with electricity for my purposes. [. . . N]o storage battery was in sight of a weight that was practical. An electrical car had of necessity to be limited in radius and to contain a large

> amount of motive machinery in proportion to the power exerted. (Ford and Crowther 1922: 25–6)

As we know today, the battery problem was only resolved recently and, during the century in between, the combustion engine had won the race, so to say, and transformed our societies and landscapes. The rise and fall of the electric car in the late nineteenth century and its return in the early twenty-first century raises many issues about the direction of technological development and diffusion, of which only two shall be addressed here because of their relevance to the overall reasoning.

With hindsight, Edison's plans for an electric car were part of an electrification trajectory that would mark twentieth-century societies, visible already in imagined futures early in the century, even without the electric car. I have already mentioned Lenin's statement that the special path of the Soviet Union meant the combination of electrification with Soviet power (chapter 5). He had possibly seen the introduction of electric street lighting in St Petersburg and integrated this technical progress into his vision of social progress. In contrast with Edison's plans for car batteries, electrification was based on electric power stations from which the energy was distributed via a grid, as such a part of the building of comprehensive infrastructures in 'organized modernity'. In much of twentieth-century economic thinking, electricity production was indeed considered to be a 'natural monopoly', most suitably handled by public enterprises because of the combination of resource-related technical requirements with the public service function that electric utilities were fulfilling. Starting in the United States, electric appliances spread very quickly in private households (while the steam engine persisted in factories and rail transportation), accounting for a considerable part of the growth in energy consumption. Another major part was played by the combustion engine for use in private motor cars. While electricity for grids was often produced in coal-fired power stations, cars were running on derivates of oil. (By implication, it should be noted, climate change would hardly have been prevented or slowed down had Edison's electric car been successful, given that electric energy was mostly generated in coal-fired power plants – and still largely is in some regions of the globe.)

The fossil fuel trajectory, fully embarked upon in the twentieth century in the global North, thus had two distinct components.

While they both contributed to the warming of the atmosphere, they were quite differently socially embedded. Electricity provided convenience through the grid in stable settings such as the household or the city, whereas the combustion engine provided convenience of movement, for private but also for commercial and military purposes. The two partial trajectories, though, have one social effect in common. Through resource input, they enable a shift in personal time use, away from necessities towards actions of choice, and an enlargement of potential personal movements in space. This observation appears to provide some basis for Dipesh Chakrabarty's assertion that 'the mansion of modern freedoms stands on an ever-expanding base of fossil fuel use' (2021: 32).

A third example of critical junctures links to this observation. As mentioned before, railway networks reached their largest extension in European societies by the early twentieth century. They served as transportation for commodities, not least coal, but increasingly also as passenger traffic, including tourism, both private and state- or company-sponsored. From the interwar period onwards, networks largely did not grow. Instead, the growth of mobility infrastructure shifted to roads for car travel, the Italian *autostrada*, the German *Autobahn* and the US highway programme serving as examples for publicly sponsored road network extension. Railways were initially run with steam engines, then with diesel engines, but the rail network could be connected to the electricity grid, thus allowing a shift to electrification. Regardless of the kind of fuel, rail traffic is much more energy efficient than car or truck traffic, measured by the energy consumption per passenger or per weight of goods transported. However, railways offer a timetabled, collective travel possibility, whereas movement by car offers greater personal opportunities for choice. Again, freedom, or a certain understanding of freedom, appears to require greater use of biophysical resources – and, until recently, these were almost exclusively fossil fuels.

The possible non-fossil bifurcation at mid-century

While having introduced the distinction between grid-based electrification and the diffusion of combustion engines as the two main components of energy use that proliferated in the twentieth century, I have characterized both components as contributing to the fossil fuel trajectory. Until now, barring still unspecified future developments, this is unavoidably the case for the combustion component. However, grid-based electrification does not necessarily require fossil fuels. From the early twentieth century, hydro energy started to be used for electricity generation, and from the middle of the twentieth century nuclear energy was strongly promoted for the same purpose. We will briefly explore if and how far these energy sources could have provided a path bifurcation away from fossil fuel intensity. I will use the examples of two European countries to explore these two possibilities.

Starting with hydro energy, let us first look at Sweden, a small, thinly populated North European country that changed rather quickly from a largely agricultural to an industrial economy during the first half of the twentieth century. In comparison with other European countries (as described in chapters 4 and 5), Sweden moved relatively smoothly through these social transformations. Democratic political participation was gradually widened; an alliance of workers and farmers was built that provided an answer to the social question, referring to the national community as the 'people's home' and building welfare institutions (against the background of which Gunnar Myrdal reasoned after the Second World War; see chapter 6). From the 1930s onwards, Sweden also developed its particular 'Fordist' trajectory towards consumer capitalism, with the industrialist Axel Wenner-Gren playing a particular role. Wenner-Gren was employed by, and later became owner of, the company Electrolux (which still exists) that supplied Swedish households with domestic electric appliances such as vacuum cleaners, refrigerators and washing machines, and later expanded globally. One might assume that Sweden, therefore, also embarked on a resource-intensive trajectory of economic growth and enhanced material well-being, not dissimilar to other western countries. While this is broadly true, Electrolux appliances used in Sweden contributed little to global warming, given that they were operated with electricity generated through water power, of which there was abundant supply. After extended government deliberation, Vattenfall, its full name then being Kungliga Vattenfallsstyrelsen (Royal Waterfall Board), was founded in 1909 as a state-owned company to exploit the hydropower potential of Sweden and, in particular, provide industry with energy. Vattenfall has remained the dominant electricity provider, strongly developing hydropower up to the middle of the twentieth century, but also getting involved in nuclear power and, more recently, wind and solar energy. The increase of nuclear energy was slowed down after conflictive political debates in the 1970s. Despite an increase in fossil fuel use between the 1960s and the 1980s, mostly due to motorization, Sweden remains one of the countries with the highest shares of its primary energy coming from renewable sources. Sweden is a rich country with high per capita energy use, but it has the lowest CO_2 emissions per capita, as well as per unit of GDP, in the European Union.

If Sweden is a useful case to study the conditions for hydropower development within western societies, France provides a similar case for nuclear power. A society with a strong industry base that had experienced political polarization more than Sweden, France had limited reserves of fossil fuels on its territory and lacked the geographical conditions for expanding hydropower use. The Groupe 1985, introduced earlier (chapter 6), foresaw significant import dependence on fossil fuels and considered the development of nuclear energy production as a significant contribution to covering energy demand. Nuclear power stations were built from 1957, with the one in Chinôn on the River Loire being the first one to go into operation in 1964. From 1974, after the first oil price hike, France's governments developed their energy strategy forcefully under the slogan '*tout électrique, tout nucléaire*' ('all electric, all nuclear'), aiming to make it part of the national identity (Hecht 2016). Even though efforts are currently made to increase the share of wind and solar energy, France remains the country with one of the highest shares of nuclear power in primary energy generation. At the same time, the share of fossil fuels is relatively low, and CO_2 emissions per capita are below the EU average.

Sweden and France participated in the high increase of per capita energy use during the post-Second World War decades, now known as the Great Acceleration. Thus their somewhat different trajectories in comparison with other western countries, such as the United States, the United Kingdom or (West) Germany, bring us a step further in exploring logics of expansion. In this light, it is important to note that the expansion of neither hydropower nor nuclear power was primarily driven by capitalist investment decisions but by state action. They were largely political projects, at times meeting commercial reluctance, in particular in the case of nuclear energy. This is well known for both rather statist France, with the then state-owned company Électricité de France as the monopoly developer, and for West Germany's supposed social market economy (e.g., Radkau and Hahn 2013). But it also holds for the liberal market economy of the United States in which the producers of nuclear power stations and the electric utilities that were to operate them required state guarantees against losses and liabilities as well as state responsibility for dealing with nuclear waste (see also Seow's [2021] notion of 'carbon technocracy' for state involvement in energy projects in East Asia).

Andreas Malm and Alf Hornborg stated some years ago: 'The succession of energy technologies following steam – electricity, the internal combustion engine, the petroleum complex: cars, tankers, aviation – have all been introduced through investment decisions, sometimes with crucial input from certain governments but *rarely through democratic deliberation*. The privilege of instigating new rounds appears to have stayed with the *class ruling commodity production*' (Malm and Hornborg 2014: 64; my emphasis). If this statement is meant to refer to energy use under capitalist conditions, it appears rather banal. Investment decisions are mostly made by the capitalist class. As the examples of hydropower and nuclear energy show, furthermore, even in societies that can be called capitalist, significant energy decisions were not made by the owners of the means of production. So the statement is not even entirely true under those conditions. Begging to differ, certainly, we need to use the term 'democratic' in a formal-procedural sense and do not consider the quality of deliberation. Nevertheless, these 'decisions' were clearly not made by the capitalist class and not driven by a straightforward capital logic. Some may want to argue that even the democratic state tends to act as representative of 'capital in general' because the energy sources were meant to cover the needs of private industry. But this assertion begs further questions and tends to merge different forms of power when it is more enlightening to keep them separate. I have here just made one further observation on an issue to which we will come back later (chapters 9 and 10).

A second question that the examples of Sweden and France raise is how far they are exemplary for avoiding the trajectory of fossil fuel intensity. Clearly, these societies improved the material well-being of their citizens under democratic conditions mostly by increasing the use of non-fossil fuels, thus contributing comparatively little – in relation to other western industrial countries – to climate change. Nevertheless, this exploration of alternatives to the fossil fuel trajectory is not driven by the assumption that water and uranium are necessarily preferable to fossil fuels as main sources of energy. Each of them has considerable problematic aspects. The use of hydropower for generating electricity requires the damming of rivers with often severe social and ecological consequences, such as the destruction of livelihoods, the appropriation of water resources by one society or group of people at the expense of others and the creation of water scarcity. In many cases, water power projects are also an expression of power hierarchies within a society, including 'colonial' attitudes to rural and sometimes remote regions and their cultures, such as those of the Sami in Northern Scandinavia.

As to the much more widely perceived potentially negative consequences of nuclear power, let me add another autobiographical note. My student years – the late 1970s and early 1980s – coincided with the high point of nuclear power station construction in West Germany and concomitantly with the rise of a strong anti-nuclear power movement. I was quite actively engaged in the latter but deviated from other activists in one respect: I did not consider the risk of a major nuclear accident as the main reason for objecting to the use of nuclear energy. Certainly, the significant accidents that did happen (Three Mile Island, United States, 1979; Chernobyl, Soviet Union, now Ukraine, 1986; later Fukushima, Japan, 2011) vindicated the arguments of the critics. But after all, air traffic has been made highly safe by a combination of engineering skills and operator training, and there is no reason why something similar could not be achieved with the 'normal' operation of nuclear power stations. What concerned me most was the arrogant assumption – now I call it hubris – that nuclear power stations and nuclear waste disposal sites could be kept safe for thousands of years, that is, time spans that go beyond our usual readings of world history and approach geological dimensions. Such misplaced trust in the durability and reliability of human-made social institutions becomes visible when one notices that nuclear power stations were technically designed to resist an aeroplane accident, but that their protection from military attack, while enshrined in international law, cannot be technically guaranteed, given the unpredictability of warfare, as the current concern over the Zaporizhzhia power plant in Ukraine, the largest in Europe, demonstrates. In this sense, the use of nuclear power shows similarities with geo-engineering, engaging long timelines with inadequate knowledge about consequences (see chapter 8). But our core concern here is with climate change, not with other negative, even disastrous, effects of human action. And from this angle, one cannot fail to notice that hydropower and nuclear power provide large amounts of energy – and, significantly, in the form of electricity – without emitting carbon dioxide.

One can recognize with hindsight, therefore, that the early post-war decades, even though they became known for the first Great Acceleration in the use of fossil fuels and the emission of carbon dioxide, witnessed a double possible bifurcation that, had alternative roads been taken, might have avoided at least the rapid move into the climate emergency. First, there was a possible bifurcation between fossil fuels and non-fossil alternatives. While the former trajectory had already been embarked upon, in particular in the United States, it was not yet that advanced that one could speak of path dependency or lock-in. The alternatives consisted in hydropower and nuclear power. By 1950, the former already was a tried and tested technology that in some countries provided a large share of primary energy, mostly dedicated to the generation of electricity. But its exploitation depended on geographical conditions, thus it was not an option for all countries. Furthermore, it did not lend itself to huge further growth, certainly not to the 'endless' growth that came to be promoted soon. This, though, was announced to be the case with nuclear energy, which was presented as the energy base of the future, the use of which would leave all social problems in the past. This 'radiant future' (Alexander Zinoviev) was pursued in some countries, but nowhere came to full realization, and was slowed down, if not halted, by techno-economic problems and sociopolitical protest. By 1980, the outcome in the high-energy countries was mostly a technical mix that included water and nuclear energy but kept making increasing use of fossil fuels.

'Development' and its alternatives

As this first bifurcation failed to be realized in the stark terms in which it had fleetingly appeared, the second possible bifurcation remained largely concealed. Resorting to hydropower and to nuclear energy meant accepting the need to face rapidly increasing energy demands. And the geographical, economic and sociopolitical limitations to pursuing these options meant a continuation on the path of increasing fossil fuel intensity. But we have seen (in the preceding chapter) that the choice of fossil fuels had been a response to a specific question in one world region, the West. This answer depended on the way the problem was identified – as consolidation of democracy in liberal-capitalist societies – and on the way it was meant to be solved – namely, by leaving the power hierarchies intact. There was no strong a priori reason why societies in other world regions should define their key problems and the solutions to them in the same way, in particular not in societies that liberated themselves from western colonial domination and claimed the right to self-determination.

Dipesh Chakrabarty (2021: ch. 4) rightly asks for a better understanding of the relation of post-colonial elites to the western notion of 'development' after gaining independence. He seems to suggest that these elites did not just emulate or imitate the western approach but that they did aim at raising the level of material well-being in their societies and to do so by increasing the use of energy. As a key example, he refers to Jawarhalal Nehru, the first prime minister of independent India, and his combination of faith in complex engineering achievements with (what one would now call) the historico-cultural identity of India. The practical core of this combination, repeatedly evoked by Nehru, was to make the water flowing from the Himalaya Mountains the key energy source for Indian development. Given that Chakrabarty's concern is with climate change, it is surprising that he does not say that hydropower does not contribute to CO_2 emissions; he remains content with underlining Nehru's commitment to scientific-technical progress.

In the absence of a more detailed analysis, some comparative observations must suffice (continuing the brief characterization of world-regional resource regimes before mid-century in chapter 5 above). The existing correlation of the global social divide with the energy divide suggested that an increase in per capita energy use was a plausible requirement for development. Furthermore, as Nehru's example shows, a new politico-technical imaginary emerged in the multiply shaped context of decolonization, the consolidation of socialism and the technical advances arising from the military sector. Even so, the interpretations of the issue varied rather widely. Broadly, three orientations can be distinguished.

First, a partial emulation of the western fossil fuel path occurred under different sets of political circumstances: in Japan as an almost direct emulation of Western Europe; in Soviet and Chinese socialism in the name of system competition and energy security; and in some 'settler societies', with conditions of high social inequality or even formal segregation, where increasing energy use, partly through fossil fuels, served more for sustaining hierarchies and privileges through an 'imperial mode of living' for a minority than for consolidating democracy. This is most clearly seen in South Africa and, in more ambivalent ways, in Latin America (for analyses of Brazil 'in the Anthropocene', see Acker and Fischer 2018; Issberner and Léna 2017).

In post-colonial societies, two other orientations can be distinguished. So, second, in some cases energy was the core of the politico-technical imaginary. India under Nehru's government, however, is one key example that shows that fossil fuels were not necessarily at the centre of the strategy. This may have been partly due to the fact that the centrality of fossil fuels was not yet absolutely evident even in the West (see the cases of Sweden and France) and partly because domestic fossil fuel reserves were insufficient or unknown, and water was a more plausible energy source. In the case of India, the nuclear option was also pursued in cooperation with Canada, and the use of coal was increased due to constraints on hydropower distribution. A similarly striking example is found in the ideas of Cheik Anta Diop, physicist, historian and activist born in today's Senegal, for the energy future of a federated post-colonial Africa. In his *Black Africa*, he asserted that 'Black Africa leads all the world in hydraulic energy', saw nuclear energy as a future means of overcoming energy limits and imagined hydrogen 'as an eventual replacement for gasoline to fuel a type of internal combustion engine to be invented' (cited by Eshun 2020: 221 and 229). Third, while Diop envisaged the use of energy for industrialization, the alternative of rural development was outlined and pursued most consistently by Julius Nyerere, president of Tanzania from 1964 to 1985 (and before of Tanganyika), who focused on a notion of self-reliance (see, e.g., Getachew 2019: 154–5).

In contrast to activist usage, these examples serve here to claim neither that these were viable alternatives to fossil fuel intensity nor that they only failed because they were actively blocked by western powers (though often they were; see, e.g., Grischow and Weiss 2019: 232, on Ghana's Volta River Project; or Hecht 2016: 166–7, on the uranium trade between Niger and France). Rather, they are intended to show that the path towards increasing fossil fuel intensity was certainly not globally entrenched during the western so-called 'thirty glorious years' between 1945 and 1975. Not only was fossil fuel use very limited across most world regions; it had also not captured the global political imagination. Even though the higher level of material well-being in the West was a point of orientation for political elites elsewhere, projects of reaching social objectives were proposed and pursued in a variety of forms. While the significance of energy supply was widely recognized, fossil fuels were not considered to be the only, or even the preferred, way to cover this supply.

The actual change of trajectory: from one Great Acceleration to another

Only shortly later, by the 1980s and more so by the 1990s, the situation had changed in several world regions. The two most populous countries on the globe, China and India, radically changed their economic policy orientations and engaged much more strongly in production or services for world trade. Slightly later, so-called transition governments in post-dictatorship Brazil and post-apartheid South Africa aimed to consolidate inclusive-egalitarian democracy by enhancing material well-being. In all these countries, as well as some others, but most markedly in China and India, fossil fuel use and CO_2 emissions increased very rapidly, whereas they stagnated and started to decline in North America and the European Union. (From being an industrial power at the time of the Soviet Union, post-Soviet Russia deindustrialized, CO_2 emissions rapidly falling during the 1990s, and turned into a major fossil fuel exporter.) Because of the size and significance of China and India, we refer to these developments as the Asian Great Acceleration. Stepwise, through chapters 6 to 10, I try to capture the social logics leading to this global socio-ecological transformation. At this point, I will just look at the issue from the angle of the Asian societies.

In the terminology of dependency theory and the world-systems approach, one can speak here of the 'dependent' economic development of countries on the semi-periphery of the world economy. If we consider China as the strongest case, the state-led strategy initially focused on existing technology and products, developed in the West, following the preceding strategies in Japan and the so-called 'Asian tigers' (Taiwan, South Korea, Hong Kong and Singapore). Rather than aiming at import substitution, as Latin American countries had done earlier, these societies aimed at producing for export, not least to the West. Key sectors were consumer goods such as textiles and household items and electronic technologies, as well as heavy industries such as steel and shipbuilding. Such production was either labour intensive or highly polluting or both. Thus it was competitive because of lower labour cost and less strict environmental regulation. At the same time, it addressed key domestic concerns in western countries: the profitability of production, from the employers' side, and rising environmental concerns from the citizens' side. By starting from a situation of dependency, therefore, Asian economies made use of opportunities provided by changes in western societies. Over the medium term, this led to interdependency, rather than one-sided dependency, and a change in the opportunity structure.

8

Enabling and Constraining Knowledge: Frontiers, Limits, Boundaries

Climate change as unanticipated consequence of human action?

Climate change has been considered as the exemplary case of unintended consequences of human action: 'Global warming is the unintended by-product par excellence' (Malm 2016: 1). In a related view, as mentioned at the outset, humanity is regarded to have 'stumbled' into the Anthropocene; 'we have slid' into it without being able to recognize, much less prevent it (Chakrabarty 2021: 40). The latter expression reminds me of Lloyd George's dictum that the European states 'slithered' into the First World War, without any one of them wanting or intending this. Making this comparison, though, one should also recall that Lloyd George tried to exonerate Imperial Germany, which in the dominant British view had been seen as unleashing the war, by claiming that no one was responsible. While Lloyd George had his political reasons, interpreting purposive action as 'slithering' with regard to a past event arguably made it more difficult to recognize the impending catastrophe of the Second World War.

A distinction needs to be made between unintended consequences and unanticipated consequences (De Zwart 2015). Future consequences of one's actions can be known, or better, known to be possible or likely, without being wanted or intended. There is a large strand of scholarship, being well received in impassioned public and political debate, which suggests that climate change as the consequence of burning large amounts of fossil fuel was neither anticipated nor intended. A rather standard view, to be detailed below, holds that global environmental consciousness arose only during the 1970s, and solid scientific knowledge about anthropogenic climate change only from the 1980s. However, it is not very difficult to show convincingly (Bonneuil and Fressoz 2016 [2013]: ch. 9 is a recent summary) that knowledge of all kinds had been available earlier and warnings had been given: knowledge about the limits of paleo-organic resources that were created over long periods and thus are 'non-renewable' for human purposes; knowledge that large-scale production and consumption based on fossil fuel use leads to dangerous pollution and environmental degradation; knowledge that burning fossil fuels releases carbon dioxide into the atmosphere which, in turn, leads to rising temperatures. Therefore, it is incorrect to claim that humanity did not know – it knew from the nineteenth century onwards, and even more so across the past century and a half.

Thus the question is not about knowledge in general. The key questions are about the kind of knowledge and about its evaluation with regard to action (or omission). If there is knowledge about adverse consequences of burning fossil fuels, first, one will further want to know how likely these consequences are, that is, the degree of certainty of knowledge, as well as when and where these consequences occur, an aspect that leads to a sociopolitical assessment. The identification of adverse consequences, second, does not immediately demand action or omission – that is, not or no longer burning fossil fuels. In many situations, one is willing to knowingly accept adverse consequences of one's actions, most broadly in all those cases in which beneficial consequences are expected to outweigh adverse consequences. Indeed, one may even say that this is exactly the situation in which the question poses itself: an intentional action is likely to be embarked upon if it is accompanied by the expectation of beneficial circumstances – at least for someone at some point. (This should not be read as a narrowly rationalist reasoning as the 'benefits' can be very broadly understood.)

In other words, fossil fuels would arguably not have been burnt at large scale if strongly negative consequences had been expected early on with a high degree of certainty and if significant benefits had not been expected by anyone. Given the situation we are in today, this sounds like an implausible statement; it can even be misunderstood as an apologetic one. But we will not be able to understand the trajectory of our societies towards ever greater use of fossil fuels if we do not take the state of knowledge and the expected benefits into account at each point of the trajectory. It is in this light that I shall now briefly review the supposed rise of environmental consciousness since the 1970s and then systematically address the questions about the kinds of knowledge and their interpretations.

From frontiers to limits, apparently

The standard narrative about the supposedly recently rising environmental consciousness is very familiar. We can be brief. The publication of Rachel Carson's book *Silent Spring* in 1962 is considered to be a breakthrough event because it pointed to an invisible yet omnipresent, as well as hitherto unrecognized, degree of environmental degradation. In short succession, it was followed by Paul Ehrlich and Anne Harland Ehrlich's *Population Bomb* in 1968, pointing in a neo-Malthusian way to the pressure on resources by the mere presence of increasing numbers of human beings on the earth, and the report *The Limits to Growth* by the Club of Rome (Meadows et al. 1972), expressing concern about the relation between available resources and increasing population in a methodologically new way. From this moment onwards, fundamental concerns about energy, environment and technology that had been raised earlier, Lewis Mumford's *Technics and Civilization* of 1934 being a major example, condensed in new scholarly fields, such as, most importantly for our purposes, 'political ecology'. The year 1972 also witnessed the United Nations Conference on the Human Environment in Stockholm, signalling the recognition of the topic in international politics. Significantly, it formally introduced the principle of 'common but differentiated responsibilities' (CBDR) into international law, as mentioned earlier, which was also taken up in the Paris Agreement on climate change in 2015. Subsequently, the so-called Brundtland Commission provided a definition of 'sustainable development' with its report of 1987 that became a reference in global public debate up to the 'sustainable development goals' of the UN in 2015 (Borowy 2013). The UN Conference on Environment and Development in Rio de Janeiro in 1992 marked the international recognition of anthropogenic climate change as an urgent global problem and led to the creation of the UN Framework Convention on Climate Change (UNFCCC) with its by now widely publicized – and increasingly criticized – Conferences of Parties (COP), the latest one of which, COP28, held in Dubai at the end of 2023, concluded explicitly, though far too vaguely, with the need for 'transitioning away from fossil fuels in energy systems'.

As can be seen, this narrative is easily written with a certain degree of prima facie plausibility, even though its baseline argument of a recently emerging and quickly spreading environmental consciousness is quite untrue. To say that our epoch is the one of global environmental consciousness is a strong statement. Implicitly, such a statement refers back to the time-honoured question of historical consciousness, of a sense of history that can be grasped (see recently, Boltanski and Esquerre 2022: 264–5). At the very least, it suggests that it is possible to situate ourselves in historical time, to catch the specificity of our moment. Trying to test this assertion, we need to explore what the significant novelty, if any, is in these recent developments.

Four aspects emerge: first, the apparently new environmental consciousness is indeed not absolutely new, but it has considerable contextual force as it is a critical reaction to decades of reasoning about the potential *endlessness* of the growth of knowledge and material production. Second, the ecological debate becomes *explicitly global* during the 1970s, underlining the planetary dimension of the key issues, which, furthermore, are recognized as such in international organizations and institutions. Third, the debate is increasingly underpinned by scientific findings, permitting at least the claim that earlier assessments lacked knowledge with a sufficiently action-guiding *degree of certainty*. In the combination of these three aspects, fourth, sharp contours of the debate emerge, now explicitly opposing a concept of 'limits' that cannot be overcome with the one of 'frontiers' that can and need to be transgressed for the benefit of humankind. Without ever having been explicitly defined as such, to the best of my knowledge, these terms come to stand for different kinds of knowledge in relation to the possibilities for action that they imply. We may call them *knowledge attitudes*.

In what follows, we will briefly explore in more detail the three specificities of the recent ecology-related debates as a basis for analysing the emerging knowledge attitudes and their impact on climate-change action.

Time: endlessness

The opposition of 'cornucopian' and 'finitarian' visions of scarcity across recent history, as presented by Jonsson and Wennerlind (2023; see chapter 2 above), ultimately confronts an idea of endlessness with one of limits. While natural resources themselves were rarely thought of as absolutely infinite (except in a particular sense to which we will come in a moment), the main reason for believing in endlessness was the trust in human inventiveness and ingenuity. This reasoning was explicitly spelled out during what came to be called the scientific revolution in the seventeenth century, supposing the capacity of the human mind, once liberated from constraints, to uncover the laws of nature and to bring such knowledge to fruition for the benefit of humankind. While getting embedded in different intellectual contexts, it has remained remarkably persistent to the present day.

Rather than in human ingenuity in general, which includes literary or artistic imagination, I am here interested in the assumption that human ingenuity can overcome the constraints posed by given resource limits. On a closer look, this assumption has two components, one about non-human nature and one about the specificities of human ingenuity. First, non-human nature is assumed to be malleable to such an extent that human intervention can transform it in successful pursuit of its purposes. The identification of such possibilities of nature – the creation of alliances with nature, following Bruno Latour – is often referred to as *scientific-technical innovation*. And second, human beings are assumed to have the capacity to detect and exploit such malleability for their purposes. Rather than being simply physically located in the human mind, this capacity has historically been considered in need of being unleashed by giving human beings autonomy in their pursuits. From this angle, human ingenuity leads to *sociopolitical innovation* based on the belief in autonomy. There are two basic ways in which such innovation can be brought about: in the form of spontaneous aggregate results from free interaction; or in the form of purposeful collective action consolidated in institutions such as states.

Let us, in a very stylized way, reconstruct the history of these two types of innovation with a view to identifying the specificity of the moment of the 1970s (for more detail, see Wagner 2016). Both scientific-technical and sociopolitical innovation may support cornucopian notions of endlessness, which in their explicitness go back to the seventeenth and eighteenth centuries. They culminated in a way of thinking about progress and the course of history as separating the horizon of expectations radically from the space of experiences during the decades around 1800, to use Reinhart Koselleck's terms (1979). These two modes of action were seen as potentially liberating humankind from constraints by non-human nature. Since then, though, experiences with these modes of action have altered the horizon of expectations. The course of scientific-technical innovation can be read as rather gradual, even though faster and altering experiences more at some times than at others. The course of sociopolitical innovation alternated between trusting in spontaneous order, on the one side, and in organized purposeful action, on the other. For both scientific-technical and sociopolitical innovation, the 1930s and 1940s marked a moment of transformation.

As we have seen (chapters 4 and 5), the crossing of the two vertical frontiers of coal, first, and crude oil and natural gas, second, enabled further technical innovations that became known as the First and Second Industrial Revolution. The 1940s witnessed the construction and use of the atom bomb and, subsequently, the programmes for the 'civilian use of nuclear energy'. The former opened the possibility for unprecedented anthropogenic destruction, whereas the latter appeared to hold out the promise of an equally unprecedented liberation from constraints. As regards sociopolitical innovation, the idea of reaching both peace and wealth through market self-regulation was opposed to a 'Jacobin' approach to purposeful social transformation from the late eighteenth century onwards, with fluctuating emphases over time and with context. But both approaches entered into a profound crisis with the Great Depression (1929–39), on the one side, and the rise of totalitarianism, on the other. Let us recall that contemporaries were aware of the depth of the crisis, as we saw in the analyses by Schumpeter and Polanyi from the 1940s (chapter 6), to whom we may add Friedrich von Hayek, Hannah Arendt and Isaiah Berlin, among numerous others.

The way out of this crisis, which was to lead into the Great Acceleration and the 'thirty glorious years', required a reconsideration of endlessness. Given the bifurcation of scientific-technical expectations between apocalypse and utopia, the compromise solution was a conscious monitoring and steering of scientific-technical innovation, as announced in *Science: The Endless Frontier* and widely practised in western countries during the post-war decades. The combination of enhanced financial support for science and some policy direction of research was meant to keep securing potentially endless progress while taming the risks. In parallel, the major sociopolitical innovation was a compromise between the two opposed models for achieving social objectives. The term 'Keynesianism' came to refer to more than a novel economic policy approach; it signalled a supposed symbiosis of trust in spontaneous order and purposeful collective action, not unlike the idea of smoothly steering the otherwise autonomous pursuits of scientific researchers. What may appear, in both cases, as a moderation of earlier radical commitments and expectations turned out to be most effective in bringing about the appearance of endlessness, namely through the enhancement of material well-being based on extraction of biophysical resources, most significantly fossil fuels. In contrast to the original expectations of endlessness to be reached through the self-directed combination of freedom and reason, this was now what we may call *directed endlessness*.

It is against this background that one needs to understand the supposed rise of environmental consciousness from the 1960s and 1970s onwards. Rather than being entirely new, the environmentalist critique was a contextual reaction against the factual radicalization of endlessness. Its two foci came to be the explicit commitment of western governments to 'economic growth' without considering the purpose of such growth and the exhaustion of natural resources combined with the hubris of claiming to have tamed nuclear power, thus the core of both pathways of scientific-technical and sociopolitical innovation.

Space: frontiers

Arguably, some notion of the endlessness of territorial space was common in early human history, not least because the limits of space were not known and not encountered. In principle, one could always go further. All frontier expansion before 1500 was based on such experience, be it by migration or by territorial expansion of empires. If we have no record of a sense of open-endedness from this period, this is probably due to the effort required and the obstacles to be overcome to move beyond the given space. The reachable spatial expansion was thus always limited, even if space appeared not to be.

This changed with the European maritime expansion from the late fifteenth century onwards, which confirmed by experience and measurement the global form of the earth and thus its finiteness and limits. From this moment onwards, expansion across frontiers was no longer a movement into the absolutely unknown but into areas that were known in principle, though not specifically and not by experience. One may well consider that the knowledge of a somewhere that exists but is not known in detail provides the background for the rise of an art form that projects human imagination and longings into this somewhere else, namely the accounts of 'utopia', beginning with Thomas More's eponymous text, but moving from another space to another time at around 1800 (Guéguen 2023). In parallel, the origins of the cornucopian vision of the world, as sketched by Jonsson and Wennerlind (2023), may well be related to the insight into the abundance of nature at the moment when the full size of the globe became known. While this meant that nature was not infinite, it also made clear that its huge resources were largely 'untapped' and thus available for exploitation.

The change of perspective around 1800 is more complex. On the one hand, the exploration and exploitation of nature's terrestrial resources were still in process, as shown by the US debates about western expansion. On the other hand, Malthus made the claim that all earth was 'already possessed', thus seeing an unsurpassable limit that demanded adaptation. It is not sufficiently clear if and how the wide opening of the horizon of expectations is historically linked not only to the promise of freedom but also to the exploration of the vertical frontier of deep coal mining, thus adding resource-rich 'space' to the limited 'already possessed' territory. One could suggest that this was the moment of confluence of the two notions of progress, the one of scientific-technical innovation with the one of sociopolitical innovation. To the best of my knowledge, though, strong evidence that this link was actually made by contemporary interpreters is lacking. Rather, as argued before in more detail (chapter 4), there is a time lag between the rise of the promise of freedom, namely before 1800, and the promise of general abundance due to fossil fuel-based technology, late in the nineteenth century. The period around 1900, *pace* Malthus, is more appropriately seen as the time when European powers, jointly with societies that emerged from European settlement, effectively 'possessed' most of the earth and exerted strong influence on the societies that were neither colonized nor settled, most importantly China. The 'scramble for Africa', made explicit by the Berlin Conference in 1884, can be seen as the high point in dividing up the earth among European powers, and the debate on imperialism accordingly shifted away from further territorial expansion to imperial competition.

Then the end of the imperial wars of the first half of the twentieth century marked a crisis point, not unlike the one of the notion of directed endlessness, and indeed related to the latter. Rather than the Westphalian peace agreement of 1648, the end of the Second World War was the beginning of the so-called Westphalian order, within which the emerging great powers agreed on the territorial division of the earth into blocs and their zones of influence. In a sense, this was a global agreement on the end of spatial expansion, but this also meant that it was the end of a mode of sociopolitical action through which elites secured and extended their power. Thus some reorientation could be expected. In point of fact, there is sufficient evidence that the moment was interpreted as such. On the one hand, the United Nations and its subsidiary organizations were founded, along with bloc-specific organizations such as NATO, the World Bank, the International Monetary Fund, the European Economic Community, as well as the Warsaw Pact and COMECON on the socialist side. On the other hand, debates about 'planetary management' were inaugurated, signalling the emergence of planetary consciousness in a still rather optimistic vein. In parallel, the earlier opening of the second vertical frontier, while confirming the perceived limitation of horizontal space, had by then provided a way out of the crisis moment of spatial expansion. After the Second World War, it was embarked upon at great speed both in the 'First' and in the 'Second World', with the Great Acceleration in carbon dioxide emissions as a consequence.

Again, as with the notion of directed endlessness, the 1940s attempt at acknowledging global spatial limits while organizing this new spatiality in the interest of the western elites started to falter from the 1970s onwards. It was contested in a pincer movement both from outside the West and from within. On the one hand, the decolonized societies demanded an end to the unequal economic relations, thus challenging the continued low-cost provision of the West with biophysical resources, most explicitly with the programme for a New International Economic Order. On the other hand, environmental degradation and the threat of resource exhaustion became a central topic of public debate. The latter occurred globally, but it was more prominent in the West and at times seen with suspicion by the South. It could appear as denying the developing countries that future resource use that the theory of modernization and development had promised them, whereas those resources had already been used up by the West.

To avoid misunderstandings, it should be underlined here (an issue to be returned to in chapter 10) that this is not to argue that the spatial limits of the planet have ultimately been reached and that there are categorically no frontiers any longer to be transgressed. Rather, the encounter with the limits provoked attempts at transgressing yet further frontiers. Since this crisis moment of the 1970s, the exploitation of oceanic resources, in terms of both fishing and ocean mining for biophysical resources, such as oil and minerals, has rapidly increased. We may call this the third vertical frontier, downwards like the preceding two but maritime instead of terrestrial. In turn, the fourth and fifth vertical frontiers are transgressed upwards. The transgression of the fourth one leads to the filling of the atmosphere with greenhouse gases, preceded by chlorofluorocarbons, the emission of which could be halted by the Montreal Protocol. And the fifth one is marked by the return to space travel. The latter indeed underlines the insight of astrophysics that there are no recognizable frontiers in the infinity of the universe. Indeed, astrophysics translates the time-honoured human awe inspired by the infinity of the sky above us into a notion of an ever-expanding universe, thus creating another sense of infinity, now based on scientific investigation and theorizing. However, certain frontiers will remain impossible to transgress, either because they are not humanly reachable, due to the relation of travel time to human lifetime, or because the benefits of transgression are scarce in terms of useful resources for humankind in general, in contrast to some small current elites. Thus, I dare call the fifth-frontier attempts grotesque and bound to fail, despite the amount of money invested in them, but the move towards transgressing the fourth frontier is highly significant, as it has led to the current climate emergency.

Certainty: towards cognitive mastery

We have already seen that it is not entirely true that the climate effect of burning large amounts of fossil fuels was not known at the time that western societies embarked on the trajectory of increasing fossil fuel intensity. But some may still want to insist that it was not known with a sufficient degree of certainty to act. There are two questions here. First, the knowledge about anthropogenic climate change was not sufficiently certain. One could not be sure whether it would happen as a consequence of burning fossil fuels. Second, even if there was a strong degree of certainty, the need to counteract climate change does not follow immediately from this knowledge. Other considerations will legitimately enter into the decision to act. I will here predominantly retrace the historical course of the certainty of knowledge about climate change – with some additional notes about the knowledge of resource exhaustion, which precedes the one about climate change but is connected to it. At the end, we will come back to the question about the link between knowledge and action.

Looking at the early scholarly contributions about exhaustion of fossil resources and warming of the atmosphere from a present point of view, one is easily inclined to see them as forerunners in an emerging research area rather than as solid findings about the matter in question. Jevons and Arrhenius had only some data about coal reserves and the relation between CO_2 concentration and warming of the air and no adequate methodology to infer their conclusions from the data. Nevertheless, one might well say that they articulated plausible hypotheses, almost trivially plausible hypotheses: when coal keeps being burnt, then the coal reserves will at some point be exhausted. If CO_2 concentration keeps heat in lower levels of the atmosphere, then further CO_2 emissions will make temperatures rise. Original at the time, these hypotheses gave rise to debates, but the debates remained inconclusive. In each case, it was easy to point to considerations not included in the hypotheses, such as the possible discovery of further coal reserves or intervening factors that lead to atmospheric cooling. In both cases, indeed, the debate remained not only inconclusive but on the contrary suspended until the 1970s. With regard to resource exhaustion, the Club of Rome report *The Limits to Growth* revived the issue and gave it much greater urgency than it had before. With regard to climate change, research confirming the initial hypothesis accumulated during the 1970s and 1980s before the creation of the UNFCCC in 1992 recognized the issue as an urgent global problem.

Assembled in the reports of the IPCC, there is now consolidated knowledge about climate change: that global warming is happening; that it is caused by human action, most importantly the burning of fossil fuels; and that it is accelerating and increasingly difficult to avoid or reverse. The increasing amount of data and the sophistication of the modelling have made it difficult, almost impossible, to deny that anthropogenic climate change is happening at a highly problematic pace. As a consequence, one main line of public debate about climate change suggests that we now know but keep failing to act. This line is repeated on the occasions of a publication of an IPCC report or of the failure of the annual Conference of Parties (COP) to reach consensus on any significant decision. Reading the IPCC reports, though, one immediately notices the emphasis on the variable degrees of certainty with which statements are made and indeed marked as such. After all, the reports outline a future on a highly complex phenomenon of global scale that we cannot know with absolute certainty (see also Hulme 2023).

Nevertheless, a new constellation of knowledge and certainty had arisen by the late twentieth century with regard to both availability of resources and climate change. This did not just mean more knowledge and greater certainty. Rather, the scope and ambition in the search for knowledge and certainty had increased. There was general awareness that these were questions of planetary scale concerning the history and future of entire humankind. Thus the question of knowledge and certainty connected with those of endlessness and frontiers. Between the 1940s and the 1970s, spontaneously generated endlessness had been abandoned in favour of directed endlessness, and the push for frontier exploration had moved towards filling the known space rather than finding new space. After the 1970s, even these options appeared to close. Now there is an identifiable specificity to the current situation, but it is misdescribed as the emergence of environmental consciousness, which in fact already existed. Rather, it is growth in the awareness of the significance of planetary space and time for the human condition.

Stabilizing the future

In West European history, there had been at least one earlier period in which a perceived uncertainty gave rise to the search for tools that could generate certainty. In the late nineteenth century, the combination of coal-based industrialization and belief in the market-based generation of spontaneous order had led to the deterioration of working and living conditions for many and widespread social unrest and protest. The social sciences emerged as a response to this situation. In particular, the creation and gathering of quantitative data and their treatment with statistical tools were developed to 'make things that hold together' (Desrosières 1991; see also Desrosières 1993; Hacking 1990; Porter 1995). These were the tools with which the institutions of organized modernity were built as a moderating response to the widely open horizon of expectations after 1800 (e.g., Evers and Nowotny 1987; Rueschemeyer and Skocpol 1996). At that time, importantly, the nation-state served as the frame within which 'things' could be held together, providing data in the form of national statistics and societal self-understanding, with the nation as the bearer of collective responsibility, while at the same time setting boundaries defining its outside.

After the end of the Second World War, the horizon of expectations appeared much less open or, maybe, problematically open, and the progressive march of history not at all assured. Rather than just allowing it to happen, the future needed to be given a direction. 'Futures studies' emerged as a field of investigation that aimed to aggregate various sets of data and information to assess the possibilities of future development. This new field of study was thoroughly interdisciplinary as well as globally oriented. It provided a space for the emerging earth and climate sciences, by their very nature planetary in scope, and within the social sciences it focused on behavioural approaches towards decision making and on the development of a systemic perspective. After the end of the war and in the context of the Cold War, it had a strong base in military research centres, such as the RAND Corporation.

Many of the reports on the future were presented in the form of prediction. Once the path of economic growth had visibly been embarked upon in the West and in Soviet socialism, extrapolation of data series was the easiest way of proposing a view of the future, with more or less nuance. Nevertheless, such reports are better seen as proposals for intervention, with a view to choosing from within the possible futures the one that was most desirable. As Jenny Andersson (2018; see also Andersson 2012) has argued, futures studies were exploring and testing the 'malleability of the world'. This knowledge interest put the field at odds with conventional understandings of scientific investigation. On the one side, the future does not yet exist, thus it is not amenable to empirical analysis. On the other side, scientific inquiry aims to identify the 'independent variables' that shape empirical phenomena, thus operating with some kind of determinism of the past and present on the future. In terms of the then prevailing philosophy of the sciences, it was difficult to sustain the notion of plural future possibilities.

Speaking in rather stylized terms, the compromise solution that prevailed between the 1940s and the 1960s was an attitude of moderate malleability of the future. More precisely, the future was seen in terms of a combination of lawlike regularities and tendencies of history, on the one side, and a possibility of intervention by using these laws and tendencies for moving in what was seen as the right direction. To illustrate this understanding of the future, I will briefly discuss three examples from this crucial period of the Western Great Acceleration and the 'thirty glorious years', focusing on the specific constellation of finiteness and endlessness, of space and time, and certainty and uncertainty.

Keynesianism

John Maynard Keynes had a keen awareness of the uncertainty of the future, theorized as constitutive for economic action by Frank Knight and visible in repeated recessions, most importantly the one of 1929. His intention was to stabilize the future by developing policies to avoid economic downturns. Like Schumpeter, Keynes saw the main challenge for capitalist societies in the unsolved social question, most clearly identifiable in the deteriorating living conditions due to unemployment. Like many economists of his time, he accepted the cyclical nature of economic development with alternating boom and bust periods. Beyond them, though, he recognized a role for economic policy in stimulating the economy during downturns and slowing it down during upturns. The means for this demand management, as it came to be called, was increasing the public debt to finance works during downturns and paying back the debt from the increased tax revenue during the following upturn. Three aspects of this economic policy approach are important for our purposes. For this approach to work, first, the self-understanding of capitalist societies as deeply class divided had to be transformed into a view according to which classes could cooperate for a common benefit. Second, this view assumed an 'economy' that had its own laws of motion, while operating within the frame of the nation-state, which had the capacity to give it direction without altering the underlying laws, that is, by steadying economic growth. And third, this approach was intended to stabilize the future by a controlled 'mortgaging' of it, as the English expression has it. By incurring debt, the state committed itself to a determined future action, namely repaying the debt. But it did so by relying on the laws of economic motion, specifically that a boom with increased tax revenues would follow upon a downturn.

'Modernization and development'

The sociological theory of modernization and development may be considered as the international counterpart to domestic Keynesianism. Indeed, it found its inspiration in the reading of economic history, promoted by Walt Rostow (1959), which saw the Industrial Revolution in Western Europe as the moment of 'take-off' for economic development that started in one region but could and would be repeated in others. Developed as a response to historical materialism, at that time the official self-understanding of Soviet-socialist societies in the form of Marxism–Leninism, the sociology of modernization accepted some degree of economic determinism by assuming that 'economic development' would lead social change in other spheres of society. Furthermore, it assumed that the direction of this social change was functional differentiation, which made modernized societies superior to others in achieving social goals. In turn, other societies would be inclined towards emulating this development precisely for reasons of this functional superiority.

For our purposes here (on the context of the 'global social question', see chapter 6), only one glaring gap in the reasoning needs to be underlined. On the one hand, the theory assumed that modern societies would stabilize and materialize their full benefits through high consumption of energy. On the other hand, the theory assumed that not-yet-modernized societies would follow the path of the advanced societies. Since the former constituted the majority of the world population by, say, 1960 and was expected to grow much faster than the latter, 'modernization' quite evidently required an enormous increase in global energy consumption. However, this issue was hardly touched upon before the early 1970s. The attitude behind modernization theory denied the majority of the global population the status of being in the same time as the West, a 'denial of coevalness', as Johannes Fabian (1983) called this attitude, and relegated them to a 'not yet'. In doing so, the West undermined the very possibility of the developing societies ever reaching the same time by itself using up limited biophysical resources and emitting large amounts of carbon dioxide into the atmosphere.

Keynesianism and the sociology of modernization and development were sociopolitical innovations that maintained the belief in endless progress by giving this progress direction and control, in the former case stabilizing the domestic economic growth path and in the latter case rearranging global space under a common though differentiated developmental perspective. Some advocates of these reinterpretations of the national and global social questions certainly believed in their viability – in their sustainability, as one would say today. However, it is also quite evident that these proposals were a way of addressing the social question without renouncing the power and privileges of the domestic elites in the former case, something of which Schumpeter was quite aware, and the global power hierarchy in the latter case, as Myrdal saw clearly.

The 'civilian use of nuclear energy'

The third example refers to a scientific-technical innovation, namely the use of a non-fossil source of energy, uranium, to generate electricity. Nuclear energy has already been discussed in its material and politico-economic aspects in the preceding chapter; here, we focus on the epistemic aspect, the idea of mastery and control of nature that goes with the use of nuclear energy. The splitting of the uranium atom to unleash enormous amounts of energy can be regarded as a frontier whose transgression was unprecedented. Because of the new kind of trace, artificial radioactivity, which it leaves as evidence of lasting human impact on the earth, some geologists consider the first controlled nuclear explosion in July 1945 as a suitable date for the beginning of the Anthropocene. After the dropping of nuclear bombs on Hiroshima and Nagasaki, the conversion of this power into the so-called 'civilian use of nuclear energy' became the scientific-technical incarnation of directed endlessness during the 1950s and 1960s.

As reported by the *New York Times*, Lewis L. Strauss, chair of the US Atomic Energy Commission, stated the expectation in 1954 that 'our children will enjoy in their homes electric energy too cheap to meter', thanks to nuclear power stations. The expression 'too cheap to meter' has since then often been referred to, in particular by opponents of the generation of nuclear energy, to indicate the illusions and exaggeration in the promotion of this new form of energy. Arguably, though, the statement was often misunderstood or misquoted (Brown 2016). The cost of building nuclear power stations was known to be high, and the problems associated with the generation of long-lasting and highly dangerous nuclear waste were not solved; they are not even now. What Strauss probably meant was that, once a nuclear power station is in operation, the unit cost of electricity is very low and not worth measuring. Thus electricity would not come for free but be charged on something like a flat rate, as is common today for the internet. And this interpretation is indeed more telling for the attitude of the time than the presumed cornucopian expectations. It suggests that a frame can be created, quite literally the actual nuclear power station, within which (almost) endless energy can be provided in a controlled way. And again, the creation of endlessness served to reject any claim that limited resources would need to be distributed and used in a more equitable way.

Like Keynesianism and the theory of modernization and development, the civilian use of nuclear energy aimed to stabilize the future by mortgaging it. Problems such as the national and global social question and energy scarcity were supposed to be solved by deferring them, or the consequences of solving them, to the future. The time frames differed widely – from the four or five years of the business cycle to the millennia of safeguarding nuclear waste passing through the unfounded expectations of decades of 'development'.

Unstable futures: predictions and scenarios

The three attempts at stabilizing the future entered into crisis during the 1970s. In all three cases, the crisis resulted from a combination of a lack of desirability and a lack of possibility of the projected future. The generation of electricity through nuclear power suffered from accidents and failure to make so-called advanced reactors work, on the one side while, on the other, an anti-nuclear power protest movement was rising and becoming influential in many countries. Increasing connectedness of national economies led to the failure of Keynesian demand management, as the left-wing French government led by François Mitterrand had to experience in 1981. In parallel, rising labour and environmental costs in western countries triggered relocation of production abroad, often to South East and East Asia, called an emerging 'new international division of labour' (e.g., Fröbel, Heinrichs and Kreye 1977). While this relocation was enacted by western companies, the NIEO was placed on the global political agenda by developing countries calling for more equitable sovereignty rights and rules of exchange.

Detailed studies now exist about how western elites viewed these challenges to their domination and control. Extending his analysis of the emergence of the 'economic growth' paradigm to hegemony (Schmelzer 2016), Matthias Schmelzer (2012) has shown that the Organisation of Economic Co-operation and Development (OECD) started to shift gear in the late 1960s due to its identification of profound 'problems of modern society', resulting from a combination of dissatisfaction and unrest in the western societies, exhaustion of planetary resources and demands from developing societies for equal treatment in global politics. Key actors within the OECD were instrumental in setting up the Club of Rome as a setting in which these 'problems' could be analysed outside of the constraints of OECD as an intergovernmental organization (Schmelzer 2017). Within a very few years, the Club of Rome published its report, *The Limits to Growth* (Meadows et al. 1972), which was widely read and debated, in public, by governments, and by scholars.

The key finding of the report about exhaustion of main biophysical resources in the face of a growing world population is known and does not need to be presented here in detail. I will briefly discuss the medium- and long-term effects of the report in chapter 10. Here, it needs to be underlined that an immediate effect was a profound transformation of the assessment of human knowledge and capacities. The report broke with three decades of commitment to directed endlessness through supposedly successful scientific-technical and sociopolitical innovations. In turn, it insisted on limits that cannot be overcome and that necessitate change in human collective action.

While the details of the report's predictions were and keep being debated, the shift from endlessness to limits was quickly recognized as the core of the report. For a short time, there was a struggle within the OECD about whether the report required a general change of orientation. After the so-called oil crisis of 1973 and the recession of 1974/5, which hit most western countries, though, the standard view regained the upper hand (Schmelzer 2012). In 1975, the OECD set up the research committee called Interfutures, whose task it was to reassess the possibilities for future development after the critical half-decade since 1968 (the following draws on Andersson 2019, as are all quotations). A key member of the committee, Jacques Lesourne, explained his own perspective on the future as a violent reaction to the impermissible determinism of the *Limits to Growth* report. 'The future is blocked by a ton of concrete called "limits"' (137). Given the circumstances, the committee felt obliged to explicitly restate what had been the view of theorists of economic growth since the 1940s, namely that there are 'no physical limits to growth' (Andersson 2019: 137). As Jenny Andersson quotes from the OECD archive on Interfutures: 'Most questions have nothing or very little to do with physical constraints to growth but seem to be much more related to political and social limits to growth' (136). As a consequence, the committee held to 'the idea that possible physical limits in natural resources over the long term could be overcome by political, social, and institutional adaptation to market mechanisms' (140), echoing a conviction that Joseph Schumpeter had already expressed more than three decades earlier.

For Lesourne and the 'dominant ideology', the key problem with the *Limits* report was that it argued for a profound societal reorientation, while being authored by a group of white scholars from western elites and using advanced tools of future prediction as developed by leading research institutions. In response both to the report and to the upheaval that had triggered it, the approach to the future was changed. The Interfutures committee resorted to scenario analysis, a tool that had been used by the research department of the Shell oil company since the late 1960s to sketch a variety of possible futures by varying key parameters.

It is inherent in the scenario technique that the ambition is no longer to 'know' the future through prediction but to survey the horizon of possibilities with regard to the future. For some time, the neologism 'futuribles' became fashionable, used for instance as the name of a journal (which still exists: https://www.futuribles.com/), to indicate the plurality of possible futures. It is telling that this pluralization occurred at a moment when the predicted future started to be seen as no longer either possible or desirable or even both. In this light, recent analyses have suggested that resorting to scenarios became a 'new tool in the management of multinational enterprises' (Andersson 2020: 729), used both as a means to avoid being constrained by the limits to action that emerged from predictions, as well as to present oneself as a responsible actor open to exploring different options for action (see also Diamanti 2021: ch. 1). While this was plausible in the early context of the 1970s, the new method is more ambivalent. To demonstrate this ambivalence, we can consider the example of the West German energy policy after the oil price rises and the emergence of the anti-nuclear energy movement.

As elsewhere up until the 1970s, West German expertise in energy economics assumed a close coupling between economic growth and energy consumption. As long as economic growth was a core policy objective, therefore, energy consumption was bound to rise. This correlation was mobilized for arguing for nuclear energy, in particular when the security of oil supply seemed threatened (Suckert and Ergen 2022). When the debate became politicized during the second half of the 1970s, though, the opponents of nuclear energy challenged precisely the predictive assumption about this correlation through the elaboration of counter-expertise. It was shown that decoupling of economic growth and energy consumption was possible, as well as that 'growth and well-being' could be reached without oil or uranium (Aykut 2019; Krause et al. 1980; Neu 1978; Wagner 1985). A controversy having opened, the West German federal parliament created an inquiry commission on 'future nuclear energy policy', which employed scenario analysis to demonstrate a variety of possible futures with and without the use of nuclear energy, thus introducing the counter-expertise into the recognized canon of policy options (Enquête-Kommission 1980). While government positions fluctuated, a decision to phase out existing nuclear power stations was (twice) taken and finally fully implemented in April 2023. Today, we see the IPCC using the scenario method for sketching a variety of pathways towards global temperature rise, of which only the one that requires rapid transformative action avoids climate catastrophe. While serving as a management tool, thus, the scenario method raises further questions about our knowledge of the future and our ways of relating to it.

Knowledge attitudes: constraint and enablement

When Jacques Lesourne of Interfutures complained about the 'impermissible determinism' of the Club of Rome report, he was inadvertently criticizing the method of predicting futures by extrapolating the past and its trends that had served to stabilize futures during the 'thirty glorious years'. His problem was that these methods did not support the belief in endlessness any longer. In substance, though, the Club of Rome report was arguing along the same lines: whatever had determined the past trajectory needed to be broken to create a viable future. In parallel, a rethinking of the ways of knowing the future was already under way. Close observers of the first half of the twentieth century were not inclined to think about historical time in linear terms. As Hannah Arendt (1961: 11–13) put it, there is an unavoidable 'gap' between the past and the future, and it is in this gap that the capacity for human action is located. The prevailing objectivism and determinism in the social sciences was increasingly challenged after the 1960s in the name of human agency and creativity and historical contingency. One strand of sociological thought focused on the construction of social facts in human interaction, the implication taken to be that the social world could have been constructed otherwise. The strong programme in the sociology of scientific knowledge went one step further and argued that even scientific findings are socially constructed and not merely mirroring nature. Building on this approach, other scholars held that the natural sciences were not analysing natural phenomena as objects from a distance but soliciting their interaction, thus undermining the common distinction between natural and social phenomena.

As a consequence, not only the future but 'reality' in general appeared more malleable than it had been considered earlier. I want to suggest that these intellectual changes were in some broad sense a reflection of, or better, occurred in interaction with, changes in the public diagnoses of the time in view of the 'problems of modern societies', to use OECD's terminology. They are an expression of doubt in the stability of the world, or at least decreasing certainty about the latter, which went along with the crisis moment in the self-understanding of western societies around the year 1970. As a result, one sees an opposing of two attitudes towards knowledge emerging with rather sharp contours. On the one hand, there appears to be knowledge that shows reality as resisting the grip of human action, as posing limits. The Club of Rome report is a key example. On the other hand, there seems to be knowledge that enables human beings to pursue actions in light of their purposes. The title of the 1945 report, *Science: The Endless Frontier*, reflects this form. The distinction between enabling and constraining knowledge resonates with the one between cornucopian and finitarian understandings of scarcity proposed by Jonsson and Wennerlind (2023; see above), as the former sees only frontiers whereas the latter identifies limits and boundaries. However, the distinction between enabling and constraining knowledge is more procedural than substantive: enabling knowledge can be mobilized for generating abundance but also for other purposes; constraining knowledge might lead to scarcity but does not have to, depending on the relation between scarcity and needs.

If there were truly two forms of knowledge, one of which is enabling, the other one constraining, human action, the choice should be obvious: who would prefer constraints over enablements? Let us come back to Henry Ford one more time. Ford said about Thomas Alva Edison, whom he held in great esteem, despite their failed cooperation on electric cars:

> [H]e recognizes no limitations. He believes that all things are possible. At the same time he keeps his feet on the ground. He goes forward step by step. He regards 'impossible' as a description for

> that which we have not at the moment the knowledge to achieve. He knows that as we amass knowledge we build the power to overcome the impossible. That is the rational way of doing the 'impossible'. (Ford and Crowther 1922: 170)

We may also recall that Max Weber, at about the same time, did not define rationalization straightforwardly as the increasing knowledge about our living conditions, but also referred to the 'belief' that one could 'if one only wanted, [. . .] master – in principle – everything'. He did not imply that beliefs are erroneous or, even less, ineffective. Rather, he referred to 'knowledge or belief' on equal terms and was certainly aware of the biblical saying that belief can move mountains so that 'nothing will be impossible for you' (Matthew 17: 20–1). Rather than two forms of knowledge, thus, we have identified two attitudes towards knowledge.

We can read Weber's reasoning in two ways: on the one side, he offers an ideational background to a historical sociology of modernity as a long-term process of intellectualization and rationalization; on the other side, he provides an epistemic-political reflection on knowledge/belief as transformative power. For our purposes, I keep the two readings together and underline that Weber thus posed the question of the relationship between the real and the possible and asked how one can access the possible from the angle of the real (Guéguen and Jeanpierre 2022). Or, in other words, while identifying knowledge attitudes as keys to transformative action, he also situates such attitudes in historical context. Such a step permits the identification of further differences between the attitudes that help us understand their social location and show that this is not a matter of 'choice' between adopting the enabling or the constraining view of knowledge.

In terms of the interaction between human beings and non-human nature, first, an ambiguity prevails. The scientific revolution is often seen as being based on introducing a separation between the natural and the social (Latour 1991) and aiming at the discovery of the laws of nature. While natural regularities could be seen as showing the resistance of nature to human intervention, this step is mostly considered, on the contrary, as enabling instrumental intervention in nature as an object exposed to human will. In turn, social constructivist approaches often start out as a critique of science, viewing scientific knowledge claims from the angle of 'symmetry' with other, 'lay' knowledge, claims. Furthermore, the interactive and interdependent understanding of the relation between knowable nature and knowledge-seeking human subject is often concomitant with an ecological orientation, but it can also be seen as leading to deeper interventions in nature, namely enlarging the space of the possible by enlisting nature and forming alliances. Strong claims on limits due to the 'laws of nature' become more difficult to sustain, while a 'frontier' attitude building new alliances is encouraged.

Second, speaking of knowledge attitudes rather than knowledge forms suggests that the knowledge does not determine the action that may be based on it. Within the same lecture on 'science as a vocation', similarly, Weber insisted on keeping some distinction between the search for knowledge and the commitment to sociopolitical transformation. But the term 'knowledge attitudes' also suggests that there is a link between the knowledge and the attitude. Whether constraints or enablements are identified is not entirely independent of the knowledge base. Views of enablements, in particular, would turn into 'empty projects' without such a base, using a terminology introduced by Michel Foucault (1984), who argued that imagined possibilities must be subjected to 'historical inquiry', that is, related to historical contexts, and pass 'reality tests'. We may say that this is what Ford called keeping one's 'feet on the ground' and moving 'step by step'. My preceding observations on the material features of energy sources (chapter 7) were meant to contribute to both such historical inquiry and reality test. Knowledge as enablement is not under any circumstances an adequate or sustainable attitude.

Third, tying knowledge attitudes to claims regarding empirical reality entails that we consider this reality as open to interpretation in view of future possibilities. The same empirical information can be associated with different attitudes, which give rise to different interpretations. Reinterpreting a given reality is indeed a way of addressing problems that appear unsolvable with the already existing interpretations. Hence reinterpretation occurs in the form of critique (see Boltanski 2009). As we have just seen, for example, the openness of a given situation to new interpretations was crucial for opening the path towards realistically imagining a no-nuclear and, subsequently, a carbon-free energy future. At the same time, this very interpretative openness enters into the existing constellation of powers and interests. While openness suggests that the future can be different from the present, this entails that no particular path to the future can be derived from the present. Rather, the determination of this path becomes part of the power struggle over conflicting interests. In other words, our reflections on 'limits' and 'frontiers' as expressing two knowledge attitudes focusing on constraints and enablements respectively have come to a double conclusion. On the one hand, they have shown that reinterpretation of reality is a way of more adequately addressing hitherto unsolvable problems. As such interpretative work takes place in contexts of power and interests, on the other hand, it is uncertain whether such a more adequate way will indeed be reached or whether, on the contrary, the reinterpretation will have consequences that are neither intended nor desired. In the following chapter, we will explore in more historico-sociological detail the issues that arise when reinterpretation of reality is located at the core of society and politics.

9

Problem Displacement: The Social Logic of Fossil Fuels

At the outset of my analysis, I claimed that the double focus on societal self-understanding and biophysical resources provides a more comprehensive analysis of socio-ecological transformation than the more standard concern with economic and political institutions in the history and sociology of modernity and capitalism (as programmatically stated in chapter 1). Towards that end, I have provided an account of world-historical transformations of resource regimes in the light of the shifting societal self-understandings that contributed to bringing them about (part II, chs 2–5). This account identified the carbon regime of democratic capitalism as the critical juncture within which climate change originated (chapter 6). Analysing this carbon regime in the light of the material features of fossil fuels and their alternatives (chapter 7) as well as the prevailing knowledge attitudes (chapters 8), I concluded that socio-ecological change needed to be understood as the reinterpretation of problems within the context of power hierarchies. In this chapter, I apply this insight and identify problem displacement as the core of the social logic of fossil fuels.

Self-understandings, forms of power and biophysical resources

At this point, some broader conceptual discussion cannot be avoided. It is needed to develop a language for speaking about the social setting in which the interpretation of problems and the recourse to biophysical resources undergo changes. Most basically, one can distinguish economic, political and cultural aspects of human social life. This threefold distinction is very common, both in the social sciences and humanities and in public debate. Maybe Ernest Gellner (1988) found the most evocative way of referring to these aspects by terming them 'plough, sword and book', using objects common from the advanced organic societies before the fossil fuel era.

In the social sciences, there has been a strong tendency to assume that 'societies' organize these dimensions of social life in the form of separate institutions, such as markets, states and – more vaguely – civil society or culture (a conglomerate of religion, science, arts and family). Most radically, it has also been assumed that 'modern' societies separate these institutions according to their functions in sub-systems that operate with specific codes in the theories of functional differentiation that emerged after the Second World War in US sociology but which keep haunting both public debate and social science scholarship. More recently, though, these ways of thinking have been recognized as being more an intellectual reflection of European nineteenth-century history and institution building in nation-states than a generalizable conceptualization of organized social life. The core disciplinary differentiation of the social sciences in economics, political science and sociology/anthropology testifies to these developments (Wagner 1990, 2001; Wallerstein 1996). Related to this insight, Anthony Giddens (1984) proposed maintaining the threefold distinction but speaking more openly about allocative practices, authoritative practices and practices of signification and legitimation, which may or may not become sedimented in separate institutions in different socio-historical contexts.

Building on this train of thought, I have proposed considering the threefold distinction as referring to the core *problématiques* that all human societies have to address: the economic *problématique* concerns the satisfaction of material needs; the political *problématique* relates to the setting of the rules for the life in common; and the epistemic *problématique* – using arguably too narrow a term – addresses the question of the certainty of knowledge that one can rely on (Wagner 2008). With the term *problématique*, functional considerations are introduced into social analysis without succumbing to a functionalist explanation. The latter would explain the emergence of social phenomena by the function they fulfil for social reproduction, whereas the former acknowledges that human social life is marked by functional requirements without suggesting either that all, or even most, human action is geared towards meeting those requirements or, even when it is, that human action is successful in meeting these requirements. Thus, despite acknowledging functional requirements, the notion of *problématique* does not at all suggest that social change achieves superior functionality.

More specifically, I suggested understanding 'modernity' as a situation in which human beings do not consider the solutions to these *problématiques* as predetermined and given, but as being open and determined through human action and interpretation. In this light, the recourse to biophysical resources can be considered as one key aspect of the economic *problématique*, arguably the most fundamental one, and the elaboration of a societal self-understanding similarly as a key aspect, the widest or most comprehensive one, of the epistemic *problématique*.

Such an interpretative approach to social analysis in general, and to social transformations in particular, has at times been criticized as neglecting or at least underestimating the role of power in society and in social change. While the reproach may have validity in some cases, there is no conceptual contradiction between, on the one hand, considering human beings as 'self-interpreting animals' (Charles Taylor) capable of creativity and agency and, on the other, identifying differences in the capacity of social groups for making their interpretations of a social situation significant for a societal self-understanding and, as the case may be, leading to social change. Basing the analysis on agency and interpretation does not rule out either that some of these power differences between social groups can be persistent. They can be entrenched in the design of institutions and/or in those most basic components of societal self-understandings that cannot easily be challenged, that is, self-understandings that in some intellectual traditions are known as ideologies and in others as social imaginaries.

The closest precedent for a long-term historical analysis of the 'sources of social power' that does not make prior assumptions about social structures was provided by Michael Mann (1986 and later), who indeed distinguishes economic, political, ideological and, additionally, military sources of social power. Linking Mann's (and Giddens's) work with my own conceptualizations, economic power can be understood as the capacity to determine the allocation of resources for securing material well-being. Political power entails the capacity for setting the rules for the life in common, which may include rules for the allocation of resources. The term 'ideational power' refers to the capacity for determining and shaping the sources of common knowledge and understanding.

By introducing the concept of power into the analysis, one raises the sensitivity for asymmetries and hierarchies in social configurations. However, one does not necessarily assume such hierarchies. One can distinguish a Weberian and an Arendtian conception of power, with the former seeing power as exercised by some over others and the latter as being increased by conjoined action (see, e.g., Lukes 2005 [1974] for further debate). Importantly, in the former case, the power of some entails the powerlessness of others, whereas in the latter case the overall capacity of human action grows. Broadly drawing on these traditions, Mann tries to develop a finer terminology for forms of power in which the distinction between authoritative – I prefer to say concentrated – and diffused power is of particular interest for our purposes. In Mann's terminology, authoritative power is conscious and willed by institutions, whereas diffused power is spontaneous, unconscious and decentred. Furthermore, in his analysis of the past two centuries, Mann tends to link the forms of power closely to institutions, for example associating the former with states as the dominant form of political power today, and the latter with markets as the dominant form of economic power under capitalism. Thus he states that 'the diffuse power of the contemporary world capitalist market outflanks authoritative, organized working-class movements in individual nation-states today' (Mann 1986: 8). However, this seems to be a misleading, overly narrow reading of history. From the eighteenth century onwards, true, the search for new sources of social order in Europe (see chapters 3 and 8 above) led to two possible solutions – centralized organization steered by enlightened reason from the top, or spontaneous order generated by the free interaction of reason-endowed human beings. But this distinction did not necessarily entail that the political *problématique* should be addressed through centralization of command and the economic one through decentralized networks, even though this was a view of significant appeal at the time. On a closer look, one recognizes that both options were considered for all three *problématiques*. As had already been recognized during the nineteenth century, market-industrial economies dealing with material needs have a tendency towards concentration of capital; democratization makes the setting of the common rules dependent on the formation of public opinion; and the determination of sources of certainty can be located in a central authority, such as a church or an authoritative academy, or it can occur through multiple interacting communicative practices.

While significant for current purposes, Mann's approach needs to be widened in several respects. First, rather than talking about authoritative power, which includes some notions of legitimacy (that Mann finds not very significant), it is more fruitful to distinguish concentrated and diffused power. Second, rather than trying to relate the sources of power directly to institutions, it is important to recognize more broadly how power sources are mobilized for addressing the *problématiques* by interpreting them with a view to possible solutions. Third, institutions can then be considered as sedimented interpretations, but the prior focus on *problématiques* makes the openness towards a variety of interpretations visible. After this sequence of steps, fourth, it becomes possible to see how unintended consequences can arise in processes of problem solving in different ways, namely ideal-typically either as consequences of purposive action by a large-scale actor, such as a state, that is, through hubris and/or lack of adequate knowledge or as consequences of the uncoordinated actions of multiple actors, such as markets, but also the formation of public opinion in processes of communication, that is, as an aggregate of actions unintended by any single actor.

With such an approach, some concept of 'elite' is required to identify positions of power in determining the interpretation of a *problématique*. The term has already been used repeatedly in the preceding historical analysis without much specification. In the given contexts, this was relatively unproblematic, as the power differential in developing and imposing interpretations of *problématiques* was rather evident. Two aspects of the use of the term should be underlined, though. First, speaking about 'elites' is a more open way of characterizing power differentials than the use of terms such as 'bourgeoisie' or 'political class', which already contain a sense of the specific *problématique* for which the interpretation held by this class prevails, and empirically such a link between social group and prevailing interpretation often does not exist. Second, this openness also allows for the possibility of conflicting interpretations held by different elite groups, or by an elite and a counter-elite, that is forming precisely because of the perceived need to elaborate an alternative interpretation. In other words, the gain in using the term 'elite' is an acknowledgement of power differentials without immediately explaining this differential and its consequences in terms of an underlying social theory. In turn, this openness demands specification of the elite position and of the interpretations they elaborate for each situation in a context-specific way (see Denord, Palme and Réau 2020 for extended discussion and analysis).

Problem displacement: the key to the social logic of fossil fuels

The preceding section has proposed key concepts for a general historical world sociology, but it has not yet focused on the issue of anthropogenic climate change that is the core concern here. In the prior historical account, which was more specifically aimed at understanding climate change, we have read socio-ecological transformations throughout world history as a series of world-regionally perceived problems, the 'solutions' to which were based on elite interpretations of the problem at hand and any subsequent action in the light of these interpretations. Now I want to suggest that a pattern of 'problem solving' emerges from this account that is best characterized as 'problem displacement'. Thus the following conceptually driven synthesis of the historical account will focus on actions of problem displacement to capture the social transformations that have generated climate change.

The term 'problem displacement' is not new in the social sciences, but it has hitherto mostly been used in psychology and organization studies. Maybe the first scholar who gave it a somewhat prominent place in the analysis of society and social change was Niklas Luhmann (1970) in a functionalist and systems-theoretical perspective. Drawing on organization studies, Luhmann defined a 'problem' precisely as an issue that requires a solution but does not have one in the form in which, and at the place where, it occurs. To arrive at a solution, therefore, the problem needs to be 'moved'. For Luhmann, thus, 'problem displacement' (*Problemverschiebung*) is a general expression for the process of making problems manageable. In our terminology, problem displacement is a reinterpretation of a problematic issue in such a way that a solution becomes possible that places the 'cost' or burden in some to-be-specified sense 'elsewhere'.

Possibly drawing on Luhmann, in his analysis of the end of the post-Second World War prosperity, Burkart Lutz (1989 [1984]: 253–7) used the term 'problem displacement' referring to a general tendency to deal with issues without any prefigured solution and, in particular, to the state capacity for solving problems (see above in chapter 5). More recently, significantly, the term is increasingly used in the context of the Great Acceleration and climate change, for instance by Pineault (2021) in one of a set of articles on growth politics in western societies (Reitz et al. 2021; see also Blühdorn 2022a; Eversberg 2021) and more loosely by Charbonnier (2020: e.g., 49, 382) in his environmental history of political ideas (see chapters 3 and 4 above). Hornborg (2006) used the term early as an almost technical metaphor of environmental 'load displacement'. Dipesh Chakrabarty (2021: e.g., 164, 166–77) refers with this expression to conceptual displacements. Adom Getachew (2019: 171) also used it to refer to the way western states countered the 'developing' countries' claim to a New International Economic Order (NIEO; see above, chapter 6). Myself, I first used it in my reflections on the history of progress (Wagner 2016) and subsequently with regard to climate change, as well as to the recent COVID-19 pandemic (Wagner 2020, 2022), but without much further elaboration. At this point, it is possible to somewhat further spell out the theoretical connections of the concept as used here (immediately below), to use it in the synthesis of the historical account (in the following section of this chapter), and to show how its use alters the understanding of climate change in comparison with the theories of modernity and capitalism (in chapter 10). Or, in short, an understanding of problem displacement provides the key to the social logics of fossil fuels.

For current use, the notion of problem displacement presupposes, on the one side, an agent with objectives and, on the other, a problem as a difficulty or impossibility to reach an objective. The agent can be an individual person, but in my analysis they are more typically a collectivity of some kind (group, organization, class, society or state). The objectives or requirements can be more or less narrowly defined, but there will always be some interpretative space to redefine them on the part of the agent. The starting situation is one in which the agent cannot reach their objectives on the basis of the interpretation that they hold. This constitutes the problem. A first step towards problem displacement is, therefore, the reinterpretation of the problem with a view to making it solvable. Such reinterpretation can, but does not have to, include a redefinition of the objectives.

Displacement, then, is a specific form of reinterpretation and related action that enables the agent to reach the objective by overcoming the difficulty. As already indicated, the specificity of problem displacement is the shifting of the burden of solving the problem to somewhere else. Within the economic sciences, the term 'negative externality' refers to a related phenomenon, namely an economic agent's causation of a loss or damage without incurring the related cost. Over the past decades, the concept has indeed often been used for gratuitous appropriation of resources, such as air or water, or for environmental damage caused by production processes without figuring this cost in the producing company's balance sheet. More broadly, Stephan Lessenich (2019) used the term 'externalization' for the way in which western societies deal with the globally negative side effects of their way of life. However, the concept of displacement is different in at least two respects. First, coming from economics, the concept of externality refers to a calculable (monetary, financial) cost (or benefit), whereas the meaning of displacement is wider and includes 'priceless' – in contrast to just 'unpriced' – phenomena such as biodiversity, ways of life or indeed the habitability of the planet.

Second, the term 'externality' presupposes a clear boundary between the agent who externalizes, which is mostly a company or an organization, and its outside. My use of the term 'displacement' does not only have a wider understanding of the relevant agents, which can be social groups, such as elites, but also entire states or societies. Furthermore, the reinterpretation of a problem with a view to displacing it may involve redefining the boundaries of agents. To use one example which stood in the background of one component of the preceding account: the Fordist–Keynesian reinterpretation of the economy transformed the class struggle between company owners and workers into a productivist cooperation within the enhanced collectivity of the nation-state, drawing on fossil fuels. Thus the term 'displacement' does not necessarily refer to a given outside of the agent. Displacement can be a reinterpretation that reshapes the configuration of relevant actors.

In comparison with the stable economic definition of the agent and their outside when assessing externalities, our wider understanding of displacement raises the question of the 'elsewhere', the other place towards which the problem is moved. From one angle, the history of frontier expansion is indeed a way of problem solving by movement in space, first mostly horizontally, then increasingly vertically, and first mostly as terrestrial, then as maritime movement, with a view to gaining access to more resources. The notion of problem displacement, though, has yet another dimension. In my usage, in contrast to Luhmann's, for instance, it suggests that the problem is indeed not solved, it is merely displaced; it is elsewhere, and it is a problem for others. In this sense, there have been three overlapping aspects to this movement. First, problems have been displaced onto other people: domestically, onto the lower classes, more specifically onto the working class in the nineteenth and the twentieth centuries; globally, onto the indigenous and colonized peoples. Second, problems have been displaced onto nature through intensification or extension of resource extraction and use. This aspect is conceptually problematic, as it is not self-evident in what sense nature has a problem once human beings have displaced theirs onto nature. Without necessarily taking an anthropocentric stand in general, it may suffice for current purposes to state that loss of biodiversity or environmental degradation alters the relation between human beings and non-human nature in often problematic ways. Third, problems can be displaced into the future, thus leaving their solution to successive generations.

With this brief discussion of problem displacement onto others, we have implicitly addressed the question of the capacity and the chances of an agent for effectively displacing a problem. In general terms, as discussed above, this capacity is related to asymmetric distributions of power – not only within but also between societies. With greater sources of power, the chances of defining the problems that are going to be addressed and solved is greater than from lower positions, and so are the chances of displacing them. With our distinction of different sources of power, we have also allowed for the possibility that the powers are variably distributed. Considering that problem solutions for one group often entail the burdening of others, attempts at resistance can be expected, drawing on other sources of power than those held by the dominating group. In turn, new problems for the dominating group can also arise because of the collective action of the dominated. In this case, problem displacement is an elite reaction to collective action – again, maybe needless to underline, this can occur both within and between societies. At this point, the distinction of 'two logics of collective action', introduced by Claus Offe and Helmut Wiesenthal (1980) for the analysis of capital–labour relations, should be recalled. In most circumstances, dominating groups dispose of a higher degree of concentrated power, whereas the power of dominated groups is more likely to be diffuse and in need of mobilization to become effective. In sum, the specific power of social groups needs to be identified for each context, and the potential of power struggle with other groups explored.

With these conceptual reflections, I claim to have, first, outlined an interpretative approach to socio-ecological transformations that sets the identification of sociopolitical problems in the historically changing contexts of functional requirements and existing power hierarchies and, second, developed the notion of problem displacement as a pattern of interpretation and subsequent action that has generated the resource-intensive trajectory on which some world regions have embarked over the past two centuries. While the approach has already been applied in the preceding historical account, its key concepts were only briefly announced at the outset (chapter 1) and have not yet been further spelled out. Without the historical underpinning, these concepts might have appeared barren or even somewhat arbitrary. At this point, their usefulness should be more evident and compelling. In the remainder of this chapter, therefore, we can synthesize the historical account by using this conceptual terminology.

Problem displacement as a historical pattern

The past half-millennium witnessed social transformations that can only be considered in highly euphemistic terms as long-term processes of modernization. Nevertheless, even some critical scholars claim to recognize a conflict-ridden path of increasing fulfilment of normative and functional requirements. The western liberal-democratic welfare states of the late twentieth century are often described as the highest point reached in those terms, and the expectation of following this path in due course is kept up, sometimes rather implicitly, for other world regions. Given that this supposed model is both struggling to survive and stands at the origins of climate change as a planetary crisis, scepticism paired with nostalgia for the 'thirty glorious years' has appeared (e.g., Offe 2009), but there has been hardly any rigorous attempt to re-analyse the past trajectory in a comprehensive way. In contrast, an understanding of the current global crisis as the outcome of long-term sequences of large-scale problem displacements provides at least elements of such an alternative account.

Taking up the more detailed analyses of the preceding chapters, as insufficient as they still are, the following paragraphs identify a historical sequence of social configurations, each of which shows a degree of correspondence of societal self-understanding and resource regime. These societal self-understandings contain an identification and interpretation of the key problems as well as of the ways to solve these problems. On a closer look, though, these solutions tend to gloss over incoherencies in the societal self-understanding and be in denial of the problem displacement that is actually undertaken.

The 'classical' organic economy

For early human societies, little evidence about explicit societal self-understandings is available, and the evidence we have is open to an enormous variety of interpretations. Thus, conclusions need to be largely based on what we can know about behaviour. Evidence of migratory movements and territorial expansion may be sufficient to assume that early societies dealt with resource scarcity by problem displacement in a literal sense, namely by movement across space in search of additional resources (chapter 2 above). In some cases, the resource scarcity will have been provoked by population growth, broadly in line with Malthus's theory, in others by the impact of hunting on animal populations or of agriculture on soil erosion. In many cases, furthermore, the climate impact on human societies, which in those periods was much higher than the human impact on the climate, will have been a main reason, with the consequences of, for instance, volcanic eruptions or cold spells on harvests. With a view to understanding later developments, it is noteworthy that expansion in space by settled societies, such as empires, occurred under conditions of social hierarchy with significant power differentials.

Commercial republicanism and the 'advanced' organic economy

The first historical constellation for which we can clearly identify the way in which a societal self-understanding guides the interpretation of key problems can be found in the era often referred to as 'early modernity'. The emerging societal self-understanding in Western Europe was commercial republicanism as the coming together of neo-Roman republicanism and the commercial society argument in the seventeenth and eighteenth centuries (chapter 3 above). It was particularly applicable to the politico-economic constellation of Great Britain and the Netherlands as liberal-oligarchic and commercial societies with an organic resource base. At the same time, it showed a considerable coherence, theorizing a well-ordered society as composed of property-owning male heads of households and claiming that the free interest-based interaction among those agents would enhance domestic peace and material well-being. In this 'advanced' organic economy, though, a problem was arising from the growth of its population and material wealth. The problem came to be perceived as the limitation of the main domestic resource, land, often first identified in the emerging scarcity of wood. Only obliquely acknowledged in their self-understanding for a long time, these societies addressed this problem in practice by appropriating external resources after having transgressed the maritime frontier. Thus this social configuration inaugurated the first global problem displacement in space. Largely in parallel, but accelerating in the late eighteenth century, these societies breached the vertical frontier of the deep mining of coal. While the transgression of the maritime frontier provided the conditions for a major socio-ecological transformation, that of the vertical frontier was crucial in shaping it and bringing it about.

Commercial republicanism was not only a theory of functional social organization; it was also a theory of justification of power, a political philosophy. With its basis in concepts such as social contracts, individual liberty and popular sovereignty, it enabled a critique of the very political order of which it supposedly formed the self-understanding. At the end of the eighteenth century, the claim for equal suffrage in the French Revolution challenged the oligarchic aspect, while the claim for independence in the Haitian Revolution challenged external domination. Thus the societal self-understanding was not only marked by a concealed incoherence with regard to its functional reliance on biophysical resources, it also contained a normative incoherence with regard to its political foundation. When these incoherencies were brought to the fore, the ideological power, while still concentrated, was no longer a monopoly of the elites.

Liberal-oligarchic empires and the coal-based industrial economy

In further response to the problems posed by the limitation of domestic organic resources, West European societies turned to fossil fuels. They became coal-based industrial and imperial-colonial societies during the nineteenth century, all the while remaining liberal-oligarchic in domestic political terms. The turn to coal and to colonial organic resources had been gradually developing during the seventeenth and eighteenth centuries, but it was fully acknowledged in a new societal self-understanding that arose after the middle of the nineteenth century, breaking with commercial republicanism. With the formalized territorial domination of major regions of Africa and Asia and the rising class divide between capitalists and industrial workers in Europe, domination was justified by technical-industrial accomplishment, based on extraction of fossil resources, and supposed cultural and, increasingly, 'racial' superiority, largely abandoning the prior justification which had combined normative arguments with functional social organization.

This, so to say, downgrading of the justification of domination generated the interpretative space in which an increasingly divided societal self-understanding emerged in the course of the nineteenth century. While economic and political power largely remained in the hands of the elites, ideological power increased on the side of the dominated groups, both domestically and globally, with the critiques of capitalism and colonialism/imperialism. In conditions of such divided societal self-understanding, a particular dynamic of social change emerged due to the critique of the dominant justification from the angle of the dominated one. Key components of this critique during the nineteenth century were the lack of an answer to the social question and the rise of the democratic political imaginary.

Luc Boltanski and Laurent Thévenot's *De la justification* (1991), the founding text of what became known as pragmatic sociology, systematically explores justifications for inequality by identifying a plurality of 'orders of worth'. While this approach has mostly been used for analyses of disputes and controversies, the authors also made a hesitant attempt to identify historically dominant constellations of 'orders of worth'. In a way that resonates with our notion of societal self-understanding, they consider most of nineteenth-century European societies as marked by a compromise between the market-based and the domestic order of worth, capturing the liberal-commercial and the oligarchic component mentioned above. By the end of the nineteenth century, this compromise gives way to a new compromise between the industrial and the civic orders of worth, pointing to the use of fossil fuels and to the widening of political participation (Boltanski and Thévenot 1991).

Within the nineteenth-century constellation, the United States already constituted a special case. World-historically marginal until the end of the eighteenth century, it apparently neither turned imperial nor strongly coal based during much of the nineteenth century. But this impression is somewhat deceptive. On the one hand, the slave-based economy of the Southern states constituted a kind of colonial domination on 'domestic' territory and polity. On the other hand, the 'western expansion' provided for land resources at the expense of the Native Americans, thus arguably slowing down the need to resort to coal.

Democratic capitalism and the 'advanced' industrial economy

Combining the notion of a civic-industrial compromise with an observation about the US trajectory helps an understanding of the path towards the subsequent socio-ecological constellation that would fully emerge in western societies after the middle of the twentieth century. It used to be quite common, as mentioned above, to consider 'democratic capitalism' as a relatively coherent societal self-understanding, in some way comparable with commercial republicanism in its heyday. Democratic capitalism apparently satisfied the democratic political imaginary by committing to equal universal suffrage at the same time as it provided an answer to the social question through the extended social policy measures known as the welfare state. Just as in the case of commercial republicanism, however, its societal self-understanding was in denial about the material foundations of social life, hidden under the neutralizing expressions 'economic growth' for domestic concerns, and 'terms of trade' and 'development' for external relations. The hidden incoherencies were formed by the almost complete reliance on external fossil fuels and even a considerable reliance on external biophysical resources in general. Compared to the eighteenth-century situation, the resource and social divide between the 'advanced' societies and all other world regions had massively increased, leading to the dependence of the former on the latter without extending the benefits. The much-praised accomplishments of western societies were achieved by displacing problems to those other world regions and onto nature.

For three decades, democratic capitalism was stabilized through major exercises of problem reinterpretation. Discussed before as knowledge attitudes (chapter 8), prominent examples were Keynesianism, the 'civilian use of nuclear energy', and the sociology of 'modernization and development'. All of them were addressing key problems of western societies: stabilizing democracy through steady economic growth and redistribution; securing energy supply as the material base for economic growth; and maintaining the asymmetric relation to the developing countries that permitted resource extraction. And all of them did so through performing, as well as justifying, problem displacement, most strongly as displacement in time, namely across the business cycle, across long radioactive half-life times and across world-historical periods of 'catching up'. But the entire strategy had also significant components of displacement in space and onto nature, namely through acceleration in the use of biophysical resources, most of which were extracted in other world regions but consumed by western societies, and in the degradation of the environment.

The Great Derangement

From our double angle of resource regime and societal self-understanding, the closing decades of the twentieth century can well be characterized as a 'Great Derangement', borrowing the expression from Amitav Ghosh (2016). I interrupted my analysis of the long duration in part II with the Western Great Acceleration (chapter 5) and addressed various aspects of the following crisis moment of the 1970s in subsequent chapters: the move in global debate from the social question to the ecological question (chapter 6); the shift in fossil fuel intensity from western to Asian societies (chapter 7); and the destabilizing of certainties of knowledge and future expectations (chapter 8). Assembling these elements, one recognizes transformative processes with regard to both resource regimes and societal self-understandings. But clear contours emerge neither for the former nor for the latter: thus a Great Derangement.

Some may want to argue, to the contrary, that ours is the global era of sustainable development. Without doubt, the adoption and diffusion of this term signals a reinterpretation of global problem configurations, or at least the need for such a reinterpretation and an attempt to bring it about. However, the term does not even seem to qualify for the constructive ambiguity that analysts of international relations have seen as opening pathways to conflict resolution. Its vagueness and the underlying tension between its two components – 'development' and 'sustainability' – point rather to its position as a stand-in, a place-holder until an effective reinterpretation is achieved (see Adloff and Neckel 2021 for aspects of the conflictive debate).

Arguably, very different elements of 'contours of an epoch' (Luc Boltanski and Arnaud Esquerre) emerged during the 1990s and were maybe still present through the early 2000s. After the collapse of the Soviet Union, the rise of neo-liberal economic policies and a supposed 'wave' of democratization across several world regions, it could have appeared as if modernization processes asserted themselves at a higher level, reaching all world regions, increasing levels of material well-being and bringing greater degrees of personal freedom and diversity. 'Globalization' and 'individualization' were the keywords of the time, both mostly interpreted positively. Significantly, from our point of view, this meant that 'sustainable development' receded into the background for a while, and climate-change concerns did not yet move to the centre of global public debate, despite the accumulation of knowledge and the agreement on the UNFCCC. But, to use an expression from business journalism, the globalization optimism was a bubble that soon burst, and the underlying tensions resurfaced.

Nevertheless, one could argue that the derangement is nothing but an unsettled interim. We may be living through a stretched-out transformation that at some point will crystallize as a new social constellation with a certain coherence. After all, clear contours of an epoch may be the exception in terms of temporal duration. Of the articulation of resource regimes and self-understandings presented above, the contours of the advanced organic economy have emerged with a certain clarity only in the late eighteenth century; those of the liberal-oligarchic coal-fired regime only during the second half of the nineteenth century; and those of the democratic capitalism of the 'thirty glorious years' only after the middle of the twentieth century. Furthermore, the current interim possibly comes more sharply into focus because our analysis is more fine-grained for the more recent past, in particular for the period after the Second World War. Earlier 'interims' may possibly have lasted much longer.

One may also ask why one should expect a striving for coherence actually to take place during 'interims'. Maybe world history is mostly composed of 'interims' whose structures or contours are barely intelligible – a view compatible with what Jean-François Lyotard (1979) called the 'postmodern condition'. From the angle of historical sociology combined with intellectual history, nevertheless, one can frequently observe work at self-interpretation of society that aims at stabilizing expectations and providing orientations for action. From the angle of political philosophy, furthermore, coherent self-interpretations can provide justifications for domination and inequality or avenues for diminishing either. In both respects, that is, the stabilization of expectations and normative justifications, as I have argued throughout, the material basis of social life in biophysical resources needs to be considered. To understand better the current interim and its possible aftermath, therefore, we need to take a closer look at the transformations since the 1970s in this light.

The western 'problem squeeze' and the Asian Great Acceleration

Scholars have analysed how the relative coherence of democratic capitalism unravelled mostly by looking at internal tensions (Crouch

2011; Harvey 2005; Streeck 2011; and including myself in Wagner 1994). By now, though, one can see much more clearly that the incoherencies that were meant to be hidden in the prevailing societal self-understanding came to the fore and could no longer be ignored.

By the early 1970s, the consciousness of a crisis in the West was widespread, both in the dominating elites and among critical scholars. The diagnoses argued that the connection between welfare state policies and mass loyalty eroded because of both a supposed fiscal crisis of the state and a rising discontent with alienation and control in bureaucratized industrial societies, as noted by the OECD (Boltanski and Chiapello 1999; Schmelzer 2012). In sum, these polities were diagnosed as facing 'legitimacy problems' (Habermas 1973) and a 'crisis of governability' (Crozier, Huntington and Watanuki 1975). Within the economic realm, even left-wing analysts observed that enterprises were facing a 'profit squeeze' due to the rising power of trade unions (Glyn and Sutcliffe 1972). There is now rather widespread agreement that this 'crisis' led into a politico-economic transformation that included neo-liberal economic policies and the increasingly global extension of economic practices, in production, in finance but also in services such as care. The signal events were the coming to power of Margaret Thatcher in the United Kingdom and Ronald Reagan in the United States. The main difference between the various diagnoses emerges from the interpretation of the underlying struggles. From one side, the transformation is seen as overcoming rigidities in western economies that threatened to endanger global competitiveness. From the other side, it is considered to be a new round of class struggle, initiated by an increasingly global capitalist class.

While not being entirely flawed, both versions of this diagnosis remain too focused on a supposed internal dynamic of western democratic-capitalist societies. They therefore underestimate the significance of two other components. When within OECD 'problems of modern society' moved onto the agenda in 1969, the diagnosis first focused on student and worker unrest and related it to dissatisfaction generated by the agenda of quantitative economic growth for growth's sake. But when working towards a more fine-grained analysis, environmental degradation and resource exhaustion as consequences of economic growth moved to the centre of attention (Schmelzer 2012). In parallel, the developing countries had mobilized for a more equitable use of biophysical resources, leading to the call for a New International Economic Order (NIEO) approved by the United Nations in 1974. In between, the United States was losing the Vietnam War and the Organization of Petroleum Exporting Countries (OPEC) raised the price of oil after the Yom Kippur War between Israel and an alliance of Arab states. As Jenny Andersson (2019: 131) succinctly put it, '[b]oth the NIEO and *Limits to Growth* were full-frontal attacks on the post-war economic order as one dominated by western resource extraction.' Or, with a focus on fossil fuels, it was 'the joint challenge of the NIEO and the *Limits* debate that posed an unprecedented challenge to the world of oil' (Andersson 2020: 732; see also Garavani 2019).

Adapting Glyn and Sutcliffe's expression, rather than a limited profitability crisis of western capitalism, western democratic-capitalist societies faced a 'problem squeeze' with multiple facets. While the neo-liberal recipe only returned to time-honoured ideas of market self-regulation that was framed by states so as to secure production and profit, the squeeze came from multiple angles and, most importantly, undermined the well-practised strategy of problem displacement towards other world regions and onto nature. Unable to address this squeeze, governments tried to lower domestic political expectations through the discourse that became known as neo-liberalism, while in parallel resource- and labour-intensive production was relocated to other world regions. These latter moves put pressure on workers' organizations and increased unemployment, but the elite expectation was that the importation of production with lower labour cost would sustain competitiveness in high-value-added production and sustain consumption levels and voter satisfaction. At the same time, domestic environmental quality was improved and CO_2 production emissions stabilized. During the 1990s and early 2000s, as mentioned above, this response seemed to work and alleviate the 'squeeze'. However, this was a short-lived illusion. This strategy divided western societies internally through rising inequality and, over time, generated a new form of citizen dissatisfaction expressed in nationalism and xenophobia. Furthermore, it increased economic dependence on other world regions, no longer only limited to primary resources but now also including industrial products. This was seen as rather unproblematic for a long time, assuming cooperative interdependence, but with the rising competitiveness of Chinese high-value-added products and Russian military aggression, this view could no longer be upheld.

In other words, when western societies first faced this combined politico-economic-ecological crisis during the 1970s, they tried to address it by the tried-and-tested mechanism of problem displacement. The accumulation of debt, as well as the hope for technical fixes for environmental issues, were ways of 'buying time' (Streeck 2013), though without any longer having at hand credible 'imagined futures' (Beckert 2016). In parallel, the relocation of major sections of industry to other world regions served to reduce local pollution and greenhouse gas emissions, as well as to limit the bargaining power of the working class. The displacement in time gambled on a highly uncertain future, defying the already available knowledge on climate change because of its overly constraining character. In turn, the displacement in space has had two unintended (and possibly unforeseen?) consequences. On the one hand, it enabled economic development in other world regions. Thus global relations of interdependence emerged for which western societies, accustomed to unquestioned hegemony, were unprepared. Looking from the perspective of those other world regions, therefore, these moves created economic opportunities, which were increasingly seized, in particular in Asia, enabling the exploitation of apparently cheaper social and biophysical resources in a more closely

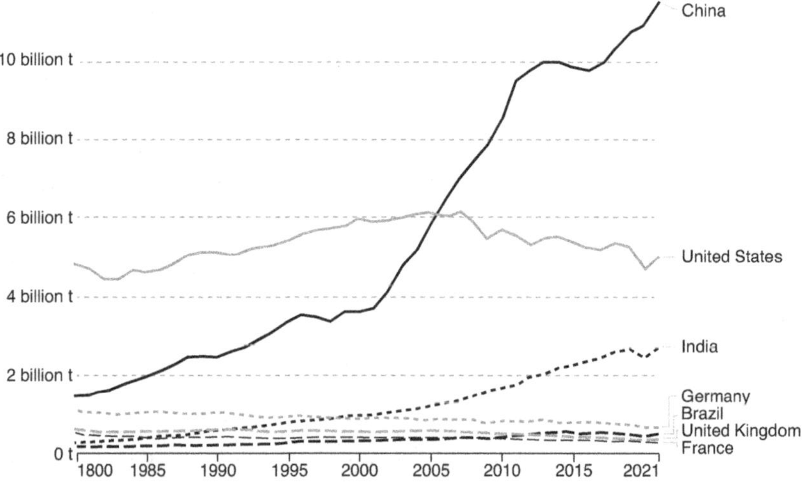

Figure 9.1 CO_2 emissions, selected countries, 1980–present

Source: Hannah Ritchie, Max Roser and Pablo Rosado, 2020, *CO_2 and Greenhouse Gas Emissions*. Published online at OurWorldInData.org. at https://ourworldindata.org/co2-and-greenhouse-gas-emissions

connected world economy (e.g., York et al. 2011). The second leap of the Great Acceleration, from roughly 1990 to the present and with its core in Asia, can therefore be seen as a regional political response to western problem displacement, given the absence of any globally negotiated solution to either social justice or environmental justice.

On the other hand, this partial globalization of resource-intensive production and ways of life accelerated climate change and, thus, limited further the option of problem displacement in time. As we now see clearly, and as was in principle known at the time, this transformation further accelerated global resource use and emissions to the degree that planetary boundaries of sustainability have been approached and partly crossed. While exhaustion of resources remains a significant issue, attention in ecological consciousness has shifted to climate change, threats to biodiversity and global environmental degradation as consequences of resource use.

The end of problem displacement?

Current analyses emphasize that 'safe and just Earth system boundaries' are increasingly reached and even exceeded (Rockström et al. 2023). Given that there is only one earth system for humankind, this could mean, in our terminology, that no further problem displacement is possible. The strategy of problem displacement has extended to almost all of planetary space; it has generated problem-increasing reactions in other world regions that had been exposed to the western displacement strategy; it has mortgaged the future to such an extent, not least through CO_2 concentration in the atmosphere, that it has run out of time. This is a very plausible assessment of the current socio-ecological constellation, based on and evermore supported by scholarly research. Nevertheless, it also is an assessment that emerges from the knowledge attitude that prioritizes limits and boundaries over frontiers still to be transgressed (see chapter 8). An attitude focusing on enabling knowledge may – and indeed does – come to a different conclusion. Thus a critical analysis of this assessment itself is needed.

Scholars writing on world-historical transformations are inclined to identify a final arrangement that just emerges and/or becomes visible and knowable at their time of writing. The entire reasoning about an 'end of history', from at least G. W. F. Hegel to Francis Fukuyama, is of this kind. Opposed to this optimistic, often evolutionist reading of history are the histories of decline, with Oswald Spengler having possibly provided the most pronounced version. This opposition of views of world history was revived at the end of the twentieth century with, on the one hand, the highest stage of progress having been reached and, on the other, the apocalyptic view of global environmental disaster, including the uninhabitability of the planet for human beings due to climate change (this opposition has splendidly been described by Vaclav Smil 2021: 251–63).

With regard to the human use of, and dependence on, biophysical resources, too, the end has already been announced several times. Scholars have cried wolf before. Again, Malthus can be seen as a threshold author: he announced limits, but they were of a persistent kind; humankind reaches them and then will be forced to recede, and this process is likely to repeat itself. Later analyses assume an expansionist process, unintentionally driven towards an endpoint. The line that leads from Jevons's analyses of coal supplies to Weber's dropped remark is an early announcement of the end of fossil fuels, and both were aware of the centrality of fossil fuels for contemporary social life. Turner's frontier thesis announces an end to horizontal frontier expansion, even though limited to one world region. The first half of the twentieth century was too occupied with catastrophes of other kinds, leading to the end of civilization as one used to know it, to be concerned with resource-focused declarations of limits. This topic returns only at the height of the Western Great Acceleration during the 1970s, now as the limited availability of resources at a planetary level. Two decades later, the consequences of resource use are the focus of attention, and now go beyond environmental degradation in the broad sense, focusing on an irreversible major alteration of the planetary condition. So, is this now truly the ultimate frontier, a frontier than cannot be transgressed? If expansion has led to the multiple displacement of the problems that it caused, is there now no further possibility of displacement? Before being fully persuaded, we should note that earlier announced ends were overcome precisely by new forms of displacement. Thus, to sustain the idea of an end today, it should provide an argument why displacement is no longer possible.

There are four reasons why one may assume that the strategy of problem displacement has indeed come to an end. Let us quickly reconsider Malthus, Jevons and the Club of Rome. In none of these cases have the predictions entirely come true. In our terms, Malthus rightly pointed to the horizontal frontier becoming a limit, and Jevons and more comprehensively the Club of Rome did so for the vertical frontier. But in all cases the pronouncements were premature and left possibilities unexplored. One can argue that something similar may happen again now, looking in particular at the maritime vertical frontier for future transgression. The debate about 'planetary boundaries', a counterargument would hold, has reached a degree of comprehensiveness that was absent in earlier reasonings about limits. But the significant change is of yet a different character: with the air, and to some extent the seas, human beings intervene in a transformative way in the very condition of their existence. They are in no reasonable way objects that human beings can purposefully transform for their benefit; they are what human beings are immersed in – 'hyperobjects', in Timothy Morton's (2013) maybe somewhat infelicitous term, because they are no object at all.

This observation leads directly to the second reason why the end of displacement may be reached. Given the dimension of the climate crisis, no trustworthy knowledge is available for achieving displacement of any kind. Of the three examples for enabling knowledge that we used before, Keynesianism was based on an elaborate reasoning on economic cycles; nuclear energy had already been proven to be accessible in the military before 'civilian use'; even the theory of modernization and development had some core of historical knowledge, although in this case belief and intention have outweighed sober reflection. Nothing comparable is the case today. While there is no reason to abandon the belief in human creativity, one also has to recognize that no innovation is currently in sight to reduce in a timely way the CO_2 accumulation in the atmosphere.

Third, the question of knowledge is closely related to the question of agency. Effective collective agency endowed with power was necessary for problem displacement. When the idea of knowledge as an endless frontier was evoked, the United States had just accomplished the Manhattan Project, an enormous collective, state-initiated effort to harness as a matter of urgency the power to create the means to win the Second World War (a thinking revived by Mazzucato 2020 and Lieven 2020 in different ways). Under this impression, the belief in collective human agency to address the core problems of society was very strong and largely stayed strong in western societies until the 1970s. Since then, however, the situation has changed in at least three significant respects. While the state has been the main container for effective collective agency, core problems have increasingly transcended state boundaries and have become global or planetary. Western states themselves have lost collective agential capacity, partly deliberately for ideological reasons, partly because of increasingly diffused political power under democratic conditions. Similarly, they have lost some of the power to impose their problem displacement on other world regions because of the empowerment of some states in those regions. The 'problem squeeze' increased the urgency for problem displacement while diminishing the capacity.

Fourth, of a somewhat different order, one can suggest that problem displacement may still be possible despite the three reasons to the contrary, but that it may radically fall short of normative justifications. True, problem displacement has always been normatively deficient. But, on the one hand, during some earlier resource regimes normative justifications were at least evoked and, on the other hand, the requirement of globally valid normative justifications may have increased. In their recent analysis, as mentioned above, Rockström and colleagues (2023) speak of 'safe and just' boundaries. By implication, this means, on the one hand, that ecological justice is being called for but, on the other, that the earth system may stay within some boundaries if the usage and distribution of resources are unjustly imposed by those with the power to do so.

These brief considerations suggest that strong reasons exist for assuming that the strategy of problem displacement has come to an end. But they also show that there is not a clearly demarcated 'boundary', all current rhetoric notwithstanding. The term 'planetary boundaries' is an interpretative device. It has its material basis in complex calculations, but it is also marked by interpretative decisions with a degree of openness. Thus it is an imagination of an endpoint, not an expression that truly serves for determining the reaching of an endpoint.

With regard to climate change, the hypothesis of approaching limits is based on the comprehensive analysis of available knowledge by the IPCC, vehemently brought into the public arena by social movements such as Fridays for Future, Extinction Rebellion and The Last Generation (e.g., Clot-Garrell 2023). While strongly knowledge based, all above actors also use the final-frontier hypothesis as a performative speech act. They draw attention to finality with a view to mobilizing action such that the announced planetary collapse will not happen. The effect of this performance, though, is limited by the fact that it is genuinely difficult to imagine the advance of environmental degradation, resource exhaustion and global warming as an absolute end. Activists of The Last Generation are well aware that they are not the last generation. They rather point to developments that are so problematic and undesirable that radical action is necessary.

Thus one cannot see the current state of ecological debate as the final sharpening of issues providing an insuperable clarity about what is at stake. On the contrary, we should guard against the temptation of thinking that no superior insights will be possible in the future. The current state of debate is likely to be temporary – like the one around Malthus about land constraint, the one around Jevons about the exhaustion of coal reserves, or the one about the general limits to growth in the early 1970s. As our analysis of knowledge claims (chapter 8) shows, however, it is unquestionable that the stakes have been raised with each new 'limit' that has been discovered, and the resulting problems have become evermore intractable. Due to this historical sequence of frontier transgression, we now know that the problems that emerge as a result of not being able to overcome limits may be less severe than the problems that arise from successfully transgressing a frontier.

Every reasoning about an end to be reached suffers from the inability to spell out what happens after the end. Philosophers may reflect on nothingness, but that option is not open to historical sociologists. The supposed end cannot be anything else than a major socio-ecological transformation. The temptation to speak about an end emerges forcefully because of the difficulties in foreseeing what this socio-ecological transformation will entail.

Principally, if we have to assume that radical action – changing power hierarchies and profoundly reinterpreting the issue – is not likely to occur, we need to explore other endings, which under given circumstances have a greater likelihood. From some interested points of view, they are also preferable to the radical transformative action asked for between IPCC and social movements.

Therefore, we need to imagine concretely the possible 'ends' (chapter 10) and then debate what we are willing and able to do to avoid them (chapter 11). This will be tried in the last part of this book.

Part IV

The Future Social Logic of Fossil Fuels

10
Other Endings: Reviewing the Logics of Expansion

Path dependency?

To recap, throughout the preceding analysis, we have aimed at understanding how the current climate emergency can be understood as the unintended outcome of sequences of attempts at solving social problems. While accepting, with the IPCC, that the resort to fossil fuels and the concomitant emission of carbon dioxide are at the core of climate change, I have embedded fossil fuel use in the broader questions of the human need for energy and for biophysical resources from non-human nature in general. Thus, I took a very long-term perspective to try to identify major transformations in human use of non-human resources across world history.

The moments of transformation that I have identified do not deviate much timewise from those emphasized in other accounts of world history: the wide opening of the maritime frontier from the late fifteenth century onwards; the systematic transgression of the first vertical frontier with deep mining of coal from the late eighteenth century; the transgression of the second vertical frontier with crude oil and natural gas from the late nineteenth century; and the shift towards a mass-consumption economy from the middle of the twentieth century. One difference between my account and others is that I have given particular attention to changes in resource use, but at first sight it may appear that the view of long-term world history is not being considerably altered as a consequence. But this only appears so at first sight.

When one looks at the long-term data series about CO_2 emissions and CO_2 concentration in the atmosphere, one is inclined to see there a path of rising emissions and, consequently, accumulation. Furthermore, there are identifiable moments at which the curve bends upwards, coinciding with the historical transformations of resource regime just mentioned, except the first one. Social scientists of our time may well be leaning towards interpreting this observation as path dependency, meaning that once human societies have embarked on such a path, the past weighs on the present in such a way that it is difficult to abandon the path or even redirect it in any significant manner (e.g., Mahoney 2000; Page 2006). The main broad-brush explanations of climate change all implicitly use a radical version of path-dependency theory. The neo-Malthusian explanation considers population growth as the driving force and sees every successful resource transformation that serves to feed a larger population as a step to further population growth, thus continuing on the path. The social theories of modernity and capitalism, in turn, assume that once human societies have made the enhancement of freedom and the pursuit of profit respectively key components of societal self-understanding, then a logic of expansion has been introduced that is impossible to abandon. But even global economic and environmental historians who emphasize long-term continuities warn that 'the tendency to stress path dependency over free agency of social groups and societies should not be exaggerated' (De Zwart and van Zanden 2018: 282; on path dependency and agency, see recently Sydow, Schreyögg and Koch 2020: 722).

My problem-oriented approach, though, slows the reasoning down and forces a more nuanced analysis. Rather than expecting that any major step on the path was taken for compelling, overarching and lastingly valid a priori reasons, one needs to take a closer look at the specific problem constellations. For certain periods, there may have been a fairly steady path that is unquestioningly pursued, suggesting that a society has stably identified its main problems and considers them as, by and large, adequately addressed. However, there are other moments, we may call them moments of crisis, in which key problems are not adequately addressed and in which there is contestation over what the key problems are and/or how they can be adequately addressed. In the light of the preceding analysis, we can now state that changes of resource regime are responses to some such moments of crisis. But rather than taking the response to a crisis for granted, based on the logic of the path, one needs to ask of each of these moments broader questions that allow recognition of possible discontinuity, if any: for whom did a problem exist; how was this problem diagnosed and interpreted; whose interpretation prevailed in cases of multiple competing interpretations; and how did a change in resource use address the problem and possibly solve it? Thus the second difference between my account and most others is that I have analysed these moments by searching for the problems to which the change in resource base was seen as an answer.

This approach entails, in other words, that any subsequent point on the timeline of carbon dioxide emissions is no longer seen as necessarily determined by the shape of the preceding line. Rather, there are moments of contingency in which the curve could go in a different direction, be it as a consequence of human action or for other reasons. This is not to say that the present is detached from the past. The timeline that displays the level of CO_2 concentration in the atmosphere, which provides a contrasting case to the one of CO_2 emissions, cannot easily be turned downwards, as this level is the result of the path taken in the past and not amenable to swift change by any human intervention now or in the near future. Such change can only happen over long periods of 'net zero' social life or, much more unlikely, through the large-scale deployment of carbon-capture measures, to use two expressions of our time. But the insight into contingency precisely invites consideration of what can change, and for which reasons, and what not.

Throughout this analysis, we have looked at resource regimes and at societal self-understanding. Much of the current debate about climate change focuses on the former, in particular on fossil fuels, contrasting their benefits with the unintended negative consequences of their use. And indeed, as argued before (chapter 7), climate change cannot be adequately understood without considering the material characteristics of fossil fuels that support their functionality or disfunctionality. An overemphasis on these characteristics, though, leads to a shortcut in the analysis. Shifts towards greater fossil fuel intensity were brought about at critical junctures in connection with shifts in societal self-understanding or, more concretely, shifts in the identification and interpretation of key problems that societies are facing, including variations in the prevailing knowledge attitudes (chapter 8). Therefore, this connection needs to be in focus in two ways. Some such junctures may be best understood as a change in problem interpretation opening the path towards a new resource regime. At others, vice versa, a prior reorientation in resource use may trigger the rise of a new societal self-understanding. As these junctures are mostly of a temporally extended nature, not literally short critical moments, there is likely to be an interrelation between changing problem interpretation and reorientation in resource use (chapter 9). At times, nevertheless, socio-historical analysis, too, may identify ‘tipping points’, after which it is difficult to revert to an earlier state, even if one wanted to (e.g., Milkoreit 2023).

Reviewing the logics of expansion

At the start of this analysis, I introduced three possible logics of expansion that other authors identified as the driving force behind the increasing use of fossil fuels and, thus, climate change. In the end, we can confirm that population growth, desire for freedom from want and profit seeking all played major roles in shaping human history. But we have also seen that there has been no inevitable drive towards heating up the atmosphere in the pursuit of social objectives. To sustain a growing population, more natural resources are required, but their use does not need to generate climate change. No logic of capital necessarily ties the search for profit to the extraction of fossil resources. No logic of modernity links freedom with a kind of material abundance that requires the burning of fossil fuels. I briefly summarize the findings in this light.

Population

So-called neo-Malthusian explanations of climate change have often been regarded with suspicion, but with the advancing climate crisis even critical thinkers cannot avoid mentioning population growth (e.g., Chakrabarty 2009, 2021; Ghosh 2016: 111–12). If we look at the curve of world population growth since 1750 together with the one representing the increase of CO_2 emissions, the parallel is striking. There is relatively slow but steady growth of CO_2 emissions during the nineteenth century, a limited upward turn at the end of the nineteenth and the beginning of the twentieth centuries, with some marked variation attributable to the world wars, pandemic and recession, and a 'Great Acceleration' after the middle of the twentieth century. World population had reached roughly one billion by 1800, two billion by 1930 and six billion by 2000 to arrive at eight billion in the present. Biologists may rightly see here the success of human beings in imposing themselves as the dominant species on the entire planet. However, historians and climate scientists need to be more cautious with the apparent correlation. While it is true that human beings need biophysical resources, the relation is not rigid, and it does not follow that a larger number of human beings will need a larger amount of biophysical resources, and even less necessarily more fossil fuels.

From a current point of view, both population growth and carbon dioxide accumulation looked relatively insignificant until the mid-twentieth century. Population growth was more rapid in Europe and North America than in most other world regions during the nineteenth century. This was due to advances in hygiene, medicine and nutrition (and in North America due to immigration), rather than to increasing fossil fuel use. Between 1950 and 1980, both population growth and fossil fuel use had become highly significant, but the former took place predominantly in Asia and Africa, whereas the increase in carbon dioxide emissions is almost exclusively confined to North America and Europe (plus the Soviet Union). Despite appearances, there is no correlation between the two. Already in 1928, Mahatma Gandhi had made a mediated connection between population growth and resource exhaustion via industrialization in his own particular way: 'God forbid that India should ever take to industrialism after the manner of the West. If an entire nation of 300 millions took to similar economic exploitation, it would strip the world bare like locusts' (cited in Ghosh 2016: 111).

Capitalism

We can take Gandhi's term 'industrialism' to refer to a mode of production based on machines operated by paleo-organic sources of energy, leaving open whether capitalism or modernity are appropriate as further defining concepts. Let us consider capitalism first.

Throughout most of the preceding account, the driving forces of fossil fuel use came from societies that had many features that can be called capitalist, in the sense of Jürgen Kocka's working definition (see above chapter 3). To be able to say, furthermore, that these developments were driven by a capitalist logic of expansion, we would need to ascertain that a dominant capitalist logic of steering existed in those societies. This was the core argument of both Marx's and Weber's diagnoses of European societies in the nineteenth and early twentieth centuries. While Marx emphasized class struggle as some kind of collective intention of a capitalist class to gain and assert its power, Weber tended to see the rise of modern capitalism as an unintended outcome of ideational change. More importantly, Marx considered that the rise of the bourgeoisie entailed the establishment of a capitalist system, whereas Weber saw the rise of capitalist institutions as generating constraints on action and life conduct. Where Marx, following classical political economy, saw an 'economy' with its own laws and regularities, Weber identified the emergence of a sphere in which economic power, the capacity to decide on the allocation of resources, was located. Ecological critics of capitalism today tend to adopt Marx's approach, often implicitly, thus seeing a possibility for combatting climate change only in a vaguely defined overcoming of capitalism. Along Weber's lines, in contrast, the task is to specify the mechanisms of power that perpetuate fossil fuel use and combat those.

If it has become clear that I tend to pursue the latter line of reasoning, then it needs to be underlined that this is not based on a prior commitment but emerges from the findings of my analysis. The expansion of commerce after the maritime expansion that entailed resource transfer to Europe and prepared the ground for extended fossil fuel use was pursued by trading companies on behalf of European governments, thus emerging from dominant groups in Europe where economic and political power were not clearly separated. Such separation became more pronounced with the crossing of the frontier of deep coal mining in parallel with the rise of classical political economy as an argument for separating economic and political power. While the fossil fuel economy arose during this period, the high intensity that led to climate change was only reached after crossing the frontiers of crude oil and natural gas. This happened during the period of imperial competition, when western governments intervened strongly in ascertaining control over resource sites outside their own territory, thus again creating close ties between economic and political power. In other words, in varying constellations, components of the dominating groups in western societies can well be characterized as 'capitalist' since the seventeenth century. However, these capitalists are better seen as holders of a significant power source than driven by a 'logic of capital'.

If no such logic was in place earlier, then the main increase in fossil fuel use during the twentieth century, in particular after the Second World War, cannot be attributed to the mere unfolding of such a logic either. Rather, the use of fossil fuels, though partly promoted by private enterprises (not exclusively; see, e.g., public electric utilities or railways), was increased due to pressure from the majority population under increasingly democratic conditions. Still, the key decisions were taken by elites, including capitalists, as the diffuse political power of the citizenry rarely takes decisions of such a kind; and citizens did not ask for more fossil fuel. However, they were taken as what was perceived as a suitable response to citizen demands without endangering the elite status. If one wanted to speak of a logic of capital when considering the interests and actions of capital owners, then one would also need to say that a logic of democratic politics unfolded in western societies across the twentieth century and needed to be articulated with the logic of capital.

Modernity

The notion that climate change has been generated due to a historically unfolding logic of modernity – an expression not commonly used as such but fruitful here – is linked to the promise of 'abundance and freedom', to use once again Pierre Charbonnier's formula. In contrast to the logic of capital, which works as a constraint even on the capitalists that benefit from it, the logic of modernity is seen as agential. Once the possibility of greater freedom and improved material well-being arises, human beings will be appealed to by it and strive for realizing it, so the – mostly implicit – argument goes. Nevertheless, this appeal is seen as (having been) so strong that it leads to some inevitability in the history of modernity; thus we can speak of a logic.

When assessing the historical account with a view to detecting any such logic at work, the first problem that arises is the dual nature of the supposed modern promises. As we have seen before (chapter 3), Charbonnier ties freedom and abundance closely together by suggesting that the promise of freedom would have been found less convincing if it had not been connected with the promise of improved material well-being. However, this is far from evident. True, one can argue that commercial republicanism linked freedom to 'wealth', most explicitly in Adam Smith. But this link expressed the self-understanding of the advanced organic economy, that is, before the massive recourse to fossil fuels. During the rise of 'industrialism' in the nineteenth century, the link did not exist for the majority of the population. A reconnection was made when the democratic political imaginary was mobilized to demand an answer to the social question in the later nineteenth century. This answer was only fully given, however, after the Second World War had tied the consolidation of democracy to 'economic development'. In turn, this was the beginning of the Great Acceleration leading to the climate crisis. In other words, there is no historical connection between freedom and wealth that lets a logic of modernity unfold. Rather, this is a history of struggle over the interpretation of modernity, in particular over the places of personal freedom, collective freedom (or democracy), (domestic and global) equality and material well-being within modern self-understanding.

One can disconnect the question of material well-being from the one of freedom and suggest that the former on its own, once seen as a real possibility, becomes a driving force for fossil fuel use and, thus, climate change. As Dipesh Chakrabarty (2021: ch. 4) suggested, inhabitants of New Delhi may well need private air conditioning in their housing to avoid suffering from heat, and they may take the first opportunity to install it, despite the fact that air conditioning further heats the air of the city and contributes to general climate change. However, observations of this kind hardly lead to the conclusion that the quest for enhanced material well-being brought 'modern' societies onto the trajectory of increasing fossil fuel intensity. Across the nineteenth and much of the twentieth centuries, most human beings, arguably, were concerned about material well-being in terms of avoiding absolute scarcity, in particular of food and shelter, which can be adequately achieved with limited biophysical resources in most circumstances. For the resource-intensive consumer society, which we know today, to emerge, an extended chain of political and economic decisions was required, as outlined above and in which the experience of scarcity played a limited role.

This reasoning can be refined, though, by noting an orientation towards emulating the higher standards of material well-being reached elsewhere. As shown above (chapter 3), a wider social diffusion of 'luxury' (Maxine Berg) occurred in the commercial societies of the seventeenth and eighteenth centuries, in particular the Netherlands and Great Britain. Recently discussed as the earliest moment of 'consumer society', these developments can also be seen as the emergence of an 'imperial mode of living' (Brand and Wissen 2017). By coining this term, Ulrich Brand and Markus Wissen aim to focus on the benefits that a capitalist economy provides to those who participate in it, and this without resorting to concepts such as 'false consciousness' or 'mass loyalty'. Because of the term 'imperial', the reasoning also touches upon problem displacement in space, resembling Lessenich's 'externalization' argument. On a closer reading, however, it considers the 'imperial mode of living', once it exists in one place, as diffusing across the globe because of its attractiveness. In this sense, it claims to uncover, in our terms, an agential logic of modernity that unfolds basically because of wealth and status differences. Again, though there may be some validity to such reasoning in our current era of global commercial mass communication, there is much less for earlier historical periods, up to even the middle of the twentieth century when the wealth and status differential was partly invisible because of its location in different world regions and partly widely considered unbridgeable in colonized and settler societies.

Beyond monocausal logics

The preceding summary discussion shows that population growth, capitalist profit drives and the striving for freedom and material well-being introduced dynamics into human history that, for different reasons, have proved difficult to stop. These elements are all relevant for understanding the rise of our resource-intensive societies that have generated climate change. But the discussion also adds important qualifications to any notion that an impersonal or systemic logic imposed itself on human history from a certain point in time onwards, for two principal reasons. First, the very plurality of 'logics' suggests that no single one of them determined the recent course of history, unless one assumes that one of them is a dominant logic, which seems difficult to sustain. Second, while each of these elements shapes conditions for human action and often can be seen as limiting options for action, none of the emerging constraints can be seen as so powerful that it necessarily imposed itself.

One can err in two ways when referring to these elements for explaining climate change. On the one hand, one can underestimate the impact of numbers (in the case of population growth), the force of desires and the wish for comfort (in the case of modernity), and the power of 'interest' in the narrow sense of the pursuit of gain (in the case of capitalism). On the other hand, mirrorlike, one can underestimate the human capacity to reinterpret one's situation in the light of problems, and thus the possibility of politics in socio-ecological transformations, both democratic domestic politics and international politics, part of which is collective work at reinterpretation.

To avoid both errors, I have explored the reasoning behind the logics and developed the historical account with a view to 'testing' the validity of those assumptions. In the way it is at times stated, the assumption of any such logic appears to reflect more the wish for a clear-cut monocausal explanation of long-term historical change than a nuanced analysis. The insistence on monocausality, furthermore, has the side effect of posing insurmountable obstacles to transformative action. 'Population', 'capitalism' and 'modernity' are elevated to the status of reified causes that are largely inaccessible to human action. This insight, though, should not lead to the assumption that the climate-changing impact of population growth, capitalist profit drives and the striving for freedom and material well-being can easily be overcome – and even reverted – by a voluntaristic belief in the creative power of the reinterpretation of our condition. The historical account needs to be scrutinized with a view to specifically identifying the constraints on, and possibilities for, action.

With this purpose in mind, I have above (chapter 7) introduced the notion of a critical juncture as a historical moment in which a socio-ecological constellation changes. A juncture separates two historical periods from one another. Each of these periods may have seen relatively smooth and gradual change, but the juncture alters the direction of change. Or from the angle of human agency, the constraints on action change during the juncture, and very often they change due to the exercise of human agency, not least a change in societal self-understanding and interpretation of key problems. I have also used above, more in passing, the notion of socio-historical tipping points, borrowing a common concept from the earth and climate sciences (Milkoreit 2023). While this may be one metaphor too many, this term suggests that there may also be moments of irreversibility in sociopolitical history. At least, the outcome of a critical juncture may make reversals of certain developments highly unlikely because of new and strong constraints on human action. As such, the notions of critical junctures and of socio-historical tipping points may provide a bridge between, on the one hand, the assumption of actorless logics of historical change that impose themselves without anyone wanting their outcomes and, on the other, a focus on a series of problem-solving situations without clear connection between them (Sydow, Schreyögg, and Koch 2020, for example, mentions critical junctures).

Examining the critical junctures in human history when resource regimes changed, this historical account aimed to identify the social problems that were meant to be solved by burning fossil fuels and the power hierarchies that shaped the decisions to use them. At this point of the analysis, we can recognize that the key choices that led to the climate emergency were made relatively recently, during the second half of the twentieth century: first, the choice to consolidate democracy by using fossil fuels to answer the social question, leading through problem displacement to the Western Great Acceleration; and second, the inability to deal with the consequences of this choice when it became unsustainable, leading to 'international disintegration' (Gunnar Myrdal) and the Asian Great Acceleration.

These decisions – or, in the second case, non-decisions – are close enough in time for us to get back to them and undo the prevailing social logic of fossil fuels. To achieve this, though, a firm understanding is necessary of the problem reinterpretations that occurred during those two junctures and the power constellations that shaped them. I have prepared the ground for this assessment through the preceding chapters of part III and can now synthesize the findings.

Power hierarchies and problem definition

My account of the 1970s western 'problem squeeze' and the subsequent Asian Great Acceleration could be said to give – and may be accused of giving – greater weight to political analysis than to any dynamics of profit, comfort or freedom seeking. But this re-emphasis should not be understood as a claim to some primacy of politics as opposed to interest-based class struggle, functional requirements or normative claims. Rather, it understands politics as the site of authoritative interpretation of the problems a social configuration faces and of collective decision making to address these problems. As such, politics is unavoidably in the centre of concerns about climate change. The common assertion that there is a glaring gap between the accumulating knowledge about climate change and the absence of adequate action is a claim about the failure of politics. Whatever forces may drive climate change, the analysis and interpretation of these forces and effective action to tackle them is a task of politics. That is why my focus on power hierarchies and problem interpretation is meant as a tool to specify how and why politics has failed over the past half-century to effectively address climate change.

Broadly in line with Michael Mann's approach, world history can be read in terms of the growth in the sources of human power. More specifically, one aspect of this growth is the planetary extension of the reach of human action. Climate change and the concept of the Anthropocene testify to this aspect of the increase in human power. One other aspect, at the centre of Mann's analyses, is the building of states and their apparatuses as power over territory and the resident population, which is the main historical form of what we here call concentrated power. But a third aspect, less frequently in focus, is the emergence of what we may call extended diffused power, starting with the rise of commercial society and its justifying notion of spontaneous order.

Two major changes in power hierarchies occurred after the middle of the twentieth century: western capitalist societies became democratic throughout, arguably in two steps: first, with the consolidation of democracies with apathetic citizenry after the Second World War; and second, with the more active citizenry creating 'governability' and 'legitimacy' problems from the late 1960s onwards. And the global political constellation became post-imperial, meaning that it came to be composed of a multitude of formally equal state actors. Without repeating the earlier account, I want to highlight the main changes.

During the nineteenth century, western societies were internally hierarchical, with the sources of authoritative power concentrated in a small part of the population, including capitalists but also aristocrats (with the exception of North America) and state officials, who exerted their power externally through colonial domination, settler elites and military threats. Given this double hierarchy, the dominant elites could reap the resource benefits of exploiting the first vertical frontier in Europe and the horizontal frontier of plantation agriculture in America without ceding significant amounts of resources to the majority of the population. This social configuration contributed relatively little to climate change, not least because the benefits of fossil fuel use accrued only to a minority population. However, the situation changed with the increasing political power of the majority population in western societies from the late nineteenth century onwards, visible in effective demands for material resources in terms of 'the social question' and for political resources in terms of suffrage extension. The dominant elites ceded somewhat to these demands, visible in slightly rising CO_2 emissions, but kept showing considerable resistance, leading in some countries to the destruction of the just-emerging democratic institutions. After the Second World War, the elite view was that a repetition of such collapse should be avoided. The complex mechanism to achieve this consisted in: providing material well-being to the population in the metropoles; extracting fossil fuels through the second vertical frontier for this purpose at low cost; and maintaining the boundaries to the population in the colonies and, internally, to the majority in the 'settler societies'. At this time, western societies were internally based on formal equality, and the elites' power of problem definition started to be limited by the power of democratic political participation. Externally, the rising claim for self-determination demanded the search for new power mechanisms, such as with oil companies in the protectorates of the Middle East, to be extended when decolonization accelerated. This new configuration of power remained rather stable through the early post-war decades (conditioned and aided by the Cold War confrontation).

In their own self-understanding, western societies were normative orders – just and democratic – whose core problems were the social and democratic questions. Both these problems appeared to be resolved owing to a high concentration of power in the state, which was aligned with an economic power elite, in which some large enterprises were central, and with an electorate that behaved politically according to an orderly cleavage structure. Furthermore, again in their own view, these societies had limited external obligations, while remaining sufficiently dominant in the global constellation to reap resource advantages.

In response to the 'problem squeeze' of the 1970s and after, as analysed above (chapter 9), the political elite in state and political parties resorted to self-abdication as holders of concentrated power, both in relation to economic elites and to the electorate, thus weakening public institutions, as became highly visible during the recent pandemic, and relinquishing the attempt to dominate processes of problem definition. The existing answer to the social question was put in doubt, and no compelling answer to the rising ecological question was elaborated. External relations became more volatile due to resource dependency on now independent states, as well as a deliberate strategy of internationalizing the division of labour, which may have somewhat stabilized the domestic power constellation but in the same move empowered actors in other world regions.

The weakening of the concentrated power of the democratic state is highly significant in two key respects: first, because the state used to be the main container of collective action both domestically and globally, and it is not replaced by any other such form; and, second, because the democratic state is – and this is what Rawls well recognized – a potential container of justice, and again there is no other such form. Thus a deliberate self-weakening of the democratic state, as it happened, without making steps towards a world order endowed with criteria of justice means a weakening of normative justifications overall.

Stating this, one should not overlook that – as has indeed been central to our analysis – the western democratic states of the post-war period were the major promoters of fossil fuel use and of climate change. In terms of self-understanding, this development was enabled by the almost exclusive focus of normative justification on domestic issues, as promoted by Rawls's theory of justice. This assumption is problematic in terms of general political theory, but it is much more so under real-world conditions in which the (majority of) existing democratic states are inheritors of colonial power and resource transfer benefits, thus capable of displacing their problems onto other world regions and onto nature. We may call this the condition of imperial democracy.

Due to the 'problem squeeze', the current global situation is different from the one of the early post-war period in terms of power hierarchies and of problem definitions. Starting with the latter, the ecological question has risen to the level of a global emergency since no significant action to combat climate change has been taken since the issue was officially globally recognized three decades ago. The social question is still considered mostly a domestic problem, and the situation varies considerably between countries. Importantly, this also entails that the problem agenda has diverged between countries. With the sole exception of climate change, and even in this case with considerable hypocrisy, there are few items on a common agenda. This divergence, in turn, is problematic for two main reasons: first, the increased degree of global connectedness leading to more problems that need to be addressed in common; and, second, because of the greater distribution of power between states.

Which leads to the question of power hierarchies. The congruence between state-based political elites, economic elites and the citizenry has strongly eroded in the West. One may be inclined to say it has disappeared. Due to the deliberate abdication from power of political elites, most importantly through financial liberalization and new kinds of free-trade treaties, western economic elites operate much more globally. The citizenry is divided over the relative significance of social and ecological questions, importantly often matching this divide on commitments to greater openness towards the outside or greater closure. Given their dependence on the vote, the political elites lack the capacity to re-concentrate power. In non-western democracies, similar divides have arisen, but they are framed by a broadly acknowledged need to improve material well-being, which nonetheless goes with a split over whether to achieve this objective by granting economic liberties or by state guidance and redistribution. In other non-western countries, those not considered to be democracies, the accountability of governments to the citizenry, while important, can be more strongly moderated by the governments, which retain a high concentration of power. Having said this, global power balances have shifted away from the West to the other two kinds of polities, mostly due to the new international division of labour in tandem with greater assertiveness. These reflections on shifting power hierarchies and changing problem definitions serve as a background for an assessment of the further course of global and planetary history.

Other endings: ways of reading the present

The Great Convergence

The rapid economic growth in China and, slightly later, India from the late twentieth century onwards has stimulated new interpretations of world history. Throughout the earlier twentieth century, as mentioned in chapters 4 and 5, a reading of world history as increasingly divided by the 'rise of Europe' or the 'rise of the West' had emerged and consolidated. By the 1980s, though, the view held in modernization theory that the 'developing' countries could and would 'catch up' with the West had become discredited on numerous grounds. The terminology of a North–South divide, the so-called Brandt Line, gave expression to the belief in an entrenched divide between a 'Global South' and a 'Global North', not subsiding but only to be overcome by global collective action. By 2000, however, when Kenneth Pomeranz's book *The Great Divergence* had provoked new debate and research about the reasons and the timing for this divergence, developmental trends in different world regions had changed. While the UNFCCC in 1992 introduced a formal division of developed and developing countries, which now proves to be an obstacle for agreement on climate-change policies (Ciplet and Timmons Roberts 2019), not much later economic historians started to speak about a 'Great Convergence' because they were seeing non-western countries approaching western levels of economic development (e.g., Grinin and Korotayev 2015; Jones 2017). In parallel, sociological modernization theory found a new lease of life by showing that indicators of development in some Asian countries were rising quickly and reaching the levels of 'advanced' western societies (e.g., Schmidt 2010). Furthermore, findings of the rise of a 'new middle class' from the poor strata of society in countries like Brazil and South Africa during the first decade of the twentieth century led to expectations of political consolidation processes in hitherto unstable democracies – to go back to Lipset's theorem and terminology (chapter 6). From the perspective of the study of international relations, these socio-economic changes might lead to a multipolar world order replacing western domination as well as the temporary bipolar world order of the Cold War period.

There are sufficient empirical indicators to take this interpretation of global change processes seriously, despite and beyond its obvious appeal to political and business elites in the West as well as in the so-called emerging countries. Drawing on earlier theories of economic take-off and social modernization, the theorem refers empirically to selected countries whose economic and social indicators can be brought in line with earlier western developments and extrapolated further. However, this approach is insufficient to sustain an argument about an impending global Great Convergence for two reasons.

First, the data only show that China, India and some other Asian countries may be 'converging' towards the West. Other large, and economically and politically powerful, countries such as Brazil, Russia and South Africa – together, with China and India, the members of the BRICS association – or Argentina, Nigeria and Türkiye have shown periods of economic growth, but not to an extent leading to convergence with the West. Rather than a confirmation of a general world-historical tendency, the Asian developments may be a world-regional specificity. More importantly, the growing wealth in China and India does lead to a statistically significant decrease in global social inequality, due to the large population of these countries (Milanović 2016). But it does not at all lead to the diminishing, much less the closing, of the global social divide; it rather displaces the boundary between its two sides. Many countries, including Brazil, South Africa and Russia, continue to show high domestic social inequality, including again rising poverty rates. And other countries, most importantly in sub-Saharan Africa, face 'double exposure' to increasing social problems and environmental degradation (Leichenko and O'Brien 2008).

Still, one could argue that the rise of Asia is only the next in a sequence of steps on a world-historical trajectory. However, second, this reasoning does not take into account that a continuation along this trajectory would further increase the global 'exposure' to climate change. As we have seen, the Asian Great Acceleration of CO_2 emissions has taken over from the preceding western one, and there is no sign of it abating. China, in particular, has emulated the early growth path of western economies based on energy-intensive industrialization both for production and consumption, and it has until now largely satisfied its energy needs with fossil fuels. Even though significant steps towards a transition to wind and solar power have been taken, the pursuit of the growth path will keep requiring fossil fuels for much longer than IPCC calculations permit.

There are only two ways of reconciling this insight with a possible sustainable global path. Drawing on Vaclav Smil (2021), first, one may consider human history across the past two centuries as going through a sequence of transitions, each of which is characterized by a period of rapid growth, a 'take-off', which then subsides and stabilizes at a lower than peak level. The first and best known of these transitions, which probably inspired Smil's presentation, is the demographic one: a period in which natality far exceeds mortality and entails quick population growth is followed by one in which mortality is stably somewhat higher than natality, leading to slow population decline. Western societies have shown declining birth rates for decades, and estimates suggest the world population may also start to decline during this century. Similarly shaped transitions may be happening for agriculture and for economic production in general, but the current challenge is to speed up the energy transition and the transition away from environmental degradation, including global warming. Smil sketches this world history of transitions eloquently and in an 'unapologetically empirical' way (Smil 2021: x), which is both refreshing and sobering. He concludes with significant doubts about the success of the environmental transition. There is just too little time.

In this light, therefore, there is a likelihood of a partial Great Convergence, but it will not address the global social question and it will considerably accelerate climate change. To continue on the path towards the Great Convergence without other major changes, in more concrete terms, may entail wars, famine and extreme weather events that can be of such an order that they radically reduce the number of human beings inhabiting the earth, even beyond Malthus's imagining, and thus decrease CO_2 emissions. Such a catastrophe possibly happened, largely unintentionally, in America during the sixteenth century. More than two centuries later, Malthus may turn out to have been right.

Self-defeating prophecy

Given this prospect on the road to the Great Convergence, many current observers prefer to look the other way, gambling on human ingenuity finding yet another solution. Earlier announcements of limits, so the argument goes, had been invalidated through technical-economic innovation. The presentation of upcoming limits to growth can serve as a performative speech act and trigger action to turn this very analysis into a self-defeating prophecy.

This is what happened with the report *The Limits to Growth*. It received great attention and a wide reception, including among decision makers at high level. At the same time, its method and findings were widely criticized (see, e.g., Nowotny 2002). Whether one approved of it or rejected it, the report's main call was to take action to avoid that which had been announced. But defeating the prophecy could be accomplished in two very different ways: overturning the predictions by decreasing resource use, as advocated by the report, or overcoming the predicted limits to growth by increasing resource availability. Facing potential shortage of principal resources, in particular oil, the exploration of new extraction sites as well as methods, for example, fracking, was intensified so that the report's conclusions could be refuted. A particular place in the attempted reinterpretation had been assigned to nuclear power, supposed to be cheap, relatively easily available, and not a contributor to air pollution or the warming of the atmosphere. It is interesting to note that the then West German head of government, Helmut Schmidt, mentioned global warming as an argument in favour of nuclear power, as it shows awareness of the latter issue among leading politicians even at that time (*Der Spiegel* 1979; Suckert and Ergen 2022 drew my attention to this interview). However, we can assume that for Schmidt this was an instrumental argument to accelerate the technology-driven 'modernization of the national economy' (Hauff and Scharpf 1975), not motivated by ecological concerns. In other words, the western elites tried everything to avoid limiting the energy supplies to their societies, having come to assume that material well-being had become a crucial 'social requisite of democracy' (Lipset).

One could argue that self-defeat is the unexplicated, and maybe at times unintended and even unconscious, effect of apocalyptic prophecies. In this sense, the response was quite successful. But if the prophecy could be denied in two ways, by limiting resource use or by searching for more resources, what happened was mostly the latter. The global exploitation of biophysical resources continues unabated, even accelerating in some world regions. Across at least the past half-century, however, this response entailed that the problem was displaced from the limited availability of resources to the consequences of resource use, from pollution and environmental degradation to climate change, which came to be globally the most important concern. And the argument about limits returned in the expression 'planetary boundaries'.

To recall the *Limits to Growth* experience is important because it carries many analogies with current debates about climate change and the respective action or inaction. In political debate, the call for 'innovation' suggests making economic growth ecologically sustainable, and economic liberals insist on maintaining 'openness to new technologies' – a choice term of the German Liberal-Democratic Party, currently in a government coalition – against possible ecologically motivated restrictions. Within the economic sciences, the commitment to 'technical progress', which as we have seen (chapter 6) supposedly secured growth in the 1960s without needing biophysical resources, was revived in a more sophisticated fashion, namely a neo-Schumpeterian emphasis on innovation as 'creative destruction'.

Philippe Aghion is a leading preacher of creative destruction, one of 'those who believe in ever-escalating inventions' (Smil 2021: 259), as the following mission statement (the term 'mission' to be taken literally) demonstrates:

> [T]he answer can be summed up in a single word: innovation. Only innovation can push back the limits of the possible. Only innovation has the potential to improve the quality of life while using fewer and fewer of our natural resources and emitting less and less carbon dioxide. Only innovation will enable us to discover new and cleaner sources of energy. (Aghion, Antonin and Bunel 2021 [2020]: 175)

Like much religious discourse, these statements are either tautological or false. If the term 'innovation' refers to all kinds of newness, they are tautological. If innovation is something more specific, namely an entrepreneurial practice, they are false. It is very possible, for instance, to 'improve the quality of life' without entrepreneurial innovation.

The point here is not to deny that entrepreneurial innovation can help, maybe is even necessary, to effectively combat climate change. The problem is that scholars such as Aghion and colleagues advocate faith in such 'innovation' without any concrete idea about which 'innovation' will reduce carbon dioxide emissions so radically within the next ten or twenty years that significant climate mitigation results. In doing so, he diverts attention away from sociopolitical changes – which one may well call 'innovations' – that could have an effect on climate change but will not be implemented against prevailing powers if influential preachers suggest they are not necessary.

The debate about geo-engineering is the most striking example for the vicious connection between power-induced inaction and innovation talk. The term 'geo-engineering' is used to refer to large-scale environmental interventions to either reduce the level of carbon dioxide in the atmosphere, so-called carbon dioxide removal (CDR), or to limit the warming of the atmosphere by reducing solar radiation, so-called solar radiation management (SRM). Both CDR and SRM refer to bundles of technologies that have largely in common that they are undeveloped; that there is no evidence that they can achieve their objectives; and that they are likely to have adverse consequences that are neither fully explored nor assessed. Not very long ago, there was consensus that climate mitigation policies, that is, radical reduction of carbon dioxide emissions, were the only way to limit global warming to 1.5°C. Given the persistent inaction in this regard, however, CDR and SRM have entered the international agenda of climate policy, including in the IPCC, even though the insecure and potentially dangerous status of these technologies remains largely the same (for recent explorations, see, e.g., Sovacool 2023; Sovacool, Baum and Low 2023, and ongoing research by Iris Hilbrich). Paradoxically, CDR and SRM are being evoked because time is running out, even though the positive effects of their deployment, if any, would arise much later than those from emission reduction.

The innovation discourse in climate matters signifies nothing other than an a priori commitment to an enabling knowledge attitude, not supported by empirical knowledge, and the, equally a priori, ideological rejection of a constraining knowledge attitude, even though the latter draws on much more compelling evidence.

Given the data and analyses that we have, it is implausible that geo-engineering can be successful in combatting climate change. But given prevailing knowledge attitudes in combination with given constellations of power and interest, it is very plausible that at least some technologies of geo-engineering will be pursued and maybe even tried. To underpin this insight, my last step in trying to read the present is a brief reassessment of the moment of the 1970s and its aftermath in terms of its impact on power hierarchies and problem interpretations.

Reassessing the moment of the 1970s

In the current debate about the Anthropocene and climate change, there is a tendency to see the early 1970s as a turning point towards greater sustainability, environmental protection and the use of renewable energies. There is no doubt that this was a moment of rethinking, and with a bit of detective work one can find the seeds of a major reinterpretation, the fruits of which may still be ripening today. But this would be a very optimistic reading. The data about carbon dioxide emissions since the 1970s, though not only those, suggest rather that the global trajectory towards increased fossil fuel intensity has remained unaltered and that all that has happened is a world-regional shift.

I have referred to the moment of the 1970s throughout the preceding chapters in its different aspects (chapters 6–9) and can now synthesize my partial analyses towards an assessment of the then emerging socio-ecological constellation. During the early 1970s, all elements seemed to be in place for a turning point in world history. After decades of fixation on economic growth sustained by enabling knowledge, a pronounced shift towards emphasizing constraining knowledge occurred. In particular in the West, where this growth occurred, vociferous discontent with an empty notion of growth arose, together with a stronger environmental consciousness, diffused quite widely in society. At the same time, claims for redistribution of power and resources were made more successfully by the developing countries and acknowledged by the United Nations.

What appeared at the time as a potential critical juncture turned into a failed moment of socio-ecological transformation. Three slogans capture the events: the New International Economic Order

(NIEO) transmuted into a new international division of labour. That is, an arrangement for enhancing global socio-economic justice in the representative organ of the formally sovereign states gave way to the exploitation of comparative advantages in a more densely connected global economy. The assessment of the planetary condition moved from the Club of Rome to the IPCC. That is, the threat of resource exhaustion transmuted into the threat of the inhabitability of the planet due to excessive resource use. The democratic welfare state transmuted from being seen as a globalizable model into an entrenched bastion of globally unsustainable privilege. That is, the notion of a political order that is both democratic and fair failed the test of expansion beyond the world region where it emerged.

I take the liberty of adding another autobiographical note. While this may raise the suspicion that I am merely reasoning from my personal experience, I do so, to the contrary, because my own changing attempts at reading the present may in some way be telling about changing societal self-understandings overall. During the 1970s, I was a young adult and involved in the larger ongoing attempt at socio-ecological reinterpretation. At the end of the 1980s, I had a sense that this attempt had failed and tried to grasp this failure in my scholarly work. My conclusions were pointing to ambiguities of transformative practices that were in part shaped by the evocation of normative principles (see Wagner 1994). But at that moment I was not yet aware that this was a failure of world-historical dimensions. Possibly, I was shying away from that insight, even though the elements for arriving at such a conclusion were all visible and identified.

These elements included centrally the alteration of power hierarchies and problem interpretations that were signalled above. It was also evident that these post-1970s changes were disabling collective communication, deliberation and action within but also between the states in the global order. It was less evident, even though not unknown by the 1980s, that a problem of the dimension and urgency of climate change would arise so very rapidly and would demand global communication, deliberation and action of higher quality and intensity than ever achieved before. In 1983, in my first academic job, I was asked to look at the final report of an investigation into global warming, pursued by Wilfrid Bach, and was surprised to see how clear and compelling the findings were that global warming was indeed measurably happening (see Bach 1982).

The problem constellation of the early 1970s as described constituted a new kind of global emergency, which was not resolved or, rather, was postponed by problem displacement practised under the hegemony of the West. Driven by climate change as the key issue among several others, the current problem constellation repeats many features of the earlier one, but it is of much greater urgency and shows higher requirements for globally coordinated action. At the same time, the half-century that has passed since has weakened and disabled many of the sociopolitical resources that were then still to some degree available.

11
What Is to Be Done?

Up to this point, I have aimed to provide a sober analysis of the trajectory of human societies that led to increasing fossil fuel intensity and, consequently, to the current climate crisis. While the sense of urgency was not meant to be hidden, it was not supposed to stand in the way of the analysis. This short last chapter now changes approach. It asks what, in the light of the preceding analysis, can and needs to be done to sufficiently mitigate the climate change that can no longer be entirely avoided.

The general answer to this question is rather obvious. The trajectory of increasing fossil fuel use was created and perpetuated by problem interpretations promoted by elites, and the imposition of these interpretations led to problem displacement with a view to sustaining and enhancing the existing hierarchies of power and privilege. Thus a change of trajectory will need to be based on developing and promoting different interpretations of what the key problems are that our societies are facing and on changing the distribution of power so that the new interpretations can determine action. The core practical conclusion of the preceding analysis is exactly this: by *redefining the key problems* that humankind is facing and *reshaping the existing mechanisms of power*, decisive action needed to reduce our dependence on fossil fuels and avert the worst consequences of climate change can be taken. But it is also a far too general conclusion, which needs to be made more specific and concrete.

In particular, there is a significant practical ambiguity in this diagnosis. On the one hand, we have shown a transformation of power hierarchies that makes it more difficult to identify a position of concentrated power towards which transformative claims can be directed and which would be capable of implementing these demands – both domestically and internationally, power is more diffused than, say, half a century ago. Furthermore, a practice of addressing problems through displacement has become so entrenched that it seems difficult to alter it. On the other hand, we have also shown that the origins of the current climate crisis are closer to us than is often assumed and that the crisis is not driven by inescapable logics. Rather, it goes back to deliberate decisions, first, to consolidate western democracies through the intensive use of fossil fuels and, second, to deal with the crisis of this approach in the 1970s by further diluting power and shifting problem definitions. These two steps of the Great Acceleration are still in sight, so to say, they are retrievable as intelligible interpretations and actions and, thus, also amenable to be undone, at least in principle. These concluding reflections are devoted to grasping both sides of this ambiguity to, possibly, show what steps need to be taken and how difficult it may be to take them.

Reinterpreting the social question: a historical analogy

The late Alain Touraine had suggested that societies are marked by a key conflict around which social movements form. In the industrial-capitalist society emerging in the nineteenth century, this key conflict was over the social question, and it was articulated by the workers' movement. Touraine was more wavering in his judgement of the key conflict in the closing decades of the twentieth century, even having doubts as to whether there was a central conflict at all any longer, but now we can justifiably say that this is the global ecological question, a key component of which is climate change. In our attempt at assessing possibilities for combatting climate change, it may be useful to take a look back at the social question, both in terms of similarities and differences, and the ways in which the problem was solved – or displaced. This is not to assume that past solutions can simply be revitalized. We have to face what Burkart Lutz (1989 [1984]: 267) called a 'present that lacks historical models'. But, as we have seen, the social question was fully addressed in western societies only after the Second World War and through the use of fossil fuels. Thus we stay close to the origins of the problem at hand.

Up until the end of the nineteenth century, the social question was inaccessible because of the widespread conviction that inescapable logics were at work, conceived either as a logic of steady material progress through science and technology or as a logic of capitalism. Gradually, though, the question came to be reinterpreted through sets of social policies, the so-called early welfare state. Let us start by considering this as a successful reinterpretation of a key problem and conflict – successful in the sense of being effective, without implying an overall evaluation.

A core component of the reinterpretation was the insight that the problem could not be directly attributed to individual or even collective actors. It was a consequence of a new kind of society – industrial society – which required a new community of responsibility to address the social issues generated by industry, a community that was found in the nation-state. To advance this new interpretation, an – unintended – alliance came to be formed between enlightened elites, often located in public administration and universities, and opposition movements, with the workers' movement at the centre. Furthermore, the reinterpretation was supported by new forms of knowledge, in particular in statistics but also in medicine and hygiene. As the reinterpretation advanced, pressure mounted on key actors in the nation-states to develop policies along its lines, such as compulsory workers' accident insurance and unemployment benefits.

In much of Europe, though, the rise of the reinterpretation had unanticipated and largely undesired consequences. As it was threatening power and privileges, elite resistance led to totalitarianism and war in the first instance. This interim outcome tended to confirm the view that nothing much can be achieved prior to a major upheaval, thus leading to further polarization. After the Second World War, as discussed in detail above, an answer was found that preserved elite privileges but operated through the intensification of resource extraction and confined the benefits to one world region.

Interpreting the ecological question

Now let us try to develop the analogy. There is a relatively broad agreement on the centrality of the ecological question, in particular climate change, which has emerged due to, and is underpinned by, ever more knowledge from the environmental, earth and climate sciences. In other words, a reinterpretation of the central conflict in our societies is well under way. As for the social question, one can also argue that there is an emerging alliance between enlightened elites and social movements, taking the government-supported IPCC and the scholars who contribute to its reports, on the one side, and Fridays for Future, Extinction Rebellion and The Last Generation, on the other, as examples.

However, there is an ongoing dispute over the identification and understanding of the community of responsibility. While the global significance of climate change is acknowledged and a general principle of common but differentiated responsibilities agreed upon, these vague commitments do not advance the matter in practice. The earlier established community of responsibility, the nation-state, which was enabling for the world-regional answer to the social question, has today become rather an obstacle to finding an operable answer to the global ecological question. There is a profound ambivalence here: on the one hand, states are and remain containers of relatively concentrated political power and agency with justifications of their own, but in global coordination efforts state power is diffused because of the large number of formally equal states with often different short- and medium-term interests in relation to fossil fuels. Unlike in the case of the social question, there is not an evident site of effective agency to answer the ecological question.

Power imbalances

This observation leads to the consideration of power hierarchies. It does not seem correct to say that the advocates for the social question then were more powerful than are those for the ecological question today. The former were opposed to an economic elite of industrial capitalism and a political elite in states in which they were largely lacking adequate representation. Theirs was an uphill struggle that in many countries kept failing until the 1950s. The struggle for an adequate answer to the ecological question has also continued to fail for more than half a century, but not exactly in the same power constellation.

Reinterpretation of key political problems entails providing justifications for collective action. In addition to our reflection in chapter 10, we can distinguish forms of power that are subject to public justification from those that are not. This distinction overlaps with the one between political and economic power, but it is not the same. In democratic states, power is subject to justification, but it is also so in states that accept the need for accountability and to some extent in business enterprises exposed to regulation and demands for transparency. The current global constellation is marked by a pronounced imbalance between power-subject-to-justification and power without. The former has become more diffused in two respects: domestically because of effective ('real') democratization, and internationally because of the increase in the number of power holders with partly diverging interests. In turn, power without justification has tended to become more concentrated, with a small number of globally operating enterprises, in particular in the areas of fossil fuels (energy), of finance and of communication – an unholy alliance.

The entrenchment of fossil fuel interests

The diffusion of power-subject-to-justification also goes along with the entrenchment of everyday interest in the continuation of fossil fuels. It is difficult to imagine how a large-scale protest by car users – of the kind the *gilets jaunes* ('yellow vests') staged in France in 2018–19 – could have occurred at the time of car-use restrictions during the first oil-price hike in 1973. The Western Great Acceleration had already generated a considerable permeation of social life with fossil fuel products, although more pronouncedly in the United States than elsewhere. The Asian Great Acceleration led to much greater entrenchment for two reasons: in the West, due to the importation of comparatively cheap consumer products, creating the discrepancy between rising consumption-based CO_2 emissions with stagnating or declining production emissions; and in Asia and in some countries of other world regions, due to fossil fuel-driven 'development' and the rising consumption levels of the 'new middle classes', emulating the western path.

As a consequence, those social groups that one used to consider as 'dominated', namely, workers in western countries and the majority of the population in 'Third World' countries, are today often – not always and not everywhere – heavy users of fossil fuel-based products. In combination with the greater diffusion of power domestically in democratic states and globally due to the greater number of states, some of which are new power holders, this makes it much more difficult to envisage a means by which a socio-ecological transformation away from fossil fuels can be brought about. As Ingolfur Blühdorn (2020: 56) puts it, we witness a 'hegemonial logic of unsustainability' (see also Blühdorn 2022a and 2022b).

Mechanisms of change

With the help of the historical analogy, I have identified three mechanisms of change that need to be operated to combat climate change: reinterpreting the ecological question as an urgent question of global responsibility; re-concentrating power-subject-to-justification to create effective agency in light of that interpretation; de-entrenching fossil fuel interests to weaken resistance to the needed socio-ecological transformation. (In broad terms, we might say that activating these mechanisms means mobilizing ideological, political and economic power respectively.)

Mobilizing processes are ongoing along all three lines, but the first is more advanced than the second, and much more advanced than the third. In other words, little effective agency has yet been created, and the forces of resistance remain in a very strong position. Or, in comparison with the critical juncture of the 1970s, the interpretation of the problem is much more adequate as well as more widely shared than it was then, but the prospect of action against resistance has diminished. These observations provide a better understanding of the supposed enigma of climate change, namely that all necessary knowledge is available, but action nevertheless fails to be taken.

As a consequence, the scenarios of partial convergence and of technologically driven attempts at self-defeating prophecy (as sketched in chapter 10) are much more likely to occur than the action-oriented re-appreciation of the 1970s moment. They will lead to a more unequal and unjust world, which will not immediately become uninhabitable for human beings in general but is already becoming uninhabitable for many. One cannot help thinking that in western societies, but not only there, an attitude has become widespread that recalls a view held within the elites of apartheid South Africa. In 1960, Helen Suzman (1993: 107), for many years the only member of the South African parliament opposing apartheid, had an argument with a government minister over the impossibility of sustaining the apartheid regime in the long run. The minister, Carel de Wet, responded to her: 'Nonsense, we can hold the situation for my generation and for my children's generation, and after that, who cares?'

These insights nevertheless do not impose a defeatist conclusion. The reactions to the recent COVID-19 pandemic and to the Russian invasion of Ukraine show that there still is a capacity for action in cases defined as emergencies. The lockdowns have demonstrated that government action is possible against vested economic interests and engrained social habits. Both the pandemic and the war have shown that dogmas of fiscal stability and government limitations can be dropped when urgencies require doing so. A main difference, of course, is that these actions could be labelled as temporary, whereas climate change requires a profound socio-ecological transformation. Furthermore, both the pandemic and the military aggression conveyed a sense of utter urgency that has not yet been widely diffused for climate change, although it should be (for a more differentiated comparison of reactions to the pandemic and climate change, see Wagner 2022).

The preceding analysis and reflections do not lead straightforwardly to a masterplan for ending our societies' dependence on fossil fuels and mitigating climate change. But they indicate directions for further thought and action.

In terms of the general diagnosis, first, it is necessary to abandon the obsessive focus on invincible enemies and inalterable logics, which one often finds in critical ecological debate. I have tried to show that such focus is based on an inadequate reading of history, arguably driven by the search for unequivocal causality. In practical terms, such a focus leads to a dead end as it cannot be specified what overcoming capitalism or curtailing human desires for freedom and comfort could mean in terms of possible and justified action, let alone the moral impossibility of insisting on reducing the global population. In contrast, I have suggested that a problem-oriented perspective be adopted in a double sense: to identify the problems that have in the past led to embarking on the fossil fuel trajectory and may still be significant today, and to reinterpret the current key social problems in such a way that their solution is compatible with, ideally even conducive to, disembarking from this trajectory. While I have tried to do the former throughout the book, the latter is the task of current analysis and action for which the preceding account may provide some guidance.

This task of reinterpreting the current key social problems should not be confused with developing lists of climate policy designs and measures, as is largely done in climate economics and climate policy analysis. While such work is important, it is insufficient to address the supposed knowledge–action gap regarding climate change because it fails to understand and address the social logics of fossil fuels. And by implication, it fails to understand the persistent attractiveness of monocausal logics and thus creates a cleavage between a piecemeal social engineering attitude and apocalyptic beliefs. While it may be true that the resort to monocausal logics is, on the one hand, a remnant from a strong European tradition of teleological and/or evolutionist thinking, it is also, on the other hand, a way to express the dimension of the challenge: If there is a strong driving force leading to climate change, then the need for radical action and for profound social change is underlined. The resort to monocausal logics misidentifies the historical dynamic but it captures the dimension of the challenge. And about this dimension there should be no doubt, even though it is expressed in apparently contradictory terms. Thus Vaclav Smil (2021: 278), for instance, sees the IPCC scenarios and its interpretations as 'wishful thinking', whereas Mark Jacobson (2023) insists that 'no miracles [are] needed' because existing technology is sufficient for bringing about a radical energy transition away from fossil fuels. On a closer look, though, both scholars – along with many others – agree that much more is possible than is actually achieved, and that most of what is possible will need to be achieved. Our analysis of the social logic suggests that this will not occur without major social reorientations.

A key component in the *struggle over interpretations* concerns the relation between enabling and constraining knowledge attitudes. The climate crisis shows that the accumulated consequences of human action have reached unprecedented dimensions and significance, and so has the increased capacity for human action, nuclear energy and geo-engineering plans being the key examples. The resulting combination of urgency and uncertainty (Nowotny 2019) often appears dilemmatic but can be addressed through a principle of prudence (Shue 2015). In practical terms, measures to phase out fossil fuels by replacing them with renewable energy sources and by changing the mode of production and consumption have certain and immediate climate-mitigating effects, whereas geo-engineering has highly uncertain consequences and no short- or even medium-term positive effects. Though the insistence on limits and boundaries is important, even essential, it is neither possible nor desirable to discard enabling knowledge entirely. But the balance between the two attitudes needs to radically change: supposedly enabling proposals can only be adopted if they are made with a high degree of concreteness in terms of effects and impact. This maxim even applies to wind and solar energy, which should not merely be seen as replacing fossil fuels, as they mostly are today, but as part of a broader strategy of socio-ecological transformation reducing energy needs. Furthermore, given that the climate crisis was generated by repeated problem displacements, future such displacements need to be ruled out, both as displacement across new planetary frontiers, vertically into the seas and the air, and into the future. Talk about 'creative destruction' as a strategy is irresponsible, given that there is no concrete feasible innovation that can be effective within a short time, and it only serves to delay necessary action.

Key components of the *struggle over economic and political power* are the justification of power, which needs to be imposed or enhanced for all sources of power, on the one hand, and the increase in the effectiveness of justified power, on the other – as follows.

The question of economic power brings us back to capitalism. During the Western Great Acceleration, economic power in the energy sector (coal, oil and gas) was already highly concentrated, but it was dependent on state policies, including foreign policy, and partly based on state ownership. Similarly, the communication sector was state dominated or even owned, as in the case of public broadcasting. The problem, therefore, was not that these two sectors could not be directed by democratic public policies, but that the main public policy directive was enhancing economic growth through fossil fuels. Today, both the energy and the communication sectors are no longer state dominated, partly due to internationalization and partly to deregulation and privatization, and, furthermore, they are closely connected to the rising separate sector of finance, previously closely tied to industry and state. Significantly, we have here now highly concentrated power, which is almost completely exempt from justification needs. At the very least, the available knowledge about imminent climate change and its consequences is to be used to impose justification needs, not only in terms of transparency requirements but also in terms of compliance with climate protection laws. Steps in this direction are being taken, but much more is needed.

In turn, the question of political power makes us return to the issue of freedom and its relation to material abundance. It has clearly distinct, though interrelated, domestic and international aspects.

Within *domestic politics* in democratic states, a diffusion – or we may even say dilution – of political power, in particular democratically justified political power, has occurred over the past half-century, which in the West was a rather conscious elite reaction to the 'problem squeeze'. While this process has had recognizable liberating aspects, not least in terms of recognition of diversity, it has had a disabling impact on the exercise of legitimate authoritative political power, enhanced by an ideology of denunciation of collective action. In this process, furthermore, an individualized understanding of liberty was connected to material abundance more tightly than ever before. To combat climate change, there is a need to re-concentrate legitimate power, an effort that has an interpretative and an institutional dimension. As to the former, the potential positive effect of purposeful collective action needs to be underlined and contrasted with the potential negative effects of the mere aggregate of individual actions. As to the latter, the capacity for agency of the democratic state needs to be enhanced, underlining institutionalized collective responsibility and renewing confidence in laws and public policies over vague 'governance' and supposed 'best practices'. Such effort will tend to be – it already is – marked as curtailing liberties by the fossil fuel-related powers. It will only be convincing if, in parallel, steps are taken to transform the diffuse power of democracy from an aggregate of individual votes and opinions voiced in surveys and social networks into a public opinion formed in communication, deliberation and mobilization. Vaclac Smil (2021: 290) recently drily remarked that effective climate policies are 'promises that yet have to win any election'. This has to occur, though, given the need for a profound change in the way of living in the rich countries. But it will not occur under conditions of civic apathy, atomization and, more recently, interest-based mobilization in favour of maintaining a misconceived understanding of liberty.

Within *international politics*, political power is today more diffused than it has been for a long time, despite persistent power asymmetries. This diffusion is a consequence of both decolonization and the 'international disintegration' (Gunnar Myrdal) brought about by western-induced problem displacement. To deal with the global ecological question, a more cooperative operating mode of international politics is essential (see recently Sharpe 2023 about the failure of climate diplomacy). Such cooperative interaction is unlikely to emerge without western societies fully recognizing their historical role in generating climate change, which needs not only to be acknowledged but also to lead to acceptance of 'differentiated responsibilities'. The recent Asian Great Acceleration cannot serve as an excuse for inadequate western action. The contributions of the early industrializing western societies to CO_2 concentration in the atmosphere will remain higher than those of all other societies combined for a long time, even if CO_2 emissions keep rising rapidly in China, India and other countries. Between 1750 and 2017, the United States, the United Kingdom and the countries of the current EU were together responsible for 47 per cent of CO_2 emissions, China for 13 per cent and India for 3 per cent. This is hard evidence of historical responsibility which no claim of being 'at the forefront' (European Commission) of climate policies can erase.

The struggle over political and economic power is much more difficult to win than the one over interpretative hegemony. It involves not only thought but also action, and it touches upon material interests. The evermore frequent practice of 'greenwashing' indicates the activity of existing economic and political powers against the risk of losing the struggle over interpretative hegemony. Furthermore, action in political power struggle needs to be collective and coordinated, whereas struggles over interpretation can have softer contours. Given the difficulties of creating effective domestic, and even more so international, coordinated action, a way of combining interpretative and political power struggle is the use of 'the force of the example' (Ferrara 2008). The creation of situated alternatives to the prevailing socio-ecological constellation may increase the unjustifiability of absence of action on the part of the powers that be.

References

Acemoglu, Daron and Robinson, James A. 2012. *Why Nations Fail: The Origins of Power, Prosperity and Plenty*. London: Profile.

Acker, Antoine and Fischer, Georg. 2018. 'Presentation: Historicizing Brazil's Great Acceleration'. *Varia Historia* (Belo Horizonte) 34(65).

Adloff, Frank and Neckel, Sighard (eds). 2021. *Contested Futures: A Sociology of Sustainability and Ecological Crisis. Social Science Information* 60(2).

Agarwal, Anin, and Narain, Sunita. 1991. *Global Warming in an Unequal World: A Case of Environmental Colonialism*. New Delhi: Centre for Science and Environment.

Aghion, Philippe, Antonin, Céline and Bunel, Simon. 2021 [2020]. *The Power of Creative Destruction: Economic Upheaval and the Wealth of Nations*. Cambridge, MA: Harvard University Press.

Aglietta, Michel. 1976. *Régulation et crises du capitalisme*. Paris: Calmann-Lévy.

Almond, Gabriel A. and Verba, Sidney. 1963. *The Civic Culture: Political Attitudes and Democracy in Five Nations*. Princeton: Princeton University Press.

Andersson, Jenny. 2012. 'The Great Future Debate and the Struggle for the World'. *American Historical Review* 117(5).

Andersson, Jenny. 2018. *The Future of the World: Futurology, Futurists and the Struggle for the Post-Cold War Imagination*. Oxford: Oxford University Press.

Andersson, Jenny. 2019. 'The Future of the Western World: The OECD and the Interfutures Project'. *Journal of Global History* 14(1).

Andersson, Jenny. 2020. 'Ghost in a Shell: The Scenario Tool and the World Making of Royal Dutch Shell'. *Business History Review* 94 (Winter).

Angeletti, Thomas. 2023. *L'Invention de l'économie française*. Paris: Presses de Sciences Po.

Arendt, Hannah. 1951. *The Origins of Totalitarianism*. New York: Harcourt, Brace, Jovanovich.

Arendt, Hannah. 1961. *Between Past and Future*. New York: Viking Press.

Arendt, Hannah. 1970. *On Revolution*. New York: Viking.

Arnason, Johann P. 1993. *The Future That Failed: Origins and Destinies of the Soviet Model*. London: Routledge.

Arnason, Johann P. and Raaflaub, Kurt A. (eds). 2011. *The Roman Empire in Context: Historical and Comparative Perspectives*. Oxford: Blackwell.

Arnason, Johann P. and Wittrock. Björn (eds). 2004. *Eurasian Transformations, Tenth to Thirteenth Centuries: Crystallizations, Divergences, Renaissances*. Leiden: Brill.

Aykut, Stefan Cihan. 2019. 'Energy Futures from the Social Market Economy to the *Energiewende*: The Politicization of West German Energy Debates, 1950–1990', in Jenny Andersson and Eglė Rindzevičiūtė (eds), *The Struggle for the Long-Term in Transnational Science and Politics*. Abingdon: Routledge.

Bach, Wilfrid. 1982. *Gefahr für unser Klima. Wege aus der CO_2-Bedrohung durch sinnvollen Energieeinsatz*. Karlsruhe: C. F. Müller.

Baldwin, Richard E. and Martin, Philippe. 1999. 'Two Waves of Globalisation: Superficial Similarities, Fundamental Differences'. *National Bureau of Economic Research (NBER) Working Papers* 6904.

Barbier, Edward B. 2011. *Scarcity and Frontiers: How Economies Have Developed through Natural Resource Exploitation*. Cambridge: Cambridge University Press.

Bayly, C. A. 2004. *The Birth of the Modern World, 1780–1914*. Oxford: Blackwell.

Beckert, Jens. 2016. *Imagined Futures: Fictional Expectations and Capitalist Dynamics*. Cambridge, MA: Harvard University Press.

Beckert, Sven. 2014. *Empire of Cotton: A Global History*. New York: Knopf.

Beckwith, Christopher I. 2009. *Empires of the Silk Road: A History of Central Eurasia from the Bronze Age to the Present*. Princeton: Princeton University Press.

Belich, James. 2009. *Replenishing the Earth: The Settler Revolution and the Rise of the Anglo-World, 1783–1939*. Oxford: Oxford University Press.

Belich, James. 2022. *The World the Plague Made: The Black Death and the Rise of Europe*. Princeton: Princeton University Press.

Bell, Daniel. 1960. *The End of Ideology: On the Exhaustion of Political Ideas in the Fifties*. New York: Free Press.

Berg, Maxine. 2007. *Luxury and Pleasure in Eighteenth-Century Britain*. Oxford: Oxford University Press.

Berg, Maxine and Hudson, Pat. 2023. *Slavery, Capitalism and the Industrial Revolution*. Cambridge: Polity.

Black, Brian C. 2012. *Crude Reality: Petroleum in World History*. Lanham, MD: Rowman & Littlefield.

Blom, Philipp. 2017. *Die Welt aus den Angeln. Eine Geschichte der Kleinen Eiszeit von 1570 bis 1700*. Munich: Hanser.

Blühdorn, Ingolfur. 2020. 'Die Gesellschaft der Nicht-Nachhaltigkeit. Skizze einer umweltsoziologischen Gegenwartsdiagnose', in Ingolfur Blühdorn et al., *Nachhaltige Nicht-Nachhaltigkeit*. Bielefeld: transkript.

Blühdorn, Ingolfur. 2022a. 'Planetary Boundaries, Societal Boundaries, and Collective Self-Limitation: Moving Beyond the Post-Marxist Comfort Zone'. *Sustainability: Science, Practice and Policy* 18(1).

Blühdorn, Ingolfur. 2022b. 'Liberation and Limitation: Emancipatory Politics, Socio-Ecological Transformation and the Grammar of the Autocratic-Authoritarian Turn'. *European Journal of Social Theory* 25(1).

Bolsinger, Eckard. 2001. *The Autonomy of the Political: Carl Schmitt's and Lenin's Political Realism*. Westport, CN: Greenwood.

Boltanski, Luc. 2009. *De la Critique. Précis de sociologie de l'émancipation*. Paris: Gallimard.

Boltanski, Luc and Chiapello, Eve. 1999. *Le Nouvel esprit du capitalisme*. Paris: Gallimard.

Boltanski, Luc and Esquerre, Arnaud. 2022. *Qu'est-ce que l'actualité politique? Événements et opinions au XXIe siècle*. Paris: Gallimard.

Boltanski, Luc and Thévenot, Laurent. 1991. *De la Justification. Les économies de la grandeur*. Paris: Gallimard.

Bonneuil, Christophe and Fressoz, Jean-Baptiste. 2016 [2013]. *L'évènement Anthropocène. La terre, l'histoire et nous*. Paris: Seuil.

Borowy, Iris. 2013. *Defining Sustainable Development for Our Common Future: A History of the World Commission on Environment and Development (Brundtland Commission)*. London: Routledge.

Bourdieu, Pierre and Boltanski, Luc. 1976. 'La production de l'idéologie dominante'. *Actes de la recherche en sciences sociales* 2(2–3).

Boyer, Robert and Orléan, André. 1991. 'Les transformations des conventions salariales entre théorie et histoire: d'Henry Ford au fordisme'. *Revue économique* 42(2).

Brand, Ulrich and Wissen, Markus. 2017. *Imperiale Lebensweise. Zur Ausbeutung von Mensch und Natur im globalen Kapitalismus*. Munich: Oekom.

Brooke, John L. 2014. *Climate Change and the Course of Global History: A Rough Journey*. Cambridge: Cambridge University Press.

Brown, M. J. 2016. 'Too Cheap to Meter?' *Canadian Nuclear Society*. https://cns-snc.ca/media/media/toocheap/toocheap.html

Burbank, Jane and Cooper, Frederick. 2010. *Empires in World History: Power and the Politics of Difference*. Princeton: Princeton University Press.

Bush, Vannevar. 1945. *Science: The Endless Frontier*. Washington, DC: United States Government Printing Office.

Castel, Robert. 1995. *Les Métamorphoses de la question sociale. Une chronique du salariat*. Paris: Fayard.

Castoriadis, Cornelius. 1975. *L'Institution imaginaire de la société*. Paris: Seuil.

Chakrabarty, Dipesh. 2009. 'The Climate of History: Four Theses'. *Critical Inquiry* 35.

Chakrabarty, Dipesh. 2021. *The Climate of History in a Planetary Age*. Chicago: University of Chicago Press.

Charbonnier, Pierre. 2020. *Abondance et liberté. Une histoire environnementale des idées politiques*. Paris: La Découverte.

Cho, Ji-Hyung. 2014. 'The Little Ice Age and the Coming of the Anthropocene'. *Asian Review of World Histories* 2(1).

Ciplet, David and Timmons Roberts, J. 2019. 'Splintering South: Ecologically Unequal Exchange Theory in a Fragmented Global Climate', in R. Scott Frey, Paul K. Gellert and Harry F. Dahms (eds), *Ecologically Unequal Exchange: Environmental Injustice in Comparative and Historical Perspective*. London: Palgrave-Macmillan.

Clot-Garrell, Anna. 2023. 'Voices of Emergency: Imagined Climate Futures and

Forms of Collective Action'. *Current Sociology*. https://doi.org/10.1177/00113921231182179

Conze, Werner et al. 1972. 'Demokratie', in Otto Brunner, Werner Conze and Reinhart Koselleck (eds), *Geschichtliche Grundbegriffe. Historisches Lexikon zur politisch-sozialen Sprache in Deutschland*, vol. 1. Stuttgart: Klett-Cotta.

Crosby, Alfred W. 2003 [1972]. *The Columbian Exchange: Biological and Cultural Consequences of 1492*. Westport, CN: Praeger.

Crouch, Colin. 2011. *The Strange Non-Death of Neoliberalism*. Cambridge: Polity.

Crozier, Michel, Huntington, Samuel P. and Watanuki, Joji. 1975. *The Crisis of Democracy: Report on the Governability of Democracies to the Trilateral Commission*. New York: New York University Press.

Crutzen, Paul J. 2002. 'Geology of Mankind'. *Nature* 415.

Crutzen, Paul J. and Stoermer, Eugene F. 2000. The 'Anthropocene'. *Global Change Newsletter* 41.

Darwin, John. 2007. *After Tamerlane: A Global History of Empire since 1405*. London: Allen Lane.

Degroot, Dagomar et al. 2022. 'The History of Climate and Society: A Review of the Influence of Climate Change on the Human Past'. *Environmental Research Letters* 17. doi.org/10.1088/1748-9326/ac8faa

Denord, François, Palme, Mikael and Réau, Bertrand (eds). 2020. *Researching Elites and Power: Theory, Methods, Analyses*. Cham: Springer.

Der Spiegel. 1979. 'Kernenergie. Der Kanzler geht aufs Ganze', 17 June.

Descola, Philippe. 2005. *Par delà nature et culture*. Paris: Gallimard.

Desrosières, Alain. 1991. 'How to Make Things which Hold Together: Social Science, Statistics and the State', in Peter Wagner, Björn Wittrock and Richard Whitley (eds), *Discourses on Society: The Shaping of the Social Science Disciplines*. Dordrecht: Kluwer.

Desrosières, Alain. 1993. *La Politique des grands nombres*. Paris: La Découverte.

De Vries, Jan. 2008. *The Industrious Revolution: Consumer Behavior and the Household Economy, 1650 to the Present*. Cambridge: Cambridge University Press.

De Zwart, Frank. 2015. 'Unintended but Not Unanticipated Consequences'. *Theory and Society* 44.

De Zwart, Pim and van Zanden, Jan Luiten. 2018. *The Origins of Globalization: World Trade in the Making of the Global Economy, 1500–1800*. Cambridge: Cambridge University Press.

Diamanti, Jeff. 2021. *Climate and Capital in the Age of Petroleum: Locating Terminal Landscapes*. London: Bloomsbury.

DiMuzio, Timothy. 2015. *Carbon Capitalism: Energy, Social Reproduction and World Order*. London: Rowman Littlefield International.

Durkheim, Émile. 1897. *Le Suicide*. Paris: Alcan.

Durkheim, Émile. 2007 [1893]. *De la Division de travail social*. Paris: PUF.

Dussel, Enrique. 2007. *Política de la liberación. Historial mundial y crítica*. Madrid: Trotta.

Ehrlich, Paul and Ehrlich, Anne Harland. 1968. *The Population Bomb*. New York: Ballantine.

Ekardt, Felix, Wieding, Jutta and Zorn, Anika. 2018. 'Paris Agreement, Precautionary Principle and Human Rights: Zero Emissions in Two Decades?' *Sustainability* 10(8).

Emmer, Piet C. 1988. *The Dutch in the Atlantic Economy, 1580–1880: Trade, Slavery and Emancipation*. Aldershot: Ashgate.

Enquête-Kommission des 8 Deutschen Bundestages. 1980. *Zukünftige Kernenergiepolitik. Kriterien – Möglichkeiten – Empfehlungen*. Bonn: Deutscher Bundestag.

Erhard, Ludwig. 1957. *Wohlstand für alle*. Düsseldorf: Econ.

Eshun, Kodwo. 2020. 'From 953 AD to 1 Gigayear: Cheik Anta Diop's Future Vector of Energy', in Eric C. H. de Bruyn and Sven Lüttiken (eds), *Futurity Report*. Berlin: Sternberg.

Evers, Adalbert and Nowotny, Helga. 1987. *Über den Umgang mit Unsicherheit. Über die Entdeckung der Gestaltbarkeit von Gesellschaft*. Frankfurt am Main: Suhrkamp.

Eversberg, Dennis. 2021. 'From Democracy at Others' Expense to Externalization at Democracy's Expense: Property-Based Personhood and Citizenship Struggles in Organized and Flexible Capitalism'. *Anthropological Theory* 21(3).

Fabian, Johannes. 1983. *Time and the Other: How Anthropology Makes Its Object*. New York: Columbia University Press.

Fagan, Brian. 2001. *The Little Ice Age: How Climate Made History, 1300–1850*. New York: Basic Books.

Farey, John. 1827. *A Treatise on the Steam Engine, Historical, Practical, and Descriptive*. London: Longman, Rees, Orme, Brown, and Green.

Ferrara, Alessandro. 2008. *The Force of the Example: Explorations in the Paradigm of Judgment*. New York: Columbia University Press.

Fichte, Johann Gottlieb. 1800. *The Closed Commercial State* [*Der geschlossene Handelsstaat*]. https://www.marxists.org/archive/fichte/1800/commercial-state.htm

Fischer-Kowalski, Marina, Krausmann, Fridolin and Pallua, Irene. 2014. 'A Sociometabolic Reading of the Anthropocene: Modes of Subsistence, Population Size and Human Impact on Earth'. *Anthropocene Review* 1(1).

Ford, Henry and Crowther, Samuel. 1922. *My Life and Work*. Garden City, NY: Garden City Publishing.

Forrester, Katrina. 2019. *In the Shadow of Justice: Postwar Liberalism and the Remaking of Political Philosophy*. Princeton: Princeton University Press.

Forster, Piers M. et al. 2023. 'Indicators of Global Climate Change 2022: Annual Update of Large-Scale Indicators of the State of the Climate System and Human Influence'. *Earth System Science Data* 15. https://doi.org/10.5194/essd-15-2295-2023

Foucault, Michel. 1984. 'What is Enlightenment?' in Paul Rabinow (ed.), *The Foucault Reader*. New York: Pantheon.

Fourastié, Jean. 1979. *Les Trente Glorieuses, ou la révolution invisible de 1946 à 1975*. Paris: Fayard.

Fröbel, Folker, Heinrichs, Jürgen and Kreye, Otto. 1977. *Die neue internationale Arbeitsteilung*. Reinbek: Rowohlt.

Fucks, Wilhelm. 1966. *Formeln zur Macht: Prognosen über Völker, Wirtschaft, Potentiale*. Stuttgart: Deutsche Verlags-Anstalt.

Fuhrmann, Uwe. 2017. *Die Entstehung der 'Sozialen Marktwirtschaft' 1948/49*. Konstanz: UVK.

Garavini, Giuliano. 2012. *After Empires: European Integration, Decolonization and the Challenge from the Global South 1957–1986*. Oxford: Oxford University Press.

Garavini, Giuliano. 2019. *The Rise and Fall of OPEC in the Twentieth Century*. Oxford: Oxford University Press.

Gellner, Ernest. 1988. *Plough, Sword, and Book: The Structure of Human History*. Chicago: University of Chicago Press.

Getachew, Adom. 2019. *Worldmaking after Empire: The Rise and Fall of Self-Determination*. Princeton: Princeton University Press.

Ghosh, Amitav. 2016. *The Great Derangement: Climate Change and the Unthinkable*. Chicago: University of Chicago Press.

Ghosh, Amitav. 2021. *The Nutmeg's Curse: Parables for a Planet in Crisis*. London: Murray.

Giddens, Anthony. 1984. *The Constitution of Society*. Cambridge: Polity.

Gilman, Nils. 2015. 'The New International Economic Order: A Reintroduction'. *Humanity: An International Journal of Human Rights, Humanitarianism, and Development* 6(1).

Glyn, Andrew and Sutcliffe, Robert B. 1972. *British Capitalism, Workers and the Profits Squeeze*. London: Penguin.

Gottl-Ottlilienfeld, Friedrich von. 1924. *Fordismus? Paraphrasen über das Verhältnis von Wirtschaft und technischer Vernunft bei Henry Ford und Frederick W. Taylor*. Jena: Fischer.

Graeber, David and Wengrow, David. 2021. *The Dawn of Everything: A New History of Humanity*. London: Allen Lane.

Gramsci, Antonio. 1971. 'Americanism and Fordism'. *Selections from the Prison Notebooks*. London: Lawrence and Wishart.

Grinin, Leonid, and Korotayev, Andrey. 2015. *Great Divergence and Great Convergence: A Global Perspective*. Cham: Springer.

Grischow, Jeff and Weiss, Holger. 2019. 'Pan-Africanism, Socialism and the Future: Development Planning in Ghana, 1951–1966', in Jenny Andersson and Eglė Rindzevičūtė (eds), *The Struggle for the Long-Term in Transnational Science and Politics*. Abingdon: Routledge.

Groupe 1985. 1964. *Réflexions sur 1985*. Paris: Commissariat Général au Plan.

Guéguen, Haud. 2023. 'Les lieux de l'utopie'. Presentation at the Centre Arts Santa Mónica, Barcelona, 13 May.

Guéguen, Haud and Jeanpierre, Laurent. 2022. *La Perspective du possible. Comment penser ce qui peut nous arriver, et ce que nous pouvons faire*. Paris: La Découverte.

Habermas, Jürgen. 1973. *Legitimationsprobleme im Spätkapitalismus*. Frankfurt am Main: Suhrkamp.

Hacking, Ian. 1990. *The Taming of Chance*. Cambridge: Cambridge University Press.

Hartz, Louis. 1964. *The Founding of New Societies: Studies in the History of the United States, Latin America, South Africa, Canada, and Australia*. New York: Harcourt, Brace, Jovanovich.

Harvey, David. 2005. *A Brief History of Neoliberalism*. Oxford: Oxford University Press.

Hatton, Timothy J. and Williamson, Jeffrey G. 2005. *Global Migration and the World Economy: Two Centuries of Policy and Performance*. Cambridge, MA: MIT Press.

Hauff, Volker and Scharpf, Fritz W. 1975. *Modernisierung der Volkswirtschaft*. Frankfurt am Main: EVA.

Hecht, Gabrielle. 2016. 'L'Empire nucléaire. Les silences des "trente glorieuses"', in Céline Pessis, Sezin Topçu and Christophe Bonneuil (eds), *Une autre histoire des 'Trente Glorieuses'*. Paris: La Découverte.

Hirsch, Fred. 1976. *Social Limits to Growth*. Cambridge, MA: Harvard University Press.

Hirschman, Albert O. 1977. *The Passions and the Interests: Arguments for Capitalism before its Triumph*. Princeton: Princeton University Press.

Hirschman, Albert O. 1991. *The Rhetoric of Reaction: Perversity, Futility, Jeopardy*. Cambridge, MA: Harvard University Press.

Hogan, J. 2019. 'The Critical Juncture Concept's Evolving Capacity to Explain Policy Change'. *European Policy Analysis* 5(2).

Honneth, Axel. 2011. *Das Recht der Freiheit*. Berlin: Suhrkamp.

Honneth, Axel. 2015. *Die Idee des Sozialismus*. Berlin: Suhrkamp.

Hornborg, Alf. 2006. 'Footprints in the Cotton Field: The Industrial Revolution as Time–Space Appropriation and Environmental Load Displacement'. *Ecological Economics* 59(1).

Huff, Amber and Mehta, Lyla. 2019. 'Untangling Scarcity', in Fredrik Albritton Jonsson, John Brewer, Neil Fromer and Frank Trentmann (eds), *Scarcity in the Modern World: History, Politics, Society and Sustainability, 1800–2075*. London: Bloomsbury.

Hulme, Mike. 2023. *Climate Change isn't Everything*. Cambridge: Polity.

IPCC (Intergovernmental Panel on Climate Change). 2021. 'Changing State of the Climate System'. *Climate Change 2021: The Physical Science Basis: Contribution of Working Group I to the Sixth Assessment Report of the Intergovernmental Panel on Climate Change*. Cambridge: Cambridge University Press.

IPCC (Intergovernmental Panel on Climate Change). 2022. 'Summary for Policymakers'. *Climate Change 2022: Impacts, Adaptation and Vulnerability. Working Group II Contribution to the Sixth Assessment Report of the Intergovernmental Panel on Climate Change*. Cambridge: Cambridge University Press.

Issberner, Liz-Rejane and Léna, Philippe (eds). 2017. *Brazil in the Anthropocene: Conflicts between Predatory Development and Environmental Policies*. London: Routledge.

Jacobson, Mark Z. 2023. *No Miracles Needed: How Today's Technology Can Save Our Climate and Clean Our Air*. Cambridge: Cambridge University Press.

Jaspers, Karl. 1968 [1949]. *The Origin and Goal of History*. London: Routledge.

Jevons, William Stanley. 1865. *The Coal Question: An Inquiry Concerning the Progress of the Nation, and the Probable Exhaustion of Our Coal Mines*. London: Macmillan.

Jones, Geoffrey. 2017. *Business History, the Great Divergence and the Great Convergence*. Harvard Business School Working Paper 18-004.

Jonsson, Fredrik Albritton. 2019. 'Growth in the Anthropocene', in Fredrik Albritton Jonsson, John Brewer, Neil Fromer and Frank Trentmann (eds), *Scarcity in the Modern World: History, Politics, Society and Sustainability, 1800–2075*. London: Bloomsbury.

Jonsson, Fredrik Albritton. 2020. 'The Coal Question before Jevons'. *Historical Journal* 63.

Jonsson, Fredrik Albritton, Brewer, John, Fromer Neil and Trentmann, Frank (eds). 2019. *Scarcity in the Modern World: History, Politics, Society and Sustainability, 1800–2075*. London: Bloomsbury.

Jonsson, Fredrik Albritton and Wennerlind, Carl. 2023. *Scarcity: A History from the Origins of Capitalism to the Climate Crisis*. Cambridge, MA: Harvard University Press.

Josephson, Per. 2017. *Common but Differentiated Responsibilities in the Climate Change Regime: Historic Evaluation and Future Outlooks*. Stockholm University, Faculty of Law.

Karagiannis, Nathalie. 2004. *Avoiding Responsibility: The Discourse and Politics of European Development Policy*. London: Pluto Press.

Khomyakov, Maxim. 2016. 'Mastering Nature: A Russian Route into Modernity?' *Social Imaginaries* 2(2).

Knöbl, Wolfgang. 2003. 'Theories that Won't Pass Away: The Never-Ending Story of Modernization Theory', in Gerard Delanty and F. Isin Engin (eds), *Handbook of Historical Sociology*. London: Routledge.

Koch, Alexander, Brierley, Chris, Maslin, Mark M. and Lewis, Simon L. 2019. 'Earth System Impacts of the European Arrival and Great Dying in the Americas after 1492'. *Quaternary Science Reviews* 207 (1).

Kocka, Jürgen. 2013. *Geschichte des Kapitalismus*. Munich: Beck.

Korzeniewicz, Roberto Patricio. 2018. 'Inequality: Towards a World-Historical Perspective', in E. Jelin et al. (eds), *Global Entangled Inequalities: Conceptual Debates and Evidence from Latin America*. London: Routledge.

Korzeniewicz, Roberto Patricio and Moran, Timothy Patrick. 2009. *Unveiling Inequality: A World-Historical Perspective*. New York: Russell Sage Foundation.

Koselleck, Reinhart. 1979. *Vergangene Zukunft. Zur Semantik geschichtlicher Zeiten*. Frankfurt am Main: Suhrkamp.

Koyama, Mark and Rubin, Jared. 2022. *How the World Became Rich: The Historical Origins of Economic Growth*. Cambridge: Polity.

Krause, Florentin et al. 1980. *Energiewende. Wachstum und Wohlstand ohne Erdöl und Uran*. Frankfurt am Main: Fischer.

Landes, David S. 1969. *The Unbound Prometheus: Technological Change and Industrial Development in Western Europe from 1750 to the Present*. Cambridge: Cambridge University Press.

Lane, Richard. 2014. *The Nature of Growth: The Postwar History of the Economy, Energy and the Environment*. PhD thesis, University of Sussex.

Latham, Michael E. 2003. *Modernization as Ideology: American Social Science and 'Nation Building' in the Kennedy Era*. Durham: University of North Carolina Press.

Latour, Bruno. 1991. *Nous n'avons jamais été modernes*. Paris: Minuit.

Leichenko, Robin M. and O'Brien, Karen L. 2008. *Environmental Change and Globalization: Double Exposures*. Oxford: Oxford University Press.

Leroy Ladurie, Emmanuel. 2004–2009. *Histoire humaine et comparée du climat, Volumes I–III*. Paris: Favard.

Lessenich, Stephan. 2019. *Living Well at Others' Expense: The Hidden Costs of Western Prosperity*. Cambridge: Polity.

Lieven, Anatol. 2020. *Climate Change and the Nation State: The Realist Case*. London: Macmillan.

Lipset, Seymour Martin. 1959. 'Some Social Requisites of Democracy: Economic Development and Political Legitimacy'. *American Political Science Review* 53(1).

Luhmann, Niklas. 1970. 'Soziologie als Theorie sozialer Systeme', in Niklas Luhmann, *Soziologische Aufklärung 1*. Frankfurt am Main: Suhrkamp.

Lukes, Steven. 2005 [1974]. *Power: A Radical View*. Basingstoke: Palgrave-Macmillan.

Lutz, Burkart. 1989 [1984]. *Der kurze Traum immerwährender Prosperität. Eine Neuinterpretation der industriell-kapitalistischen Entwicklung im Europa des 20. Jahrhunderts*. Frankfurt am Main: Campus.

Luxemburg, Rosa. 1951 [1913]. *The Accumulation of Capital: A Contribution to an Economic Explanation of Imperialism*. London: Routledge and Kegan Paul.

Lyotard, Jean-François. 1979. *La Condition postmoderne*. Paris: Minuit.

Mahoney, James. 2000. 'Path Dependence in Historical Sociology'. *Theory and Society* 27.

Maier, Charles S. 1970. 'Between Taylorism and Technocracy: European Ideologies and the Vision of Industrial Productivity in the 1920s'. *Journal of Contemporary History* 5(2).

Malm, Andreas. 2016. *Fossil Capital: The Rise of Steam Power and the Roots of Global Warming*. London: Verso.

Malm, Andreas and Hornborg, Alf. 2014. 'The Geology of Mankind? A Critique of the Anthropocene Narrative'. *The Anthropocene Review* 1(1).

Malthus, Thomas Robert. 1798. *An Essay on the Principle of Population*. London: J. Johnson.

Mann, Michael. 1986. *Sources of Social Power, Vol. 1*. Cambridge: Cambridge University Press.

Mannheim, Karl. 1935. *Mensch und Gesellschaft im Zeitalter des Umbaus*. Leiden: Sijthoff.

Marklund, Carl. 2020. 'Double Loyalties? Small-State Solidarity and the Debates on New International Economic Order in Sweden during the Long 1970s'. *Scandinavian Journal of History* 45(3).

Marks, Robert B. 2020. *The Origins of the Modern World: A Global and Environmental*

Narrative from the Fifteenth to the Twenty-First Century, 4th edn. Lanham, MD: Rowman & Littlefield.

Marshall, T. H. 1950. *Citizenship and Social Class, and Other Essays*. Cambridge: Cambridge University Press.

Marx, Karl and Engels, Friedrich. 1948. *The Communist Manifesto*. https://www.marxists.org/archive/marx/works/1848/communist-manifesto/

Maslovskiy, Mikhail. 2018. 'Russia Against Europe: A Clash of Interpretations of Modernity?' *European Journal of Social Theory* 2(4).

Mayer, Arno. 1981. *The Persistence of the Old Regime*. New York: Pantheon.

Mazzucato, Mariana. 2020. *Mission Economy: A Moonshot Guide to Changing Capitalism*. London: Allen Lane.

McKeown, Adam. 2004. 'Global Migration, 1846–1940'. *Journal of World History* 15(2).

McNeill, J. R. and Engelke, Peter. 2014. *The Great Acceleration: An Environmental History of the Anthropocene since 1945*. Cambridge, MA: Harvard University Press.

Meadows, Donella H., Meadows, Dennis L., Randers, Jørgen and Behrens, William W., III. 1972. *Limits to Growth*. Washington, DC: Universe.

Merton, Robert K. 1936. 'Unanticipated Consequences of Purposive Social Action'. *American Sociological Review* 1(6).

Milanović, Branko. 2012. 'Global Inequality: From Class to Location, from Proletarians to Migrants'. *Global Policy* 3(2).

Milanović, Branko. 2015. 'Global Inequality of Opportunity: How Much of Our Income is Determined by Where We Live'. *Review of Economics and Statistics* 97(2).

Milanović, Branko. 2016. *Global Inequality: A New Approach for the Age of Globalization*. Cambridge, MA: Harvard University Press.

Milkoreit, Manjana. 2023. 'Social Tipping Points Everywhere? Patterns and Risks of Overuse'. *WIREs Climate Change* 14(2).

Mintz, Sidney W. 1985. *Sweetness and Power: The Place of Sugar in Modern History*. New York: Viking.

Mitchell, Timothy. 2011. *Carbon Democracy: Political Power in the Age of Oil*. London: Verso.

Mokyr, Joel. 2016. *A Culture of Growth: The Origins of the Modern Economy*. Princeton: Princeton University Press.

Moore, Jason W. 2003. '"The Modern World-System" as Environmental History? Ecology and the Rise of Capitalism'. *Theory and Society* 32(3).

Moore, Jason W. 2015. *Capitalism in the Web of Life: Ecology and the Accumulation of Capital*. London: Verso.

Morton, Timothy. 2013. *Hyperobjects: Philosophy and Ecology after the End of the World*. Minneapolis, MN: University of Minnesota Press.

Mota, Aura and Wagner, Peter. 2019. *Collective Action and Political Transformations: The Entangled Experiences of Brazil, South Africa and Europe*. Edinburgh: Edinburgh University Press.

Mouzakitis, Angelos. 2014. 'Creation Ex Nihilo', in Suzi Adams (ed.), *Cornelius Castoriadis: Key Concepts*. London: Bloomsbury.

Moyn, Samuel. 2010. *The Last Utopia: Human Rights in History*. Cambridge, MA: Harvard University Press.

Moyn, Samuel. 2018. *Not Enough: Human Rights in an Unequal World*. Cambridge, MA: Harvard University Press.

Mumford, Lewis. 1934. *Technics and Civilization*. New York: Harcourt, Brace, and Company.

Muraca, Barbara and Schmelzer, Matthias. 2017. 'Sustainable Degrowth: Historical Roots of the Search for Alternatives to Growth in Three Regions', in Iris Borowy and Matthias Schmelzer (eds), *History of the Future of Economic Growth*. Abingdon: Routledge.

Myrdal, Gunnar. 1956. *An International Economy: Problems and Prospects*. New York: Harper & Brothers.

Myrdal, Gunnar. 1960. *Beyond the Welfare State*. London: Duckworth.

Narr, Wolfdieter and Offe, Claus (eds). 1975. *Wohlfahrtsstaat und Massenloyalität*. Cologne: Kiepenheuer and Witsch.

Neu, Axel D. 1978. 'Entkoppelung von Wirtschaftswachstum und Energieverbrauch: Eine Strategie der Energiepolitik?', *Kieler Diskussionsbeiträge* no. 52. Kiel: Institut für Weltwirtschaft (IfW).

Nowotny, Helga. 2002. 'Vergangene Zukunft: Ein Blick zurück auf die "Grenzen des Wachstums"', in Michael Globig (ed.), *Impulse geben – Wissen stiften. Vierzig Jahre Volkswagenstiftung*. Göttingen: Volkswagenstiftung.

Nowotny, Helga. 2019. 'Embracing Uncertainty', in Shalini Randeria and Björn Wittrock (eds), *Social Science at the Crossroads*. Leiden: Brill.

O'Brien, Patrick. 2010. 'Ten Years of Debate on the Origins of the Great Divergence'. *Reviews in History*. https://reviews.history.ac.uk/review/1008

O'Brien, Patrick. 2022. 'Was the British Industrial Revolution a Conjuncture in Global Economic History?' *Journal of Global History* 17(1.)

O'Connor, James. 1973. *The Fiscal Crisis of the State*. New York: St Martin's Press.

Offe, Claus. 1972. *Strukturprobleme des kapitalistischen Staates*. Frankfurt am Main: Suhrkamp.

Offe, Claus. 2009. 'Was (falls überhaupt etwas) können wir uns heute unter politischem Fortschritt vorstellen?' *WestEnd. Neue Zeitschrift für Sozialforschung* 7(2).

Offe, Claus and Wiesenthal, Helmut. 1980. 'Two Logics of Collective Action: Theoretical Notes on Social Class and Organizational Form'. *Political Power and Social Theory* 1(1).

O'Neill, Daniel W., Fanning, Andrew L., Lamb, William L. and Steinberger, Julia K. 2018. 'A Good Life for All within Planetary Boundaries'. *Nature Sustainability* 1.

Osterhammel, Jürgen. 2009. *Die Verwandlung der Welt. Eine Geschichte des neunzehnten Jahrhunderts*. Munich: Beck.

Packard, Vance. 1957. *The Hidden Persuaders*. New York: McKay.

Pagden, Anthony (ed.). 2000. *Facing Each Other*. London: Ashgate.

Page, Scott E. 2006. 'Path Dependence'. *Quarterly Journal of Political Science* 1.

Palmer, Robert R. 1953. 'Notes on the Use of the Word "Democracy"', 1789–1799'. *Political Science Quarterly* 68(2).

Palmer, Robert R. 1959. *The Age of the Democratic Revolution: A Political History of Europe and America, 1760–1800, Vol. 1: The Challenge*. Princeton: Princeton University Press.

Parker, Geoffrey. 2013. *Global Crisis: War, Climate Change and Catastrophe in the Seventeenth Century*. New Haven: Yale University Press.

Parsons, Talcott. 1964. 'Evolutionary Universals in Society'. *American Sociological Review* 29(3).

Parthasarathi, Prasannan. 2011. *Why Europe Grew Rich and Asia Did Not: Global Economic Divergence, 1600–1850*. Cambridge: Cambridge University Press.

Pauw, Pieter, Mbeva, Kennedy and van Asselt, Harro. 2019. 'Subtle Differentiation of Countries' Responsibilities under the Paris Agreement'. *Palgrave Communications* 5. https://doi.org/10.1057/s41599-019-0298-6

Pineault, Eric. 2021. 'The Ghosts of Progress: Contradictory Materialities of the Capitalist Golden Age'. *Anthropology Today* 21(3).

Polanyi, Karl. 1985 [1944]. *The Great Transformation*. Boston: Beacon.

Pomeranz, Kenneth. 2000. *The Great Divergence: China, Europe, and the Making of the Modern World Economy*. Princeton: Princeton University Press.

Porter, Theodore M. 1995. *Trust in Numbers: The Pursuit of Objectivity in Science and Public Life*. Princeton: Princeton University Press.

Procacci, Giovanna. 1993. *Gouverner la misère. La question sociale en France (1789–1848)*. Paris: Seuil.

Przeworski, Adam, Alvarez, Michael E., Cheibub, José Antonio and Limongi, Fernando. 2000. *Democracy and Development: Political Institutions and Well-Being in the World, 1950–1990*. Cambridge: Cambridge University Press.

Radkau, Joachim. 2012 [2007]. *Wood: A History*. Cambridge: Polity.

Radkau, Joachim and Hahn, Lothar. 2013. *Aufstieg und Fall der deutschen Atomwirtschaft*. Munich: oekom.

Rajamani, L. 2016. 'Ambition and Differentiation in the 2015 Paris Agreement: Interpretative Possibilities and Underlying Politics'. *International and Comparative Law Quarterly* 65(2).

Rawls, John. 1971. *A Theory of Justice*. Cambridge, MA: Harvard University Press.

Rawls, John. 1993. 'The Law of Peoples'. *Critical Inquiry* 20(1).

Reitz, Tilman, Schulz, Peter, Schütt, Mariana and Seyd, Benjamin. 2021. 'Democracy in Post-Growth Societies: A Zero-Sum Game?' *Anthropological Theory* (special issue) 21(3).

Richards, John F. 2003. *The Unending Frontier: An Environmental History of the Early Modern World*. Berkeley, CA: University of California Press.

Ritchie, Hannah, Roser, Max and Rosado, Pablo. 2020. 'CO_2 and Greenhouse Gas Emissions'. *OurWorldInData.org*. https://ourworldindata.org/co2-and-greenhouse-gas-emissions

Rockström, Johan et al. 2009. 'Planetary Boundaries: Exploring the Safe Operating Space for Humanity'. *Ecology and Society* 14(2).

Rockström, Johan et al. 2023. 'Safe and Just Earth System Boundaries'. *Nature*. https://doi.org/10.1038/s41586-023-06083-8

Rosanvallon Pierre. 2011. *La Société des égaux*. Paris: Seuil.

Rostow, Walt W. 1956. 'The Take-Off into Self-Sustained Growth'. *Economic Journal* 66(261).

Rostow, Walt W. 1959. 'The Stages of Economic Growth'. *Economic History Review* (New Series) 12(1).

Ruddiman, William F. 2003. 'The Anthropogenic Greenhouse Era Began Thousands of Years Ago'. *Climatic Change* 61.

Ruddiman, William F., He, F., Vavrus, S. J. and Kutzbach, J. E. 2020. 'The Early Anthropogenic Hypothesis: A Review'. *Quaternary Science Reviews* 240.

Rueschemeyer, Dietrich and Skocpol, Theda (eds). 1996. *States, Social Knowledge, and the Origins of Modern Social Policies*. Princeton: Princeton University Press.

Rueschemeyer, Dietrich, Stephens, Evelyne Huber and Stephens, John D. 1992. *Capitalist Development and Democracy*. Chicago: University of Chicago Press.

Sahlins, Marshall. 1972. *Stone Age Economics*. New York: Aldine.

Schmelzer, Matthias. 2012. 'The Crisis before the Crisis: The "Problems of Modern Society" and the OECD, 1968–74'. *European Review of History (Revue europeenne d'histoire)* 19(6).

Schmelzer, Matthias. 2016. *The Hegemony of Growth: The OECD and the Making of the Economic Growth Paradigm*. Cambridge: Cambridge University Press.

Schmelzer, Matthias. 2017. '"Born in the Corridors of the OECD": The Forgotten Origins of the Club of Rome, Transnational Networks, and the 1970s in Global History'. *Journal of Global History* 12.

Schmidt, Volker H. 2010. 'Modernity and Diversity: Reflections on the Controversy between Modernization Theory and Multiple Modernists'. *Social Science Information* 49.

Schumpeter, Joseph A. 1976 [1942]. *Capitalism, Socialism and Democracy*. London: Allen & Unwin.

Seow, Victor. 2021. *Carbon Technocracy: Energy Regimes in Modern East Asia*. Chicago: University of Chicago Press.

Sewell, William H., Jr. 2005. *Logics of History: Social Theory and Social Transformation*. Chicago: University of Chicago Press.

Shapin, Steven and Schaffer, Simon. 1993. *Leviathan and the Air-Pump: Hobbes, Boyle, and the Experimental Life*. Princeton: Princeton University Press.

Sharpe, Simon. 2023. *Five Times Faster: Rethinking the Science, Economics, and Diplomacy of Climate Change*. Cambridge: Cambridge University Press.

Shue, Henry. 2015. 'Uncertainty as the Reason for Action: Last Opportunity and the Future Climate Disaster'. *Global Justice: Theory, Practice, Rhetoric* 8(2).

Sieferle, Rolf Peter. 2010 [1982]. *Subterranean Forests: Energy Systems and the Industrial Revolution*. Winwick: White Horse Press.

Silva Pinochet, Beatriz. 2017. *Conflicto y democracia en la historia de Chile*. PhD thesis, University of Barcelona.

Smil, Vaclav. 2021. *Grand Transitions: How the Modern World Was Made*. Oxford: Oxford University Press.

Smith, Julia M. H. 2005. *Europe after Rome: A New Cultural History, 500–1000*. Oxford: Oxford University Press.

Sovacool, Benjamin K. 2023. 'Expanding Carbon Removal to the Global South: Thematic Concerns on Systems, Justice, and Climate Governance.' *Energy and Climate Change* 4. https://doi.org/10.1016/j.egycc.2023.100103

Sovacool, Benjamin K., Baum, Chad M. and Low, Sean. 2023. 'Beyond Climate Stabilization: Exploring the Perceived Sociotechnical Co-impacts of Carbon Removal and Solar Geoengineering'. *Ecological Economics* 204. https://doi.org/10.1016/j.ecolecon.2022.107648

Steffen, Will, Broadgate, Wendy, Deutsch, Lisa, et al. 2015. 'The Trajectory of the Anthropocene: The Great Acceleration'. *Anthropocene Review* 2(1).

Stoll, Mark. 2023. *Profit: An Environmental History*. Cambridge: Polity.

Stone, Christopher D. 2004. 'Common but Differentiated Responsibilities in International Law'. *American Journal of International Law* 98.

Stråth, Bo. 2023. *The Brandt Commission and the Multinationals: Planetary Perspectives*. Abingdon: Routledge.

Stråth, Bo and Wagner, Peter. 2017. *European Modernity: A Global Approach*. London: Bloomsbury.

Streeck, Wolfgang. 2011. 'The Crises of Democratic Capitalism'. *New Left Review* 71.

Streeck, Wolfgang. 2013. *Gekaufte Zeit. Die vertagte Krise des demokratischen Kapitalismus*. Berlin: Suhrkamp.

Strong, Tracy B. 2012. *Politics without Vision: Thinking without a Banister in the Twentieth Century*. Chicago, IL: University of Chicago Press.

Suckert, Lisa and Ergen, Timur. 2022. 'Contested Futures: Reimagining Energy Infrastructures in the First Oil Crisis'. *Historical Social Research* 47(2) (ed. Philipp Degens, Iris Hilbrich and Sarah Lenz, special issue, *Ruptures, Transformations, Continuities. Rethinking Infrastructures and Ecology*).

Suzman, Helen. 1993. *In No Uncertain Terms: Memoirs*. London: Sinclair-Stevenson.

Sydow, Jörg, Schreyögg, Georg and Koch, Jochen. 2020. 'On the Theory of Organizational Path Dependence: Clarifications, Replies to Objections, and Extensions'. *Academy of Management Review* 45(4).

Tilly, Charles. 1984. *Big Structures, Large Processes, Huge Comparisons*. New York: Russell Sage Foundation.

Toulmin, Steven. 1990. *Cosmopolis: The Hidden Agenda of Modernity*. Chicago: University of Chicago Press.

Turner, Frederick Jackson. 2014 [1893]. *The Significance of the Frontier in American History*. Mansfield Centre: Martino.

Umar, Ahmad Rizky Mardhatillah. 2019. 'Rethinking the Legacies of Bandung Conference: Global Decolonization and the Making of Modern International Order'. *Asian Politics and Policy* 11(3).

Urry, John. 2011. *Climate Change and Society*. Cambridge: Polity.

Van Parijs, Philippe. 1982. 'Perverse Effects and Unintended Consequences: Analytical Vindication of Dialectics?' *British Journal of Sociology* 33(4).

Verne, Jules. 1889. *Sans dessus dessous*. Paris: Hetzel.

Vries, Peer (P. H. H.). 2001. 'Are Coal and Colonies Really Crucial? Kenneth Pomeranz and the Great Divergence'. *Journal of World History* 12(2).

Vries, Peer. 2012. 'Challenges, (Non-)Responses, and Politics'. *Journal of World History* 23(3).

Wagner, Peter. 1985. 'De la "scientification de la politique" à la pluralisation de l'expertise', in CRESAL (ed.), *Situations d'expertise et socialisation des savoirs*. St Etienne: Dumas.

Wagner, Peter. 1990. *Sozialwissenschaften und Staat. Frankreich, Italien, Deutschland, 1870–1980*. Frankfurt am Main: Campus.

Wagner, Peter. 1994. *A Sociology of Modernity: Liberty and Discipline*. London: Routledge.

Wagner, Peter. 2001. *A History and Theory of the Social Sciences: Not All That Is Solid Melts into Air*. London: Sage.

Wagner, Peter. 2008. *Modernity as Experience and Interpretation*. Cambridge: Polity.

Wagner, Peter. 2010. 'The Future of Sociology: Understanding the Transformations of the Social', in Charles Crothers (ed.), *The History and Development of Sociology*. Paris: UNESCO.

Wagner, Peter. 2012. *Modernity: Understanding the Present*. Cambridge: Polity.

Wagner, Peter. 2016. *Progress: A Reconstruction*. Cambridge: Polity.

Wagner, Peter. 2020. 'Das Haus der Freiheit und die fossilen Brennstoffe', in Frank Adloff et al. (eds), *Imaginationen der Nachhaltigkeit*. Frankfurt am Main: Campus.

Wagner, Peter. 2022. 'Neuartige Probleme und die Widerständigkeit der Realität. Über das Ausbleiben angemessener politischer Entscheidungen', in Karl-Rudolf Korte et al. (eds), *Heuristiken des politischen Entscheidens*. Berlin: Suhrkamp.

Wagner, Peter. 2023. 'Theories of the Political', in William Outhwaite and Laurence Ray (eds), *Teaching Political Sociology*. Cheltenham: Elgar.

Wagner, Peter and Zimmermann, Bénédicte. 2004. 'Citizenship and Collective Responsibility: On the Political Philosophy of the Nation-based Welfare State and Beyond', in Lars Magnusson and Bo Stråth (eds), *A European Social Citizenship?* Brussels: PIE – Peter Lang.

Walker, Gordon. 2009. 'Globalizing Environmental Justice: The Geography and Politics of Frame Contextualization and Evolution'. *Global Social Policy* 9(3).

Wallerstein, Immanuel. 1974–1989. *The Modern World-System, Volumes I–III*. New York and San Diego: Academic Press.

Wallerstein, Immanuel. 1996. *Open the Social Sciences: Report of the Gulbenkian Commission on the Restructuring of the Social Sciences*. Stanford, CA: Stanford University Press.

Weart, Spencer R. 2008. *The Discovery of Global Warming*. Cambridge, MA: Harvard University Press.

Webb, Walter Prescott. 1952. *The Great Frontier*. Boston: Houghton & Mifflin.

Weber, M. 2002 [1904/5]. *The Protestant Ethic and the Spirit of Capitalism*. Los Angeles: Roxbury.

Welzel, Christian. 2013. *Freedom Rising: Human Empowerment and the Quest for Emancipation*. Cambridge: Cambridge University Press.

Wittrock, Björn. 2000. 'Modernity: One, None, or Many? European Origins and Modernity as a Global Condition'. *Daedalus* 129(1).

Wrigley, E. A. 2010. *Energy and the English Industrial Revolution*. Cambridge: Cambridge University Press.

Wrigley, E. A. 2016. *The Path to Sustained Growth. England's Transition from an Organic Economy to an Industrial Revolution*. Cambridge: Cambridge University Press.

York, Richard and Bell, Shannon Elizabeth. 2019. 'Energy Transitions or Additions? Why a Transition from Fossil Fuels Requires More than the Growth of Renewable Energy'. *Energy Research and Social Science* 51.

York, Richard, Ergas, Christina, Rosa, Eugene A. and Dietz, Thomas. 2011. 'It's a Material World: Trends in Material Extraction in China, India, Indonesia, and Japan'. *Nature and Culture* 6(2).

York, Richard, Rosa, Eugene A. and Dietz, Thomas. 2003. 'Footprints on the Earth: The Environmental Consequences of Modernity'. *American Sociological Review* 68(2).

Zalasiewicz, Jan et al. 2015. 'Colonization of the Americas, "Little Ice Age" Climate, and Bomb-Produced Carbon: Their Role in Defining the Anthropocene'. *Anthropocene Review* 2(2).

Index